Here's what professionals are saying about this book.

"Several years ago, there was a comedian who always said, "Thanks, I needed that" upon being slapped. Those were exactly the words that came to mind as I read Stephen Rosenberg's book. There is an unbelievable amount of information that anyone can use. It is presented in a very practical manner. The investment in the cost of this book should be returned many times."

> *W. Carl Joiner, Dean*
> *Eugene W. Stetson School of Business & Economics*
> *Mercer University*

"Keep Uncle Sam (and Cousin George) From Devouring Your Estate is a very useful resource for seniors doing financial planning. It helps clarify concepts and terminologies. Easy to read and understand."

> *Robert O. Redd, author, Achievers Never Quit,*
> *(a life planning book for seniors)*

"This book is the most helpful I have seen. It factually states the advantages and disadvantages of various alternatives. The information on tax impact, as well as IRS imposed structure requirements and limitations on alternatives, is particularly clear, concise, and free of "legalese." It should be required reading for anyone even considering estate planning. It will provide an excellent base of information from which to develop an estate plan."

> *Bryan W. Ziegler, Accredited Tax Advisor, Louisiana*

"I've been using these simple and incredible concepts, which Steve Rosenberg has pulled together and explained so well, to help save my clients hundreds of thousands of dollars. This book is must reading for anyone who wants to protect their assets and save money"

> *G. Peck Moxley, Estate and Business Consultant, Florida*

"Keep Uncle Sam (and Cousin George) From Devouring Your Estate is a dynamic book with great appeal for persons of all financial levels, not just the wealthy. It takes the whole complex picture and fine tunes it into alternatives that appear personalized and obvious."

> *Steven J. Finkle, President, National Financial Firm*

Here's what a cross-section of citizens say about Stephen Rosenberg's methods and this book.

"A straight forward explanation of many concepts which have been unfamiliar to me for so long."
Stuart T. Weinberg, MD, Pittsburgh, PA

"You have covered each point in a short, clear manner in readable English free from technical jargon. Your examples help explain the subjects in concrete terms that I can relate directly to. It is easy for me to say frequently, 'Hey, that could be me.'"
K. L. Campbell, Hudson, OH

"This one book helps one understand the many aspects to consider and eliminates confusion. If we only had this book in hand, it would have been very helpful and would have saved us time and money."
Albert & Joyce Legg, Ponce Inlet, FL

"I congratulate you on your frankness. It was instructive and helpful."
Eugene T. Tompane, Tempe, AZ

"The chapter on nursing home insurance is the best we have seen on this subject. The book is certainly a worthwhile purchase for anyone interested in estate planning."
Emily and Donald Sheets, Annapolis, MD

"I will recommend your book to friends because it is valuable to those who know they should have a plan but don't know how to go about it."
David H. Pottenger, Cohassett, MA

"This book is a 'must read' for anyone with an estate. People who have been successful in their vocational lives can now, by reading this book, learn how to become successful in controlling the estate they have acquired."
William C. Simmer, Blue Springs, MO

"As we talk to a trust officer and lawyer in the near future, it will serve as the source for the points to be covered. We consider ourselves fortunate to have this resource available as we go into these discussions."
Alan McAllister, Terrace Park, OH

KEEP UNCLE SAM
(AND COUSIN GEORGE)
FROM DEVOURING
YOUR ESTATE

Stephen M. Rosenberg, CFP

CAPITAL PUBLISHING
ATLANTA, GEORGIA

Additional copies of this book may be ordered through bookstores or by sending $19.95 plus $2.50 for postage and handling to:

Capital Publishing Company
2221 Peachtree Road, Suite 103
Atlanta, GA 30309

or by calling:

(800) 847-4483
(800) VIP-GIVE

Special discounts are available for bulk purchases.

PUBLISHER'S CATALOGING-IN-PUBLICATION DATA

Rosenberg, Stephen M., 1944-
     Keep Uncle Sam (and Cousin George) From Devouring Your Estate: your guide to controlling your estate and preserving your wealth / by Stephen M. Rosenberg. Atlanta, GA: Capital Publishing Co., 1992.
     xvi, 320 p. cm.
     ISBN 1-880380-11-0
     Includes index.
1. Estate planning - United States
2. Living trusts - United States
3. Finance, personal - United States

KF750.R67 1992   332.024'01'0973-dc20   91-75531

Printed in the United States of America

DEDICATION

This book is dedicated to my wife, Nancy, for her continuous love and support, my mother, Anne, my sister, Gay, and my children, Jeffrey and David, all of whom are so special to me.

This book is also dedicated to all my fellow citizens who have worked so hard to build a good life for themselves and their families, only to see "The System" devour it. It's time to protect your assets for yourself and your loved ones!

A NOTE FROM THE PUBLISHER

Case Studies: This book contains a number of situational examples. These cases, in which the author has participated, is familiar, or has combined or condensed for educational purposes, are not meant to represent recommendations for any particular situation. Rather they are merely examples intended to illustrate a point. All cases have been reviewed by a practicing attorney. All names have been changed.

Legal Disclaimer: This book is neither an attempt to provide legal advice nor a substitute for the same. It is intended to provide accurate and authoritative information in regard to the subject matter covered. It is provided with the understanding that the publisher is not engaged in rendering legal, accounting, or other professional service. If legal advice or other expert assistance is required, the services of a competent professional should be sought.

Insurance Rates: Insurance premiums and face values used in cases are based on the current projections by the representative insurance companies. Company projections are, in turn, based on current interest rates and mortality assumptions, which will fluctuate over the years.

ABOUT THE AUTHOR

Stephen M. Rosenberg, CFP, is president of Rosenberg Financial Group, where he devotes a major portion of his practice to estate planning. In addition to being a recognized authority on matters dealing with estate planning, he teaches graduate level finance courses for a major university. After working for a leading financial firm, he moved to Atlanta in 1972, where he began his work in the estate planning arena. He recently relocated his practice to the nearby community of Warner Robins to have more time to devote to his priorities. His proximity to Atlanta allows him to travel throughout the United States to work with clients and speak to organizations and groups on a variety of financial topics. Mr. Rosenberg can be reached at (800) 777-0867 (toll-free) or (912) 922-8100.

CONTRIBUTORS

The author wishes to thank the following attorneys (in alphabetical order) for their assistance and counsel in reviewing this book.

Steven R. Bone, J.D., CLU, is the director of Legal Support Services for an Indianapolis, Indiana firm that specializes in the implementation and third-party of administration of charitable remainder trusts.

Kelly R. Burke, J.D., is a practicing attorney who devotes a substantial portion of his practice to estate planning and asset protection. He is a member of the Estate, Probate and Tax Section of the Georgia State Bar and makes himself available as a spokesperson on matters of estate planning.

Gregory Diefenderfer, J.D., CFP, is a former bank trust department officer who is currently a legal consultant for a major life insurance company located in Farmington Hills, Michigan.

In addition, I would like to thank the following members of my staff who have spent endless hours helping me on this book.

Janet Peters, my Administrative Assistant, has spent immeasurable hours combing over this book for grammatical errors, misspellings, and the dreaded "dangling participle", which I still don't understand. Her input has been invaluable.

Ann Peterson, a financial consultant with my firm, has taken precious time from working with her clients to make a tremendous contribution with ideas and thoughts, not to mention restructuring parts of the book. I couldn't have done it without her.

And last, but not least, I would like to thank my wife, Nancy, who not only has helped proofread, but has spent countless evenings and weekends alone as I worked on this book. Her constant love and support are what make her so special.

TABLE OF CONTENTS

Preface   xi
Rosenberg Planning Path   xiv
Introduction   xv

PART I - TRADITIONAL PLANNING

1.   What Is Estate Planning, And Why Is It Important?   3

2.   Why Is It So Important To Set Financial Goals?   9

3.   What Are The Ways Of Holding Title?   13

4.   What Are The Problems With Joint Tenancy?   27

5.   What Are The Advantages And Disadvantages Of Wills?   35

6.   How Does The Probate System Work?   45

7.   How Do Estate Taxes Affect Me?   53

PART II - CONTROLLING YOUR ESTATE

8.   What Is A Revocable Living Trust?   65

9.   What Are the Ways Of Structuring A Living Trust?   79

10. How Can I Save Estate Taxes And Care For My Family?   87

11. How Can I Provide For My Minor Children?   103

12. What Other Types Of Trusts Are Available For Minors?   115

13. How Can I Provide For My Adult Children?   121

14. How Do Testamentary And Living Trusts Compare?   125

15. How Do I Know If I Need A Living Trust?   133

16. How Do I Live With My Living Trust?   141

PART III - REDUCING YOUR ESTATE TAXES

17.   How Can Gifting Reduce Estate Taxes?   155

18.   How Can I Avoid Paying Estate Taxes
      On My Life Insurance?   165

19.   How Can I Substantially Reduce My Estate Tax Cost?   183

20.   What Should Be My Concerns When
      Buying Life Insurance?   197

21.   How Can Charitable Giving Reduce My Taxes
      and Increase My Income?   205

Part IV - PROTECTION DURING YOUR LIFETIME

22.   How Can I Protect Myself If I Become Disabled?   221

23.   How Can I Handle The Nursing Home Problem?   233

24.   How Can I Protect My Assets From A Nursing Home Stay?   241

25.   What About Living Wills And Health Care Powers?   253

26.   How Can I Protect My Assets From A Lawsuit?   257

PART V - SPECIAL PLANNING SITUATIONS

27.   What Happens To My Business Upon My Death?   267

28.   How Can I Provide For My Handicapped Child?   289

29.   What Are The Rules For Non-U. S. Citizens?   297

30.   How Can I Protect My Family In A Second Marriage?   301

Conclusion   305
From The Publisher   307
Financial Analysis Form   311
Rosenberg Planning Path   313
Index   315

PREFACE

I consider myself very fortunate to be working in a field where I can help people accomplish their financial goals. Other than saving people's lives or improving their health, I can think of no profession more satisfying.

Helping people control their estates using the easiest and least costly methods provides a tremendous service to the public. As a result of these efforts by myself and others in my field, Americans can leave more to their families by reducing the amount that is confiscated by Uncle Sam. They can take care of their loved ones upon their death or disability. They can provide for their minor children, adult children, and grand-children in the manner they choose. They can meet their charitable goals using methods that are advantageous to themselves and their favorite charities. And they can accomplish all this, and more, at minimum cost.

Unfortunately, the people who plan are in the minority, and that is what concerns me the most. It's no secret that most people have done no planning at all. So the obvious questions are: Why would anyone **knowingly leave** his or her children in the hands of the probate court? Why would they **pay more** estate taxes than necessary? Why would they **incorrectly structure** their life insurance? Why would they put themselves in a **difficult position** in the event of their disability or mental incapacity? Why would they **tie up their estates** for years in the court system? Why would they **pay unnecessary** capital gains tax on the sale of assets? Why would they **subject their family** to needless publicity? They wouldn't. But they do. They refuse to solve those problems that are so easily solvable. They complain when their spouses waste a few hundred dollars, but they let the courts and taxes take thousands, and in some cases millions, of their dollars. I get so frustrated because these human tragedies are totally avoidable. Proper planning can resolve most of these problems. This isn't a life-threatening disease. It's not cancer of the pancreas. It's not AIDS. It's a problem that has a solution. Yet most people ignore or deny the problem. Instead, they let the dragons grab and pluck pieces of their estates. Like a fast-spreading cancer, the damage is irreversible before they finally face the issues.

It's a known fact that the lack of planning results in extra expense and aggravation to individuals and families. Why does this go on? I believe one reason is due to a general lack of useful estate planning information. Sure, there are magazine articles here and there. And there are a slew of books on living trusts. But there has been no single source devoted to explaining the various concepts in simple, everyday language that you can understand.

As a result, people make decisions based on suggestions from friends and neighbors, and bits of information they pick up in the paper. To make it even worse, there are a number of well-intentioned "professionals" who make recommendations to clients based on information that is outdated, incomplete, or just plain wrong. So you and your family suffer.

I believe the best way to counter bad advice is through education. And since I am not an attorney, I have deliberately avoided legalese and confusing terminology. Rather I have set forth, in simple, easy to understand language, the various estate planning methods and the advantages and disadvantages of each. I have put before you most of the problems you will face in your planning, and some thoughts toward working to solve them. But, and this is very important, the purpose of this book is not to give legal advice by providing counsel and "do-it-yourself" forms. It is not aimed at teaching short cuts to avoid "The System" and save legal fees.

Rather, it is to provide, in an easy-to-understand format, valuable information to assist you in your long-range planning. Unlike many people who author financial books, I am not an advocate of do-it-yourself planning. Rather, I am a strong believer that good legal work by a competent attorney is vital to your financial security. Estate planning is not the same as fixing a leaky faucet or wallpapering your home. This is serious stuff that must be handled by professionals. Do-it-yourself estate planning is like trying to slay a dragon - you'll probably end up getting burned.

This book will prepare you to move forward toward meaningful planning. It will help you get your thoughts together. And you will have an opportunity to receive an estate plan that reflects your situation and provides specific recommendations. This will be explained in the section entitled "From The Publisher" at the end of the book. By reading this book and following through with meaningful planning, you can accomplish your goals and avoid doing to yourself and your family what the majority of Americans do to theirs.

One final point. The largest obstacle we face in estate planning is that *we don't think we have a problem until we have a problem.* While that might sound confusing, it's not meant to be. The fact is, it doesn't matter how your property is owned until you need to sell it. It doesn't matter who you name as guardian of your children as long as you or your spouse are alive. It doesn't matter who your insurance company is until you have a claim. It doesn't matter what your estate tax liability is until you die. Until you become disabled or die, you have no problems. But once that occurs, the problems present themselves. By then, it's usually too late.

Rather than waiting for disaster to strike, we are going to look at these problems in advance. We are going to investigate the various planning methods and see how they might be used to save you and your family time, aggravation, and expense. Please join me as we travel through the maze of estate planning. It is with confidence I can state that it will be one of the most profitable journeys of your entire life.

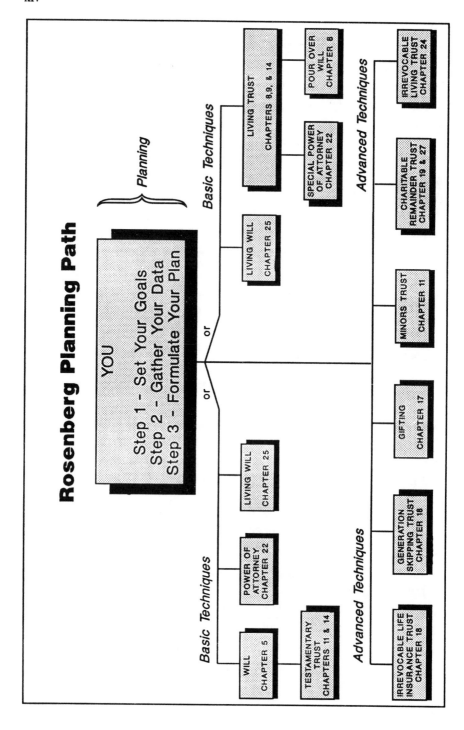

INTRODUCTION

WHO ARE UNCLE SAM, COUSIN GEORGE, AND THE DRAGONS?

Uncle Sam, Cousin George, and the Dragons! What better way to describe all the pitfalls faced in our attempts to plan?

You know who **Uncle Sam** is. You pay taxes to the federal government every single day of your life. To make matters worse, Uncle Sam is always looking for more ways to get his hands into your pockets.

But who is **Cousin George?** He represents the other people who, subtly or not, are also trying to get your money. Cousin George is the relative who wants you to finance his new venture; the ex-spouse who wants everything you have; the child who only knows how to take; the attorney who wants to profit from your problems; the insurance agent who is interested only in selling you a policy; the planner who wants to put you in a questionable investment; the court system that wants to squeeze you. Cousin George is all the people and institutions which are trying to take a piece of your estate for themselves.

All these people together, Uncle Sam and Cousin George, are the **dragons** who are seeking to devour your estate, the estate you've spent a lifetime to create. But it doesn't have to be that way. There are defenses against these dragons, and that's what this book is all about...protecting your estate from being needlessly devoured.

So let's get started and slay that dragon!

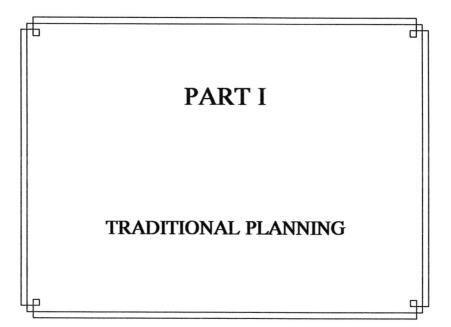

PART I

TRADITIONAL PLANNING

1

WHAT IS ESTATE PLANNING, AND WHY IS IT IMPORTANT?

One of my professors once told me that when discussing a complex subject, start from the beginning so everybody knows specifically what you're talking about. Define the terms you are using so there can be no doubt.

So let's start by defining estate planning. You've heard it used by many people, but the definition always seems to vary depending upon the intentions of the speaker. If we are going to accomplish our goals in this book, we must start from common ground.

Definition

Let me give you the definition of estate planning that I developed for my use in working with clients. In my opinion, it expresses exactly what ideal estate planning should accomplish.

Estate planning is the process by which, during your life and after your death, you can control your property in the manner you desire, minimizing all fees, taxes and court interference, preserving for yourself, your family, and those you choose, the estate you have worked so hard to create.

That's a long definition that says it all. But this is your book, and any planning should meet your goals. So let's take that definition and restate it in the form of a goal:

> *"During **my** life and after **my** death, **I** want to control and distribute **my** property in the manner **I** desire, minimizing all fees, taxes and court interference, preserving for **myself**, **my** family, and those **I** choose, the estate **I** have worked so hard to create."*

Read that definition again. Notice the emphasis. It is on "me" and "my", unlike so much planning that seems to have no direction. My definition gives you the opportunity to take care of **your** concerns, not anybody else's. And if this sounds a bit selfish, so be it. You deserve to be the master of your own estate.

Read the definition once more. Notice it doesn't just say "I want to pass my estate to my family." Estate planning is much more involved than that. Proper estate planning takes care of you and your family **while you are alive, as well as after your death.** Isn't that what you really want? Don't you want to take care of yourself while you are alive? Don't you want to control the distribution of your assets after your death? Don't you want to eliminate all the costs and taxes you can? And don't you want to stay out of court? Don't you really want to keep the dragons away? Yet, I would bet that if I reviewed your current estate plan, it wouldn't satisfy the conditions of my definition.

Let's make it "our" definition

During the course of the book, we are going to cover important estate planning concepts. I will refer often to those concepts as they relate to my definition of estate planning. At this point, I am going to make the assumption that my definition makes sense to you. Therefore, from now on, I will refer to it as "our" definition of estate planning.

Simplistic approach

Many people will tell you the purpose of estate planning is to pass your estate in an organized manner to your heirs upon your death. In my opinion, that is much too simplistic. While utilizing proper strategies at your death is important, there are many problems that you face during your lifetime that can only be solved through proper estate planning. Additionally, there are steps that can be taken to help you reduce the cost, pain, and uncertainty of the entire process.

Nevertheless, in spite of the more sophisticated methods available, the average person with whom I consult has a simple will and not much more. No thought has been given to problems that might occur before death. No thought has been given to consequences after death. Not much attention is paid to the problems which the surviving spouse and children may face. Just a simple will. Period. Nothing more, nothing less. Unfortunately, this type of plan doesn't protect you against all the dragons that are out there waiting to devour or play havoc with your estate.

Wait a minute! Haven't we been taught all our lives that as long as we have a will everything will be okay? Haven't we been told that the only reason most people run into problems is because they don't have a will?

Yes, that's exactly what we've been taught. But in my opinion, wills alone are not the answer. *Simple wills are a simplistic attempt to solve a complex problem.* Estate planning is a complex issue requiring complex solutions.

Poor planning

Having spent many years in the financial industry, I have seen the results of inadequate planning. The devastation wrought on families is shocking. It is sad to see widows and children left in the lurch, not necessarily by lack of planning, but due to improper planning. You see, the desire was there, but the strategy was faulty.

Problems you can face

Let me share with you a few of the dragons that can devour your estate.

- A disability which keeps you from handling your finances.
- A surviving spouse who can't handle money.
- Minor children who inherit money.
- An heir who contests your will.
- Relatives who fight over custody of your children.
- Attorney's fees that eat up the estate.
- Time delays in transferring your assets.
- Adult children who fritter away their inheritance.
- Handicapped children who need long-term care.
- Estate taxes which gobble up to 55% of your estate.
- Probate judges who make rulings affecting your children.
- A nursing home stay which consumes your assets.
- Business interests that can't be sold.
- Lawsuits that need to be settled.
- Property titled incorrectly.
- Fire sales to come up with estate taxes.

This list could go on for pages and pages. These are just a few of the problems that this book will address. What it all means is that the dragons are out there looking for the opportunity to take pieces of your estate. In my experience, traditional planning doesn't address these problems; it may even help create them.

Conclusion

If we are going to keep the dragons away from your estate, we must work toward creating the proper estate plan that will achieve your financial goals. Remember our definition:

> *"During my life and after my death, I want to control and distribute my property in the manner I desire, minimizing all fees, taxes and court interference, preserving for myself, my family, and those I choose, the estate I have worked so hard to create."*

Proper estate planning can provide tremendous benefits to you and your loved ones. You can feel good about the planning you have done. Proper planning can help you rest easily knowing that you have taken care of your family. And as a bonus, it can save you and your family thousands, and in some cases millions, of your hard earned dollars.

Nothing is more rewarding than being able to help a client resolve his or her potential problems. When it's over, everybody feels good. I'll never forget one situation in particular when a client grabbed my hand and said, "Now I can sleep at night knowing my children will be taken care of." Isn't that what it is all about? Isn't proper estate planning an extension of your concern for your family?

As you continue through this book, I hope that you will remember this story and relate to that person's feelings. Nothing can replace the emotional warmth you feel when you have done something good for others, especially when those others are your own family.

2

WHY IS IT SO IMPORTANT
TO SET FINANCIAL GOALS?

Why do most people fail financially? Two reasons: procrastination and failure to set goals.

PROCRASTINATION

Estate planning is a very difficult process because it requires so many decisions, several of which often stop the planning process entirely. Consider the question, "Who should be the guardians of our children?" I would venture to say the primary reason that most people don't even have a will is that they can't agree on the guardians for their children. They can't concede that anybody will do as good a job parenting as they can. This is probably true. But the result is they do nothing.......and leave the decision in the hands of the court.

We will discuss the results of dying without a will (called dying intestate). This effectively leaves all your decisions to the court. Why do people die intestate? Because they haven't gotten around to drawing up a will. They haven't made the tough decisions.

It is my hope that by purchasing and reading this book, you will put to use some of the ideas presented; you will not be one of the many people who will cause their families undue hardship because you procrastinate. In medicine, it's procrastination that causes death. In dentistry, it is procrastination that results in rotten teeth. In my practice, it is procrastination that devours estates.

As you read this book, highlight those points that are important to you and refer to them. And, then, most importantly, take action before it is too late.

GOAL SETTING

Goals are mentioned often throughout this book. Goals are so important to the estate planning process that nothing can be accomplished without them.

It is a fact that people can't be successful without goals. The achievers in our society are those who continually establish goals. Business leaders will tell you that they attribute their success to setting and achieving goals. Yet, when we are dealing with finances, we ignore goal setting and instead tend to leave things to chance.

I believe that the general public makes poor financial decisions because they fail to work toward a definite goal. As a result, they have no idea if a particular strategy is suitable for their situation.

Determining your goals

This is equally true with estate planning. However, you can avoid mistakes by determining the goals you want for yourself and your family.

- How do you want to take care of your spouse?
- How do you want to take care of your children?
- How do you want to fund their college education?
- How soon after your death do you want them to begin receiving their inheritance?

- At what ages and in what percentages do you want them to receive it?
- Do you need to care for handicapped children?
- Do you want to provide for your parents? Other relatives? Any special charities?
- Do you want any restrictions if your spouse remarries?
- Is there a potential for a lawsuit?
- Are you involved in the ownership of a business and/or any other venture? How will you dispose of them?
- How can you best reduce your estate tax cost?
- Who should manage your estate upon your death?
- Are you concerned about nursing home care?
- What provisions have you made for a potential disability?

If a plan is going to be designed to meet your particular goals, then these questions, and more, must be answered. In my profession, as in medicine, *prescription without diagnosis is malpractice.*

How can a professional help you design a plan without fully comprehending your goals? How can you possibly know how to get where you want to go if you don't know the direction you are headed in the first place?

Would you set out on vacation with no destination in mind? Of course not. But I see financial meandering along that line every day in my business. As motivational speaker Zig Ziglar says, "How can you possibly hit a target you can't see?"

You're not expected to know the questions that should be asked to help you accomplish your financial goals any more than you should be able to diagnose your own illness. That's why you need a competent advisor - one who will ask the right questions and, more importantly, listen carefully to your answers before recommending solutions.

The Rosenberg Planning Path

Setting goals is only the first step toward total estate planning. Pages xiv and 313 contain a chart entitled the "Rosenberg Planning Path". This is the road map my firm uses with our clients in their comprehensive estate planning. If you review the chart, you will see it involves three initial steps: setting your goals, gathering your data, and formulating your plan. These steps are accomplished as a result of your input.

Once that has been done, your planner and attorney can help recommend the various techniques available to help you accomplish your goals. "Basic techniques" include the use of either a will or living trust. Each alternative is covered in detail in this book. Depending on your particular situation, more "advanced techniques" might be required. Some of the more common ones are listed on the chart.

If you don't currently have advisors with whom you can work, I have agreed to make some arrangements that you might find helpful. They are explained in the section entitled "From The Publisher" at the end of the book.

Conclusion

Keep in mind our definition of estate planning:

"During my life and after my death, I want to control and distribute my property in the manner I desire, minimizing all fees, taxes and court interference, preserving for myself, my family, and those I choose, the estate I have worked so hard to create."

If it doesn't fulfill that definition, then the plan is not complete.

3

WHAT ARE THE WAYS OF HOLDING TITLE?

As stated previously, proper planning requires addressing a multitude of issues and answering many questions. It also involves gathering data concerning your present financial situation. And in that process, the question of ownership arises. How is your home titled? In whose names are your bank accounts? Who owns your stocks and bonds? How are your brokerage accounts titled?

Most people give little or no thought as to how they title their assets. It is usually done as a matter of convenience. Nevertheless, the consequences of your actions can be enormous, and can leave the door open for the dragons.

Holding title to property, such as real estate, securities, bank accounts, automobiles, etc. seems so simple that we hardly give it a second thought.

Attorney: How do you want your new home titled?

Client: In both of our names.

Attorney: No problem.

It is so simple, it's scary. Unfortunately, it's too simple. When decisions as important as this are made without sufficient

13

thought, it can result in mistakes that create future hardships.

Let's review the various ways to hold property, along with the workings and ramifications of each.

SOLE OWNER

How titled - As a sole owner, you hold the title in your name:

"William S. York."

Control during life - Since you are the only owner of the property, you maintain 100% control over it. You can do whatever you desire with that property: sell it, use it as collateral, or give it away. You, and you alone, have complete control.

Disposition upon death - As sole owner of this property, you can pass it in any manner you desire. While many of the other forms have built-in procedures upon death, this passes one of two ways: according to your will or according to the rules of your state (if you don't have a will).

Advantages - Sole ownership has the following advantages.

- It is simple to establish; it doesn't require anybody's signature but your own.

- It is easy to control; you don't have to worry about the approval of other parties.

- The property receives a "stepped-up" basis upon your death. This subject will be discussed in Chapter 17.

- It passes according to the terms in your will.

Disadvantages - Sole ownership also has disadvantages.

- Since you alone control the property, transfers during a period of disability are difficult, and often require living probate.

- The property must go through probate upon your death.

- You must make specific arrangements for the property to pass upon death.

- The entire value is included in your estate upon death.

- There are higher settlement expenses upon death than other methods of ownership.

TENANTS IN COMMON

How titled - As tenants in common, you own the property with some other person or persons:

"William S. York and Allen M. Hutchins."

Control during life - If there are two owners, you each own half. Many people refer to this as an undivided interest. Even though there may be several owners, you alone have control over your own portion to do as you want. You can sell or pledge your portion, but you have no control over the entire property. Total control is possible only when all parties agree.

Disposition upon death - Upon your death, you can leave your portion to whomever you desire in your will, if you have one. Otherwise, it will pass according to the laws of your state.

Advantages - Tenants in common has several advantages.

- You have complete control over your interest.

- It is an effective technique for income splitting.

- It passes according to your instructions in your will.

- It receives a "stepped-up" basis on the decedent's share (see chapter 17).

Disadvantages - Tenants in common also has its disadvantages.

- It can get cumbersome if there are many tenants.

- Transfer of your share is difficult if you become disabled.

- Your share of the property must go through probate upon your death.

- You have control over only your interest; you have no voice in what your co-tenants do.

- You can easily end up with an incompatible co-owner upon either the death of the present co-owner or upon the sale of his or her share.

- It is subject to administrative expenses upon your death.

JOINT TENANTS WITH RIGHTS OF SURVIVORSHIP

How titled - With joint tenants with rights of survivorship, you own the property with another person or persons:

"William S. and Patricia F. York, JTWROS."

Control during life - Each of the joint tenants owns 100 percent of the asset. Yet neither tenant alone has control over the property. Make sense? I hope not because it shouldn't. It's one of many contradictions in the law - some call it a legal fiction. It is a difficult issue when dealing with control. If you want to sell your share, while it is cumbersome and difficult, it possibly can be done with the court's intervention. As a rule, it is easiest to sell when all parties sign. But as an individual tenant, you are limited by the realities of law. While you might be able to sell your portion, the person buying it may never realize anything, because the last survivor gets it.

Disposition upon death - The factor that separates this type of property from all other types is what happens upon death. When this type of property is properly titled, which means including the phrase (or similar phrase) "Joint Tenants With Rights of Survivorship", the last surviving tenant gets the property. If you, your husband, and your brother own an office building in this form, and you and your husband die, then your brother will automatically end up with the property. It is a classic case of whoever lives the longest wins.

Advantages - The advantages of joint tenancy are as follows.

- It is easy to establish; no special paperwork is required.

- Joint tenancy is inexpensive to set up.

- Property avoids probate until the death of the last tenant.

- The property automatically goes to the surviving tenant(s).

- There are no administrative expenses at death of the first tenant.

Disadvantages - The disadvantages of joint tenancy are many.

- Neither tenant has full control over the property.

- Neither tenant has control over the disposition of the property at his or her death.

- It can create potential gift problems except when the joint tenant is a spouse.

- All the property is at risk in the event of a judgment against any of the joint tenants.

- The property has to go through probate at the death of the last tenant.

- Only part of the property receives a "stepped-up" basis upon the death of the first joint tenant. (See Chapter 17.)

- The property has to go through a living probate in the event of mental incapacity of one of the tenants.

While joint tenants with rights of survivorship is a very popular form of ownership, it is also potentially the most dangerous. The next chapter is devoted entirely to a discussion of this form of ownership.

TENANTS BY THE ENTIRETY

How titled - Tenants by the entirety is used in a limited number of states and is only for titling property between husband and wife.

"William and Patricia York, Tenants by the Entirety."

Control during life - Neither tenant alone has any control during his or her life. This type of ownership can only be severed with the consent of both parties.

Disposition upon death - Like joint tenants, this form of ownership allows for the survivorship feature that automatically passes the property to the surviving spouse.

Advantages - Tenants by the entirety has several advantages.

- It is easy to establish.

- The property automatically passes to the surviving spouse upon death.

- It avoids probate at first death.

Disadvantages - There are also several disadvantages.

- You have no control over the property without the approval of your spouse.

- The property goes through probate upon the death of the second spouse.

- You have no control over the disposition of the property at your death; it automatically goes to the survivor.

- Only half of the property receives a "stepped-up" basis at the first death.

- This ownership form provides no planning flexibility.

LIFE ESTATE

How titled - The life estate is unique to certain states. With this form of ownership, one person leaves another person, usually a spouse, a right to live in and enjoy certain property, after which it goes to a named party, usually children.

Control during life - The party with the life estate has no control over the property during his or her life, only the right to use it.

Disposition upon death - The property automatically passes to the beneficiaries of the life estate.

Advantages - There are only two advantages to a life estate.

- It provides the life tenant with a place in which to live.

- It avoids probate at death.

Disadvantages - There are several significant disadvantages.

- The life tenant must be prudent in the care of property in order to remain in it.

- The life tenant is responsible for any expense in maintaining the property.

- The life tenant cannot borrow against the property for maintenance, or any other emergency.

- The life tenant is at the mercy of the heirs.

For these reasons, most attorneys avoid the life estate and instead recommend some form of trust to provide more flexibility.

REVOCABLE LIVING TRUST

How titled - A Revocable Living Trust is a special form of ownership in which property is titled in the name of the trust.

A single trust might be titled:

> "William S. York, trustee, or his successors in trust, under the William S. York Living Trust, dated October 10, 1991."

A joint trust might be titled:

> "William S. York and Patricia F. York, trustees, or their successors in trust, under the William and Patricia York Living Trust, dated October 10, 1991."

Control during life - The trustees (presumably the husband and wife), have complete control over the property during their lives. They can cancel or amend the trust anytime they desire. If they are joint trustees, transactions will require both signatures. A single trust operates like "sole ownership" property; a joint trust operates like "joint tenancy" property.

Disposition at death - The property in the trust will pass according to the instructions contained in the trust document itself.

Advantages - The living trust has several advantages.

- It cares for you while you are alive; no special arrangements need be made in the event of your physical or mental incapacity.

- You name your own trustees.

- Property titled in the trust avoids probate upon all deaths.

- You can leave your own set of instructions in the trust for the care of yourself and your family.

- It is difficult to contest.

- It is a good vehicle for caring for minor and handicapped children.

- It can help save estate taxes for married couples.

- It keeps your affairs private.

Disadvantages - The living trust also has several disadvantages.

- Initially, it is the most expensive form of property ownership.

- You must transfer your property into the trust in order to avoid probate.

- It is more complicated in its operation than other forms.

- A joint trust requires the approval of both trustees before disposing of property.

- In a joint trust, only half the property receives a stepped-up basis at the first death.

IRREVOCABLE LIVING TRUST

How titled - An Irrevocable Living Trust is a special form of ownership in which the property is titled in the name of a trust:

"Robert Hayes, trustee, or his successor in trust, under the William S. York Irrevocable Trust, dated October 10, 1991."

Control during life - The property in the trust is under the control of the trustee, who cannot be the grantor (trustmaker).

Unlike the revocable living trust, where you can be the trustee of your own trust and have complete control over the property, the irrevocable trust is just the opposite. While you can name the trustees initially, you have no control whatsoever over your property. As the name implies, the trust cannot be revoked.

Disposition upon death - The property in the trust will pass according to the instructions contained in the trust document.

Advantages - The irrevocable trust has several advantages.

- It reduces the size of the estate (and thus the taxes) of the trustmaker by removing the property from his or her estate.

- It further reduces those potential taxes by removing the growth on those assets from the estate.

- The trust can be drawn to provide income for the trustmaker.

- Depending upon state law, the property is protected from creditors of the grantor.

- Depending on its provisions, it could be used to protect assets in the case of a nursing home stay. (See Chapters 23 and 24.)

- An irrevocable trust can be used to hold assets for minors.

Disadvantages - The irrevocable trust has several disadvantages.

- Once the trust has been established and funded, you have no control whatsoever over any aspect of the property in the trust.

- In case of emergency, the trust cannot be revoked.

- Because you are irrevocably transferring the property, it is subject to gift tax implications.

COMMUNITY PROPERTY

Not to pick on my friends out west, but there are always some people who like to gum up the works. That is what we face in community property states. There are a handful of states that have a different set of rules when it comes to property. Therefore, such issues as property ownership, trusts, gifts, life insurance, and gifts to minors need to be addressed for those folks. Even though all these states are considered community property states, each one has its own particular rules. Check with your estate planning attorney and other professionals to determine how your respective state's rules apply to you.

The community property states - The following states have special rules which dictate the ownership rights of property between husband and wife:

Arizona	New Mexico
California	Texas
Idaho	Washington
Louisiana	Wisconsin
Nevada	

The rules of ownership - The basis of ownership in these states is determined by when the property was acquired. Whereas in most states, property can belong to one or the other spouse, it is a bit different here. Two kinds of property are involved.

- **Separate property** is that property which was acquired prior to the marriage. As long as it remains titled in one spouse's name, it retains separate property status. Additionally, if one spouse inherits property or receives it as a result of a gift, it is separate property belonging to that one spouse.

- **Community property** is that property which was acquired after marriage. In this case, each spouse owns a 50% undivided interest in the property. It doesn't matter who earned the money. It doesn't matter which spouse made the purchase. It belongs equally to each spouse. In addition, if separate property is sold and the proceeds are added to community property, then it takes on the characteristics of community property and is owned 50/50 by each spouse. If the title of separate property is eventually titled in the name of both spouses, it becomes community property.

Passing property at death - Unlike joint tenancy property which automatically passes to the other spouse, community property operates like tenants in common. Each party can pass his or her interest as he or she desires. As a result, community property passes according to the deceased spouse's will. If you haven't taken steps to express your wishes in a will (or a trust), the property will pass according to the intestate laws of your state. Since the surviving spouse already owns half of the property, the deceased spouse has the right to leave his or her half to anyone he or she chooses. But if he wants it to go to the surviving spouse, it is imperative that he has a will (or trust) stating those intentions.

Gifting - While a spouse in a non-community property state can make a separate gift out of his or her own property, in community property states gifts made from community property are considered joint gifts. In fact, some states prohibit one spouse from making a gift from community property without the consent of the other spouse. One major difference between community and non-community states comes in the paperwork for joint or "split" gifts. In non-community property states, a split gift of $20,000 from both spouses requires a federal gift tax return, although no tax is due. However, in community property states such a gift is considered a $10,000 gift from each spouse. Therefore, no gift tax return need be filed. If a gift exceeds the $10,000 exclusion, their lifetime exemption will be reduced by one-half of the gift over the $10,000 exemption. (Gifting is covered in Chapter 17.)

Revocable Living Trusts - Whereas in non-community property states separate trusts can be used for married couples, in community property states joint trusts are almost always used. Remember, the community property belongs to both spouses. You cannot split the property and put it in separate trusts. As a result, a joint trust is used with both husband and wife as trustmakers. Additionally, the trust will include language to the effect that in the event of divorce or revocation of the trust (and each spouse should have the right to revoke), the property will come out of the trust as it went in, thus protecting the interests of each spouse.

Conclusion

Review your property and make sure that the form of title coincides with your goals. Think about why the property is titled the way it is, and ask yourself if that is what you really want. As you can see, the ramifications are many.

4

WHAT ARE THE PROBLEMS WITH JOINT TENANCY?

To the average couple, joint tenancy is the best way to hold property. It is popular because it's easy and inexpensive. However, knowledgeable planners know there are dragons waiting to pounce.

JTWROS (Joint Tenants With Rights Of Survivorship) is so simple because it sounds so good.....''I love you, honey, and I want you to own this stock when I die.'' But it can also create some problems. It has been called the poor man's estate plan because it costs nothing to establish and it avoids probate, and thus attorneys. Unfortunately, in their desire to save attorney's fees, many people take the wrong steps - cutting off their noses to spite their faces. And the dragons are waiting.

Let's go back to our definition of estate planning.

"During my life and after my death, I want to control and distribute my property in the manner I desire, minimizing all fees, taxes and court interference, preserving for myself, my family, and those I choose, the estate I have worked so hard to create."

Does joint tenancy fulfill this definition? It might save attorney fees and avoid court interference since it bypasses probate (at least at the first death). But does it really allow you control over your property during your life and after your death? You would probably answer "yes." I disagree.

PROBLEMS WITH JOINT OWNERSHIP

No control over property at death - One of the major disadvantages with joint ownership is one that most people never consider: you have no control over the ultimate disposition of the property. Sure, you can assume the other joint tenant will receive it. But what you can not be certain of is who will ultimately end up with it.

> *Bob Miller and JoAnn Sullivan, brother and sister, owned a condo on the Gulf that both families shared. For convenience, they titled it "Bob Miller and JoAnn Sullivan, JTWROS". Two years after it was purchased, Bob died. Who got Bob's half? His wife? No. His kids? No. His sister, JoAnn, became sole owner. Remember, it passed to the surviving tenant.*

● ● ●

> *Three businessmen owned a building together. It was titled "Bob Miller, and Bert Levine, and Ted Lee, Joint Tenants." Who owned that property? Remember in the last chapter I said that they each owned 100% of it! What happened when Bob died? Did his wife then own his share? No! Bert and Ted then owned the entire building. And if Bert dies, Ted will own the whole thing. What a deal! What a disaster!*

No control over property while you are alive - Another problem with joint tenancy is you have no control while you are alive. Because there are at least two tenants, all must sign before doing anything. This can be a blessing or a problem. If the joint owners don't trust each other, then it is helpful to require both signatures. However, if only spouses are involved, we hope there is a trusting relationship.

Since every transaction requires all tenants to sign, what happens if one is unable to sign due to a physical or mental disability? The other must go to through a process known as "living probate." This is discussed in detail in Chapter 22.

> *Bob and Mary Bork owned their home together. Bob was in an accident and ended up in a coma. Mary wanted to sell the house. Enter the dragon. Both names were on the deed, and Bob couldn't sign. Mary visited her attorney. He informed Mary that she should apply for guardianship of Bob (called the conservator in some states). This caused her to go through a process that was not only embarrassing, but expensive as well.*

• • •

> *Julio and Maria Gonzales had a brokerage account as joint tenants. While Mr. Gonzales was out of the country attending a convention, Maria needed some money. She called her broker and requested a check from their joint money market account. It arrived in the mail, payable to "Julio Gonzales and Maria Gonzales, JTWROS." Maria went to the bank and explained to the teller that her husband was out of the country. The teller politely informed her that the check could not be cashed unless it was endorsed by both parties.*

Now, I am not so naive as to think that spouses don't sign each other's names on checks. Nevertheless, it's not legal. A bank won't cash a check if they are aware of the forgery.

Much of this is probably news to you. Joint tenancy is so common that most people don't think that there can be any problems. But as you will see throughout the book, proper planning involves identifying potential problems in advance, and then taking the necessary steps to avoid them.

Doesn't avoid probate - only postpones it - One of the main reasons clients tell me they hold property as joint tenants is that they want to avoid probate. Again, this sounds good. But is it true? Does joint tenancy property really avoid probate? Yes and no. While it does avoid probate at the death of the first spouse, the property will have to go through probate at the second death. So you have not avoided probate, you have just postponed it.

Jane and Ralph McCall owned their home and a brokerage account as joint tenants. They had 4 children. Jane was killed in an accident. The property automatically passed to Ralph at Jane's death. At that point the property was in Ralph's name alone. Upon his death, it will pass according to his will. But whether he dies with or without a will doesn't matter. The property must still go through probate.

You can see that although joint property avoids probate, it only does so when at least one joint tenant survives. At some point, the last tenant is going to die, and the property will go through probate. Joint tenancy, therefore, only postpones the inevitable.

Property can pass to unintended heirs - An additional problem with joint tenancy is your heirs may not end up with your property.

Bob and Susan Miller owned their home as Joint Tenants. Bob died, and Susan became sole owner. Two years later she remarried. After a few more years, her new husband suggested that she put the house in both their names. After all, "You do love me, don't you, honey?" "Of course, I do." At that point, the owners of the house were Stan and Susan Johnson, JTWROS. Then Susan died. Who owned the house? Bob's kids? Not on your life! Stan owned it, and Bob and Susan's kids were left out. I am sure that is not what Bob would have wanted.

Results in problems in the event of disability - One of the problems often overlooked is what will happen in the event of mental incapacity of one of the tenants. What happens if you own your home jointly with your spouse and he or she becomes mentally incapacitated? This is a subject in itself and will be covered in detail in Chapter 22.

Can result in estate taxes for party not receiving property - This can be one of the cruelest problems of all. Let's review our first case:

Bob Miller and JoAnn Sullivan, brother and sister, owned a condo on the Gulf that both families shared. For convenience, they titled

*it "Bob Miller and JoAnn Sullivan, JTWROS". Two years after it
was purchased, Bob died and his sister, JoAnn, ended up with all
the property. In addition to the fact that Bob's family did not
receive his share of the condo, there was another problem: his
half of the condo was included in his estate for estate-tax
purposes. Talk about a kick in the head!*

JOINT TENANCY WITH A CHILD

Anytime I discuss the problems of joint tenancy, there is
always the client who says, "That's no problem. When my
husband dies, I'll just put this property in joint tenancy with my
daughter, Jill. Then when I die, she will automatically receive
it without going through probate."

Sounds great. Of course, this assumes that you and your
husband won't die together. But I'll give you the benefit of the
doubt and follow through with your scenario.

*Ralph and Carol McNeil maintained several brokerage accounts
as joint tenants. Ralph died and left the accounts to Carol, free
of probate. Carol, wanting to make sure the accounts would
avoid probate at her death, then changed the title to "Carol McNeil
and Jill Baker (her daughter), JTWROS."*

Are there potential problems here? I can think of a few.

Creates a potential gift - By titling the accounts in joint tenancy
with Jill, Carol has made a gift to Jill. Now I don't want to get
ahead of myself because gifting is discussed in Chapter 17. But
when you put property into joint ownership with someone other
than your spouse, there are potential gift tax problems.
According to the IRS, Carol made a gift of 50% of the value to
Jill when she put her name on the title, assuming it was a
completed gift at the time.

Opens property to lawsuit against either party - What if Jill gets
sued? Okay, Jill is a model citizen. She is so perfect, she didn't
even need braces. But something bad could happen. Let's

imagine the following scenario.

> *One rainy day Jill is driving down the street, hits a deep puddle, and her car spins into the path of a school bus full of cute elementary kids. The bus comes to a sudden halt in a ditch and a dozen kids are hospitalized. About a month later, the lawsuits come rolling in. Poor Jill, model citizen, perfect wife and mother, is the defendant in a dozen lawsuits. Now her assets are at risk, and guess what are some of her assets? That's right! The brokerage accounts on which she is a joint tenant with her mother are included. And not just 50% of the value is at risk, but all of it. Carol risked losing all of her money by putting it in a joint account with Jill.*

Property at risk in divorce - What happens to the money if Jill gets divorced? Her husband can claim (and probably rightly so) that the money is part of the marital estate.

Passing property to siblings - Let's assume none of that happens. Everything goes according to plans. Carol holds the property jointly with Jill, and then Carol dies. Again, it's imagination time.

> *Upon Carol's death, Jill receives the money. She remembers her mother's wishes. Carol wanted her to share the proceeds with her brothers. Now Jill could be mean and say to her brothers, "Where were you when Mom needed help? Where were you when Mom had to be driven to the doctor? Where were you when I had to pay for a nurse? I deserve all the money." Jill could do that because the money is all hers. Carol left it to her as the surviving tenant. (Since a will doesn't control joint tenancy property, it doesn't matter what instructions the will contains.)*

> *But wait, Jill is the model daughter, so she gives her brothers their shares. Another dragon. Know what it is? Since the money belongs to Jill, she makes a gift when she gives her brothers their shares.*

Inadvertent gifting between family members happens all the time. The problem is that most people don't realize that transferring property can create problems. However, it can, as we will see in Chapter 17 when we discuss gifting.

Conclusion

The fact is that joint tenancy, that bastion of American estate planning, can be a disaster waiting to happen. This is one of those areas of estate planning in which people blindly act without considering the consequences, because they don't realize that there might be unfavorable repercussions. But there can be, and you should be aware of them.

And, by the way, there is another potential disaster: minor children ending up with the property. That subject is covered in Chapter 11.

Let's go back to our definition now.

"During my life and after my death, I want to control and distribute my property in the manner I desire, minimizing all fees, taxes and court interference, preserving for myself, my family, and those I choose, the estate I have worked so hard to create."

Is there much about joint tenancy that meets this definition? I don't think so, due to all the potential problems.

5

WHAT ARE THE ADVANTAGES & DISADVANTAGES OF WILLS?

As far back as I can remember, attorneys and estate planners have preached the importance of wills. Publication after publication has exhorted the general public to make a will. They have told us the problems of dying without one and indicated that prudent planning requires a will.

That theory was shattered in 1965 when Norman Dacey wrote the best seller, *How to Avoid Probate.* His book started a revolution away from probate that, if anything, is even stronger today.

Dying without a will

As often as we've been told that wills are necessary, only thirty percent of the population has one. The vast majority die "intestate", which means without a will. But not to worry. Even if you die intestate, you do technically have a will:

> *"I, being of questionable mind, hereby instruct the legislature of my state, in it's infinite wisdom, to determine where my assets should go upon my death. I fully understand that this will occur because I have chosen not to make that decision myself."*

As you can see, if you don't have a will, your property passes according to the laws of your state. I'm sure it's a comforting thought to know that your state legislature has a plan for the distribution of your assets.

The intestate laws of virtually every state provide that the spouse and children get shares of the estate. The makeup of that split depends upon the state and number of children. If there are no children, then the surviving spouse may have to split the estate with the deceased's parents or siblings.

One of the real problems, as we see throughout this book, is the fact that minor children often inherit property. Unfortunately, or fortunately, minor children cannot own property. The mere fact that they are left part of your estate, under the watchful eye of the probate court, means that your spouse, or the guardian, might not be able to do what he/she wants. This puts quite a burden on that person. The following case illustrates much of what is bad about intestacy.

> *Robert Ellsworth died without a will (intestate). He left a wife, Betty, and four children, along with a home and some certificates of deposits (registered in his name alone). Where Betty lived, since she was just one of five remaining beneficiaries, she was only entitled to receive 20% of the intestate property. The remaining 80% was divided equally among her four daughters.*
>
> *Betty was appointed guardian of her children. The probate court had very definite limitations on what could be done with their share of the money. It could be invested only in government bonds or FDIC insured accounts. If her children had needs that required large expenditures, she had to get the approval of the court, which in her county was difficult. Plus, she needed an attorney every time she went to court. She was also required to provide an annual accounting of the funds. Her late husband had promised her oldest daughter a car when she reached sixteen. The court said no. In fact, the court said no to a lot of things.*
>
> *Early on, she thought about putting the daughters' shares of the home into her name in case she wanted to sell it. But her state laws required petitioning the court, advertising it, and waiting a specified period of time. It also would have resulted in significant*

attorneys fees. She couldn't afford to spend the money, so she decided not to change the title until the time came to sell.

When that time came, her children's ages were eighteen to twenty-three. She went to each of the children and asked them to sign over their respective shares of the house. All agreed except the oldest child, Pat. She maintained that she was entitled to 20% of the proceeds of the house and refused to sign.

To make matters worse, Pat threatened to get an attorney and sue Betty for her share of the social security benefits that had been paid over the years. Betty had no choice but to give Pat 20% of the proceeds. They haven't spoken since.

This is but one tragic case illustrating how the lack of proper planning can be disastrous for the surviving family members. It illustrates but a few of the problems that can be caused by dying intestate.

Remember what was said in the preface: *we don't think we have a problem until we have a problem.* As long as Robert was alive, everything was fine. It didn't matter that he didn't have a will. How the house was owned was irrelevant. However, once his death occurred, the entire picture changed.

One of the purposes of estate planning is to ensure that your assets are distributed the way you want, not in some arbitrary manner. Dying intestate is like trying to walk through a mine field blindfolded. You might get to the other side, or you might get blown up along the way.

What is a will?

Back to the beginning. We all know what a will, or Last Will and Testament as it is officially titled, does. It is a written, properly witnessed and notarized document in which you express exactly how you want your property to pass. You also name an executor (or executrix if female) whose job it is to make sure that your wishes are followed and that your property is disposed of as you desire.

One confusing aspect of wills is that each state has its own complicated set of rules that must be precisely followed for a will to be valid. There are regulations concerning when and how the executor needs to be bonded, nominating guardians for minor or disabled children, laws of succession, disinheriting spouses and children, contesting wills, holographic (handwritten) wills, the effect of divorce, changes in the wills, etc. You should consult your attorney for information regarding your state.

ADVANTAGES OF WILLS

Vehicle for passing property - A will gives you a means for passing your property to the people you desire. You can leave your assets to a spouse, children, charity - virtually anyone you desire. However, there are some limits. Different states have varying laws on the treatment of a spouse and children.

Can provide interim funds - In some states, a will can provide for interim funds for your family during probate. This can, to a limited extent, ensure that the family has money with which to pay their living expenses while the estate is in probate.

Care for minor children - A testamentary trust within the will can be used to care for minor children or to provide a stream of income for family members. Since children cannot own property (minor children are covered in Chapter 11), the trust will name an individual or individuals (known as trustees) to handle the funds for the children's benefit. The remaining funds will be distributed to the children either at the age of majority or at the ages specified in the trust.

Reduce estate taxes - A properly drawn testamentary trust can help a married couple reduce estate taxes. Estate taxes are covered in detail in Chapters 7 and 10.

Leave property to charity - A will can specify property to a charity or charitable organizations. Chapter 21 covers Charitable Remainder Trusts, a preferred way for donating property.

Nominate guardians - A will allows you to name guardians to care for your minor children. If you have minor or handicapped children, you need to ensure that the person of your choice will rear them. Without a will, this choice is in the hands of the court. Note, however, that while the court gives consideration to your preference, it is possible that you may be overruled.

> *Donna McGee was a divorcee with custody of her two children. Five years after she remarried, she was killed in an accident. In her will, she named her current husband as guardian of her minor children. However, her ex-husband decided he wanted custody of his children. His argument was that he was the natural father, and there was no valid reason to deny him custody. The court agreed, and set aside the desires of the mother.*

The courts try to give custody to the natural parent whenever possible. Even though the court may, for what it considers valid reasons, go against your choice, you should still express your desires in your will.

Inexpensive to prepare - As a rule, wills tend to be inexpensive to prepare. I always get a kick out of picking up a paper when I'm traveling around the country and seeing advertisements for low-cost wills. I don't know how attorneys make a profit preparing wills for fifty or one-hundred dollars. There are some who say the only reason the attorney can afford to do so is that he or she hopes to make up the loss by probating the will. Different attorneys have told me different things, so I can only guess each individual attorney's motive.

DISADVANTAGES OF WILLS

A will, however, has several disadvantages. But understand that the following are not disadvantages compared to dying intestate, but disadvantages relative to other types of planning that will be discussed later.

Won't help in the case of your disability - Since a will only takes effect upon your death, it can't take care of you during a period of disability. In this case, we are talking about a mental instability that would preclude you from handling your own financial affairs. This is discussed in detail in Chapter 22.

Guarantees probate - Contrary to what many people believe, a will has to be probated, which can be time consuming and costly. For a married couple, it can mean two probates (covered in the next chapter). If you add two possible living probates, (discussed in Chapter 22), you could end up with four probates.

Doesn't control all your property - A will usually doesn't control all of your property. Certain holdings pass outside your will.

- **Jointly owned property** automatically passes to the other joint tenant, no matter what your will says.

- **Life insurance** automatically passes to the named beneficiary. The only way your will would control life insurance proceeds is if the beneficiary of the insurance is your estate.

- **Retirement plans** automatically pass to the named beneficiary. As with insurance, only retirement benefits payable to your estate would pass according to your will.

- **Living trust** property passes according to the instructions in the trust, as covered in Chapters 8 and 9.

Takes your family public - Wills take your family public. If you have any doubt about this, just go down to your local probate court and review the wills on file. They are available to the media, the curious, or anyone who might want to take advantage of circumstances.

Joanne and Roger Walker owned what they considered a modest farm. Over the years, they had purchased substantial equipment, thanks to their friendly banker. When Roger died, their banker became not-so-friendly. It seems the banker didn't have much confidence in Joanne's ability to continue the operation. With great reluctance, he called the loans. This made it necessary for Joanne to sell some equipment and land. However, because Roger's will was public, people interested in buying were able to go to the courthouse and learn the details of his finances. The end result was that Joanne received only a fraction of the value and had to sell the bulk of the equipment and property to repay the banks. If the information hadn't been public, this might not have happened.

Different interpretation in different states - Moving to another state can create problems. Although your will is probably valid in any state, its interpretation depends on the state where it is probated. What "share and share alike" means in Colorado may be different from what it means in Pennsylvania.

Easy to contest - Wills can easily be contested. The two D's, death and disability, seem to bring out the worst in people. I think it was Benjamin Franklin who said that you never really know what a person is like until you share an inheritance with him. We have all heard the horror stories of family members who have successfully contested a will. When a will is probated, the executor or executrix notifies potential heirs. This opens the door for a will contest. There are several grounds that can be used in contests, such as undue influence over the maker, improper execution, fraud, unsound mind, mental instability, etc. In many cases, it is irrelevant whether the contest is valid. The rightful heirs, not wanting to take the time and money to fight a will contest, may settle just to get the matter concluded.

John and Elizabeth Benson had two sons, Chad and Randy. While Chad had given them no problems, Randy was always in trouble. In addition, he was extremely cruel to John and Eliza-beth, to the point that they had ceased trying to continue a relationship with him. In their wills, they left virtually all their estate to Chad, with only 10% going to Randy. Upon their deaths, Randy contested the will. He said that his parents were unduly influenced by Chad and didn't understand what they were doing. He told Chad that he would tie up the estate in court for years if he didn't share a larger portion with him. Chad, not wanting to go through the time and expense of fighting his brother, agreed to give Randy 25% of the money.

What most people don't realize when it comes to a contested will is that the validity of the case is not necessarily relevant. The fact is that frequently, as illustrated above, the rightful heirs settle only because it will be cheaper and less time consuming.

The experience with contested wills is similar to that of a lawsuit. Many insurance companies agree to settle a case rather than fight it in court. The reason is that it can cost more to defend than to settle. The same is true with will contests.

MAKING YOUR WILL MORE EFFECTIVE

There are several steps you can take to make sure your will doesn't come up against one of these planning problems.

Noncontest clause - You might consider a "noncontest" clause to take care of the problem mentioned above. This clause effectively eliminates an heir's inheritance if he or she contests the will. In spite of this, however, a probate judge can still allow the contest by ruling that the "noncontest" clause is "contrary to public policy."

Keep your will current - Throughout our lives, changes occur. In most cases, people don't think to update their wills. But there are changes that need to be reflected in your will.

- Divorce is rampant in this country. In some states a divorce invalidates a will. In others, it has no effect. In either case, the result is bad. In the first, property passes according to intestate laws. In the second, property can go to the ex-spouse.

- Grown children become disabled. This can make it impossible for him or her to handle property.

- Children or other heirs die. This can, in some states, invalidate the will. At a minimum, it can result in changes in the distribution provisions.

- People move to different states. This can result in different interpretations of the will.

- Children are born. Again, this can require changes in distribution plans.

- The size and makeup of assets change. You may be able to include more people in your will, or you may have to take into consideration estate taxes.

- Executors and guardians die. This will leave those important decisions up to the court.

You can handle these changes one of two ways: either by drawing up a new will or by adding a "codicil" which amends your current will. Discuss this with your attorney to determine the best route for you.

Self proving will - One of the inconvenient steps during probate is proving that a will is valid. This can involve having to contact those individuals who witnessed the will.

One way around this problem is with the "self-proving" will. With a self-proving will, when the original document is drafted, the testator (person who makes the will) and the witnesses also declare and sign before a notary public that they did, in fact, witness each other signing and witnessing the will. While this sounds a little convoluted, it should have the effect of preventing the time-consuming and costly process of dragging in the original witnesses. It boils down to taking a few extra minutes when the will is prepared to avoid possible major headaches for the executor later.

Careful choosing of executor - The natural tendency of most people is to pick his or her spouse to be the executor or executrix of the will. While this is the easiest, and initially least costly because it will save executor fees, it could cause problems down the road. The job of executor is not one to be taken lightly. An unsophisticated executor, one who has no business or financial experience, can be taken advantage of by someone during the probate process. This can result in unnecessary fees and expenses which milk the estate of valuable funds. In the course of trying to save a few dollars in executor fees, thousands can be lost to inexperience.

Old wills interpreted under old laws - Before the Economic Recovery Tax Act of 1981 (ERTA), only one-half of your estate could be passed to your spouse estate-tax free. ERTA provided for the 100% marital deduction, under which you can pass 100% of your property estate tax-free to your spouse. However, if you have a will drafted prior to September 13, 1981, chances are that it will be interpreted under the old rules. To remedy this potentially costly hazard, see your attorney and bring your estate plan up-to-date.

Conclusion

How do wills fulfill our definition of estate planning?

"During my life and after my death, I want to control and distribute my property in the manner I desire, minimizing all fees, taxes and court interference, preserving for myself, my family, and those I choose, the estate I have worked so hard to create."

Not too well, in my opinion. They alone don't take care of you during your life, they don't guarantee you will be able to distribute your property as you desire, and they certainly don't minimize fees and court interference.

6

HOW DOES THE PROBATE SYSTEM WORK?

If there is one subject that has caused controversy in modern estate planning it is probate. In the mid-1960's, Norman Dacey's book, *How to Avoid Probate*, was a best seller. It struck a chord that is still resounding today. He initiated a change in the way Americans viewed probate. Suddenly, they wanted to avoid probate at all costs.

Since then, a number of states have instituted changes in the probate system. Many have adopted the Uniform Probate Code, which made probate laws somewhat uniform in those states. Nevertheless, probate avoidance is still one of the main advantages expounded in the marketing of living trusts. "Avoid the Evils of Probate" shout the advertisements. And people, having heard of or personally experienced how bad probate can be, flock to these seminars.

What probate is

Probate is the process by which the debts of the deceased are paid, and the title to his property is changed to the heirs specified in his will. If there is no will, the property will pass according to state law. All property, other than that listed above, goes through probate, whether or not there is a will. This process is performed under the watchful eye of the probate judge, who may have been appointed or elected, and who may or may not have a law degree.

Is probate so bad?

That's the $64,000 question. If you listen to some of the doomsayers, it is terrible. If you listen to some advocates, there is nothing to it. Obviously, the truth lies somewhere in between. It depends on your jurisdiction, type of property you own, etc. Nevertheless, probate is only one issue in planning and should be viewed with all the other matters affecting your estate.

Assets avoiding probate

Before initiating our discussion of probate, let's review the assets that automatically avoid probate.

- Assets held in joint tenancy.

- Life insurance proceeds when they are paid to a named beneficiary and not to the estate of the deceased.

- Proceeds from a qualified retirement plan (pension, profit sharing, IRA, Keogh, SEP, etc.) when the funds go directly to a named beneficiary.

- Property titled in a trust.

The parties

Although the probate judge presides over the process, your estate needs an executor (executrix, if female). This is the person you name who is responsible for handling the paperwork for the estate. If you have no will, the court will make this decision for you, as well as other decisions you have chosen not to make. The job of the executor or executrix is to get your estate to the point where it can be closed and your assets distributed. Of course, since you are working through the courts, the executor or executrix probably needs an attorney to assist him or her. This can be costly.

The process

While the stated purpose of probate is to properly distribute the property of the deceased to the rightful parties, that is only the end result of an entire process. There is a chain of events that must occur first. The exact order of those events will depend upon the particular state.

Without going into great detail, the first thing that must be done is to have the **will read and filed** in the probate court. This filing can be done immediately or at a convenient time. However, if an interested party (creditor, heir) is in a hurry, he or she can petition the court to begin the process. Otherwise, the executor/executrix will petition the court to have the will admitted. Once that is done, the process starts and the fun begins.

The property must be **inventoried and appraised.** This is laborious at times because some property is difficult to value. Additionally, people sometimes die with piles of old securities. Most times, obtaining the value is easy. In many cases, however, name changes or mergers can make it difficult. Most investment professionals know that US Steel is now USX Corporation, and International Harvester is Navistar. But many obscure companies have changed their names and become difficult to trace.

While publicly traded stocks and bonds are the easiest to value, obtaining the value on privately held companies, where no active market exists, is extremely difficult. Medical practices, partnerships and business ventures are also difficult to value. (This is covered in Chapter 27.)

Newspaper notices in the local legal publication must be run to allow creditors and heirs the opportunity to file any claims they might have against the estate. This is the opportunity for disgruntled heirs to contest the will. The heirs and creditors have a certain period of time (usually six months) to submit their claims and/or challenge the will. Talk about dragons!

The **validity** of the will must be ascertained. Each state has its own set of rules concerning the way a will must be drafted. It is at this point that it will be determined if those rules were properly followed. Was the will properly drafted? Was it duly witnessed? Is it, in fact, the last will, or are there others? Was the deceased of sound mind?

By now, all the inventories should be completed, valuations ascertained, creditors verified, disgruntled heirs heard. Although it might sound simple here, in some estates it can go on for years. Once this is completed, and assuming there are no problems, it is time to begin **settling the estate.**

The final steps

Taxes and debts must be paid. There are income taxes that must be filed for both the deceased and his estate. It might be necessary to file estate tax returns.

A **final accounting** is filed with the court along with the executor/executrix's **petitions** to allow for final distribution. (What happens in the event property is left to a minor is covered in Chapter 11). Once accomplished, a **final discharge** can be obtained.

The probate process, although long and costly for some, does have advantages along with the disadvantages.

ADVANTAGES OF PROBATE

Court supervision - The court oversees the entire process and provides some protection to the heirs of the estate. Court approval must be secured before disbursements are made. In many cases, bonds must be obtained by the executor/executrix, thus providing the heirs some protection against dishonest acts by the representatives of the estate.

Court helps settle disputes - If there are disputes between the heirs, the court can serve to settle them. Earlier I stated that probate is the perfect forum from which disgruntled heirs or family members can attack the will. If there are family members who feel they have been wronged, the probate court will resolve that dispute.

Limits time of claims against estate - Probate limits the amount of time in which creditors can make claims against the estate. This can be especially important in the case of a doctor, because future malpractice claims can arise. Lack of proper planning can create a situation in which a suit filed years after your death leads to claims against your estate.

Post mortem planning - Post-mortem (after death) tax planning techniques can be used since the estate is a separate tax-paying entity. In some cases, there are opportunities for postponing income and moving it from one tax-paying entity to another.

DISADVANTAGES OF PROBATE

Expense - It is a well known fact that probate can be expensive. A recent issue of *Changing Times* reviewed a report prepared for The American Association of Retired Persons (AARP) which indicated that legal fees often amount to 5% or more of an estate's value and sometimes exceed 20%. The report further revealed that fees "are often arbitrary, being only tenuously connected to the actual effort an attorney expends."

Time consuming - Probate can also be time consuming. The same AARP study said it takes a year or more, on average, to settle uncomplicated estates. A number of my clients wish their cases had been settled that quickly. In some cases, it can drag on for many years.

Slows liquidation - The probate process can make it difficult to sell investments quickly. An executor wishing to sell stock or real estate in an estate must wait for court approval.

> *John Martin's father died September 20, 1987. His assets included a substantial stock portfolio which he had accumulated over the years. John, as executor of the estate, felt uncomfortable with so much invested in the stock market. He had recently liquidated his own portfolio and felt he should do the same in his father's estate. However, the probate process required a notification period which precluded his liquidating any of the investments. When the stock market crashed on October 16, 1987, it severely reduced the value of the estate.*

Public process - When a will is probated, the records are public information, unless steps have been taken to avoid it. This means that anyone can go down to the court house and look at your will, see what you owned and to whom you were indebted, and take advantage of that situation. We saw the problems that created in the previous chapter.

Forum to contest - While the probate court can resolve disputes, the process also invites conflicts. Because you have to advertise, and the court provides the forum, you are inviting disgruntled heirs to contest the will. Even though the contesting party may have no right to any of the money, the rightful heirs may settle rather than fight.

Lack of flexibility - There is a general lack of flexibility. For example, many courts limit how money under their jurisdictions may be invested, thus limiting potential returns. Another problem might occur when post-mortem planning needs to be done, but is thwarted due to lack of knowledge on the part of the judge or probate attorney.

Multiple probates - If you own property in different states, then you must go through probate in those states. If you are married, depending upon how your property is owned, you may have to go through probate twice. And if you become disabled, that's even more probate problems. All of these can obviously be expensive propositions.

Conclusion

Being totally objective about probate is impossible. Opinions depend upon the persons to whom you are speaking and their biases. It also depends on their past experiences....or how they earn their living. In many cases, probate is not a problem at the death of the first spouse. This is because most of the property is jointly titled or passes directly to a beneficiary, thus automatically avoiding probate. At the death of the second spouse, however, things can be different.

Nevertheless, the difficulty with probate is that it is the perfect example of *we don't think we have a problem until we have a problem. We have no idea how much of a problem probate might be until it's too late.*

Once again, look at our definition of estate planning.

"During my life and after my death, I want to control and distribute my property in the manner I desire, minimizing all fees, taxes and court interference, preserving for myself, my family, and those I choose, the estate I have worked so hard to create."

How does probate fit in? If you truly want your affairs to comply with that definition, then probate can be a definite hinderance. How much is something that will not be known until your death.

Personally, I have chosen to structure my estate to avoid probate. I prefer to keep my family and affairs out of court.

But I also had other reasons for choosing the type of planning I did, and those will be discussed in upcoming chapters.

Probate is just one part of the planning puzzle. Some people say that a little probate is no problem. Well, maybe a little cancer is no problem, also. But wouldn't we all like to avoid it if we could?

7

HOW DO ESTATE TAXES AFFECT ME?

Uncle Sam has his ways. He gets you while you are alive, and he gets you when you're dead.

I think it was Will Rogers who said, "There are only two things in life that are certain: death and taxes. The only difference is that death doesn't get worse while Congress is in session!" It's only funny because it's true.

Taxes. Taxes. Taxes. I am constantly meeting and talking with clients whose main goal is to save income taxes. You can probably relate to that. People put a lot of their time and energy into finding ways to reduce their taxes. They purchase tax-free bonds. They contribute to retirement plans. They acquire rental property. They chase tax credits. They buy tax-deferred annuities. They make charitable contributions. They try different business structures. They put their children on the payroll. They establish leasing companies. They defer compensation. They combine business trips and vacations. But no matter how they try, they still pay more taxes. And it can only get worse - taxes **will** continue to increase.

And, then, the final insult: estate taxes. This is Uncle Sam's last shot. This one combines the two certainties: death and taxes. For you, estate taxes may or may not be a problem. But if they are, it could very well be that **you are worth only 45-**

65% of what you think you are worth.

In spite of an estate tax that can take up to 55% of your assets (and more if pension excise, generation skipping, and state inheritance taxes are included), it truly amazes me how few people have taken any meaningful steps to reduce those taxes. This is hard-earned money just being thrown away.

Before going further, let's make sure you are up-to-date on the current law. Many aspects of this discussion involve U.S. citizens only. For issues involving individuals who are not citizens of the United States, see Chapter 29.

The Rules

In 1981, Ronald Reagan gave us tax reform, and with it an increase in the amount of wealth United States citizens could pass tax-free to their heirs. That amount increased annually from the equivalent of $225,000 in 1982 to $600,000 in 1987, where it stands today. In addition, an unlimited marital deduction has been included. That means:

> *If you are **married**, you may leave the equivalent of $600,000 free of federal estate taxes to any person or combination of persons you desire. In addition, you may pass an unlimited amount to your spouse federal estate tax free (U. S. citizens only). No federal estate tax is due until the death of the surviving spouse.*

> *If you are **single**, you may pass the equivalent of $600,000 free from federal estate taxes to any person or combination of persons you desire.*

Of course, even though there is an unlimited marital deduction, your estate does get taxed when the surviving spouse dies. So while it's not a free ride, it is an improvement over the previous law.

We are talking here only about federal estate taxes. There are quite a few people who think that income taxes are due when you inherit money. That is not true. Only estate taxes are due, and they are paid by the estate of the deceased, not the recipient of the property.

Calculating your estate

Since most people in this country assume they don't have an estate tax problem, they never bother to consider it. Nevertheless, it is important to determine for sure whether or not your estate is facing any potential taxes. The first step in order to do that is to determine the make-up of your estate. What does Uncle Sam include and exclude in determining the value of your estate? Let's look.

Step 1. Add the value of the following assets:

a. Your home.
b. Securities (stock, bonds, etc.).
c. Real estate.
d. Retirement plan.
e. Bank accounts (savings, CD's, checking).
f. Life insurance you own.
g. Your business interests.
h. Personal property (jewelry, furnishings, automobiles, boats, etc.).
i. Accounts and/or notes receivable.
j   Jointly owned property.
k. Investments held in custodial accounts for minors
l. Property located outside the United States.
m. Partnership interests.
n. Other assets.

Step 2. From this figure, deduct the following:

    a.   Accounts and loans payable.
    b.   Mortgages payable.
    c.   Funeral and administrative expenses.
    d.   Liens against property.
    e.   Unpaid taxes.
    f.   Other liabilities.

Step 3. This figure represents your **adjusted gross estate**.

Step 4. From this figure, you deduct the following:

    a.   Marital deduction.
    b.   Charitable deductions.

Step 5. This figures represents your **taxable estate**.

If you leave everything to your spouse, then your entire **adjusted gross estate** will be deducted as the marital deduction in 4(a) above. As a result, your **taxable estate** will be zero, as will your taxes.

If you are not married, or if you are the second spouse to die, then we must continue the calculation. It can get complicated with regard to various credits and adjusted taxable gifts, so we will assume that you have nothing that would further adjust your estate or taxes.

Step 6. Compute your **gross federal estate tax** using the following table. (These are the federal estate and gift tax rates until 1993. They change at that point.) Any state inheritance taxes are in addition to these figures.

Taxable Estate	Tax Owed	Plus %	On Amount
$0-10,000	0	18	0
10,001-20,000	1,800	20	10,000
20,001-40,000	3,800	22	20,000
40,001-60,000	8,200	24	40,000
60,001-80,000	13,000	26	60,000
80,001-100,000	18,200	28	80,000
100,001-150,000	23,800	30	100,000
150,001-250,000	38,800	32	150,000
250,001-500,000	70,800	34	250,000
500,001-750,000	155,800	37	500,000
750,001-1,000,000	248,300	39	750,000
1,000,001-1,250,000	345,800	41	1,000,000
1,250,001-1,500,000	448,300	43	1,250,000
1,500,001-2,000,000	555,800	45	1,500,000
2,000,001-2,500,000	780,800	49	2,000,000
2,500,001-3,000,000	1,025,800	53	2,500,000
3,000,001 and up	1,290,800	55	3,000,000

Step 7. From that figure (your gross estate tax), subtract the **unified credit of $192,800.** Remember earlier we said you can pass $600,000 free of estate taxes. The figure $192,800 is the amount of tax on that $600,000 transfer. So while it is said everyone has a $600,000 exemption, what they really have is a $192,800 tax credit. That's why we call the $600,000 a **credit equivalent or exemption equivalent** rather than an exemption.

However, for easier reading, we will refer to the $600,000 credit equivalent and $192,800 tax credit as a $600,000 exemption.

Although the above chart indicates that estate tax rates start at 18%, because of the way the $192,800 tax credit is calculated, the first dollars over $600,000 are actually taxed at 37%. That means that when your taxable estate gets above $600,000, the excess is taxed at 37% or higher!

Traditional planning

To review, you have two tax breaks: the unlimited marital deduction, by which you can leave an unlimited amount of property to your spouse; and the $600,000 exemption, by which you can leave that amount to any other person or persons. However, it takes special planning to take advantage of both of these breaks.

Most people don't do this planning. In the vast majority of cases I have reviewed, the couple's estate has not been structured to take advantage of the first-to-die's $600,000 exemption. Instead, the husband has left everything to the wife, and vice versa. If this is the way your estate is structured, you will lose your $600,000 exemption, and this can result in substantial, unnecessary estate taxes.

Let's look at some numbers and see what we're talking about.

Donald Purcell was 48, his wife Rebecca was 46. They had three children, ages 21, 18, and 16. They had a total net estate of $2,000,000, including the value of their home, stocks and bonds, retirement plans, personal property, his business, his life insurance, and the custodial accounts they had established for their minor child. They each had simple wills leaving their assets to each other, if living, otherwise to their children. They each owned one half of the assets. He died in an automobile accident. She died a week later from injuries sustained in the same accident.

Calculating the tax (Exhibit 1)

Let's calculate the estate taxes on the Purcells' estate.

- Mr. Purcell's adjusted gross estate was $980,000 after probate and administrative expenses of 2%.

- There was no tax at Mr. Purcell's death since everything went to his wife under the unlimited marital deduction.

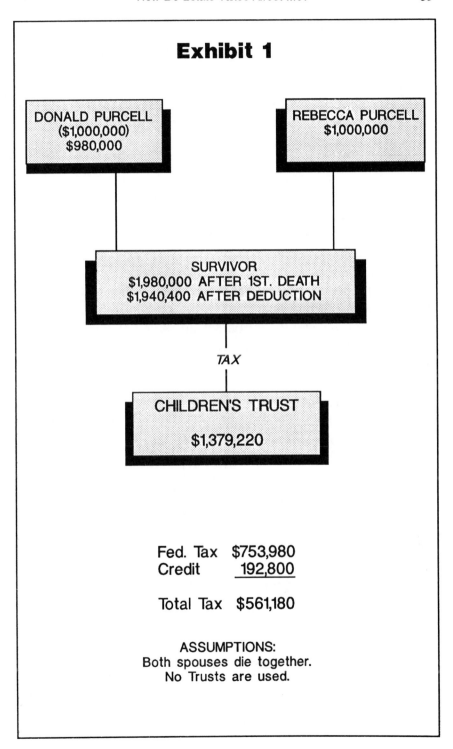

Exhibit 1

DONALD PURCELL
($1,000,000)
$980,000

REBECCA PURCELL
$1,000,000

SURVIVOR
$1,980,000 AFTER 1ST. DEATH
$1,940,400 AFTER DEDUCTION

TAX

CHILDREN'S TRUST

$1,379,220

Fed. Tax $753,980
Credit   192,800

Total Tax $561,180

ASSUMPTIONS:
Both spouses die together.
No Trusts are used.

- Mrs. Purcell's adjusted gross estate was $1,940,400. This consisted of her $1,000,000, plus her husband's $980,000, less 2% expenses.

- The gross estate tax on the $1,940,400 (after the deductible expenses) estate that Mrs. Purcell left was $753,980.

- After her $192,800 tax credit (the amount of tax on her $600,000 exemption), the estate taxes were $561,180.

- Their children received $1,379,220.

The estate tax return was filed. **The children paid $561,180 in taxes** to Uncle Sam within nine months, **all in cash.** As a result, only $1,379,220 passed to their heirs. In this case, it didn't matter who died first or how the assets were divided. The results would have been the same.

The Purcells structured their estate the way most couples do. The first to die leaves all of his or her property to the spouse under the unlimited marital deduction. As a result, he or she **never uses, and thus loses, his or her $600,000 exemption.** This means that at the death of the surviving spouse, the heirs will have to pay more estate taxes than would have been necessary with proper planning. This alternative planning is discussed in Chapter 10.

STATE INHERITANCE TAXES

In addition to federal estate taxes, your heirs may have to pay state inheritance taxes. Generally, there are two ways that states handle inheritance taxes.

Approximately half of the states are called "federal credit" states. They receive a portion of the federal estate taxes you pay, but have no inheritance tax of their own. Thus, by using the estate tax schedule printed in this chapter, you can calculate your total estate taxes.

The balance of the states have some form of "inheritance tax" in addition to the federal estate tax. Therefore, you can assume that you will have to pay more in the form of total estate and inheritance taxes than is reflected in the schedule. Included in this group are Connecticut, Delaware, Indiana, Iowa, Kansas, Kentucky, Louisiana, Maryland, Massachusetts, Michigan, Mississippi, Nebraska, New Jersey, New York, North Carolina, Ohio, Oklahoma, Pennsylvania, Rhode Island, South Carolina, South Dakota, Tennessee and Wisconsin. Since the rules for each taxing state are different, and constantly changing, it is impossible to include all the rules for each state in this book.

PENSION "SUCCESS" TAX

Face it. Congress doesn't like people with money (except themselves). So in addition to all the other taxes with which you are faced, the government penalizes you for having a successful retirement plan.

You may be subject to a **15% excess distribution penalty** if you withdraw the greater of $150,000 (or $112,500 indexed for inflation) from your retirement plan. However, if you take your retirement in a lump sum and qualify for averaging, that amount increases to $750,000. Without getting into detail, there was a "grandfather" election available in 1987 or 1988 that could have softened the blow.

Leaving your money in your retirement plan is no answer, because there is also a **15% excess accumulation penalty** if you die with over the $150,000 or $112,500 figure above. This amount is in **addition** to any estate taxes and not reduced by the unified credit or deductions.

What all this means is that if your pension and/or profit sharing plan contains an amount above the stated amounts, you must do some planning. In the worst case, you could have to pay **income taxes** when you receive the money, **estate taxes** when you die, plus the **success tax**. I have seen large pensions reduced to one-third of their former value! This is not what you worked so hard to achieve.

However, it is not all bad news. This is a specialized area that can be resolved with proper planning. Chapter 21 on Charitable Remainder Trusts provides you with an alternative type of plan that can avoid these problems. But that's not the entire answer. It takes special planning in this area that cannot be adequately discussed in this forum. Everybody's situation is so different that to generalize would be a disservice to you. Suffice it to say that you need to talk with an expert who can help you in this area.

Conclusion

Estate taxes are usually ignored because most people don't think they have a problem. And while this is statistically true (only a relatively small percentage of estates do have to pay estate taxes), you must include this as part of your planning. We will see in the following chapters that when you do have an estate tax problem, there are various methods to help you reduce these costs.

PART II

CONTROLLING YOUR ESTATE

8

WHAT IS A
REVOCABLE LIVING TRUST?

So far, we have looked at the traditional forms of planning. Methods of ownership and potential problems have been discussed. Wills and probate have been covered in detail. Let's move to a unique form of planning that can help solve many of the problems that have been raised: the revocable living trust.

Why all the fuss about living trusts?

Everywhere you look there seems to be something about living trusts. Seminars are being offered coast to coast. Books are being written. Financial publications, and non-financial publications, are carrying articles. All of a sudden, living trusts are hot. Why?

This special type of plan has finally come into its own. It is a way for people to accomplish many of their goals in a way that, due to the cost, was unattainable to all but the wealthy in the past. But as with many things, the computer age has brought the living trust into the financial range of the masses.

Plan for the best?

In estate planning, as in life, most people live their lives hoping for the best. This is what I call the "Ostrich Syndrome." They bury their heads in the sand and hope bad things won't happen. This thinking is a blueprint for disaster.

Does Apple design a computer and hope it will work? Does Boeing design an airplane, sell it to United without testing and hope it will fly? Of course not! So why does it make any more sense to hope everything will work out with your estate? Hope you won't die while your children are minors? Hope you and your joint tenant won't die together? Hope that probate won't be a problem? Hope nobody will contest your will? Hope you won't become disabled? That just doesn't make sense.

Things go wrong everyday. You are probably familiar with Murphy's Law: "anything that can go wrong will go wrong." Remember the dragons. They are just waiting to pounce on your estate.

Anticipate the problems

Proper planning involves anticipating potential problems and taking the necessary steps **in advance** to avoid them. In my experience, very few people plan in this manner. Instead, they use traditional planning methods and hope things will work out. If you are going to plan at all, doesn't it make sense to do it right the first time and eliminate the potential problems and hassles before they occur?

We have the opportunity in this age of computers to do state-of-the-art planning which can help you avoid the dragons and keep Uncle Sam and Cousin George from devouring your estate. One of the better tools to help accomplish this is the "inter vivos" trust, better known as the revocable living trust.

When you mention trusts, one of the biggest fears that arises in people's minds is that they will end up like the widow in the old movies. Remember the 85-year old banker who refused to give her any money? That's not what we're talking about here. This modern type of trust allows **you** to maintain complete control over **your** property as long as **you** choose.

Why wills are emphasized

Although most people think that wills are old and trusts are new, the opposite is true. Wills are relatively new while trusts have been around for longer than most of us realize. Nevertheless, wills have been the favored method of passing property. Some say this is due to the fact that attorneys like the fees that probate generates. Others say that law schools tend to emphasize wills rather than trusts.

I like to think it's the latter case. I hate to think that attorneys recommend wills because of the money they will eventually make from probate. But I have heard of attorneys who brag about the wills they have in their files. They are anticipating that the clients' families will use their services to probate those wills.

But whatever the reasons, trusts are becoming more popular. Although there is a concern about those attorneys and planners who are more interested in drafting trusts than properly planning for their clients, let's not throw out the baby with the bath water. A living trust is a good vehicle **in the right situation** as part of the estate planning process.

Definition of a trust

A trust is like a legal box which holds assets. Within the trust, there are three parties:

1. The trustmaker (also called the settlor or grantor).
2. The trustees.
3. The beneficiaries.

The **trustmaker,** or grantor, is the person or persons who create the trust and transfer his and/or her assets into it. The **trustees** are the people who manage the trust. The **beneficiaries** are the people who benefit from the trust.

Setting up the trust

Setting up a trust is not difficult, but there are important decisions that must be made. In the following chapters, we will discuss choosing trustees and distributing the funds. At this point, let's look at the basics of a living trust.

Most individuals and couples with whom I work name themselves as initial trustees of their own trust. As such, they have complete control over their trust and the property in it. They can add or sell property, amend or revoke the trust. They usually name themselves as lifetime beneficiaries of their trust. They can do whatever they desire as trustees to take care of themselves, the beneficiaries.

After much discussion with their attorney, Robert and Mary Jones decided to establish a revocable living trust. Their attorney drafted the document, and it was duly signed and notarized. Mr. and Mrs. Jones then transferred their assets into the trust. Did they have to transfer all their assets in the trust? No. They could have put in as many or as few of their assets as they desired. Some assets, such as professional corporation stock, normally can't be owned by a trust. But, the Joneses, for reasons we will see shortly, decided to transfer all their assets into the trust.

Mr. and Mrs. Jones wanted to maintain control over the assets in the trust. Since they didn't want a third party involved, they named themselves as trustees. As trustees, they can do whatever is necessary to follow the guidelines they have set up for the beneficiaries. Who are the beneficiaries? Mr. and Mrs. Jones. It is for their benefit that the trust was established. In other words, they set up the trust, they control the assets in the trust, and they benefit from it. They hold all three positions.

The Jones don't have to occupy all three positions (trustmakers, trustees, beneficiaries). They can, if they wish, name a financial institution, a relative, or any third party of their choice to be the trustee. They don't have to be the beneficiaries. They can name their children, their parents, or anyone they choose as beneficiaries.

A living trust has a great deal of flexibility. In fact, there are only two major limitations. First, the trust cannot contain illegal provisions. Second, the trust can not last forever. The "rule against perpetuities" limits the length of time a trust may remain in effect. This law is designed to keep wealthy people from controlling their assets forever by passing it from generation to generation without taxation. The only exception to this rule is if the beneficiary is a qualified charity.

Transferring property into the trust

For a variety of reasons, as we will see shortly, you will want to title your property in the name of the trust. For example, in the case of Mr. and Mrs. Jones above, their trust was titled:

"Robert C. Jones and Mary F. Jones, trustees, or their successors in trust, under the Robert C. and Mary F. Jones Living Trust, dated April 4, 1991."

The ways to transfer property are covered in Chapter 16.

ADVANTAGES OF A LIVING TRUST

Takes care of you while you are alive - Unlike a will, which doesn't become effective until you die, a living trust can take care of you during your life in addition to providing for your family after your death. In the event of a disability which precludes you from handling your financial affairs, the successor trustee(s) you name can handle your business without going through any court procedures. This is covered in Chapter 22.

You name your own trustees - A living trust allows you to name your own trustees. The initial trustees can, and probably will be, you and your spouse. If either of you becomes unable to handle your financial affairs because of death or disability, the other spouse can automatically take over. If your spouse is unable to carry on, the successor trustees you named in your trust will carry on. This is certainly better than going to probate court and having a guardian or custodian named.

Avoids probate - Property titled in the name of a living trust avoids probate. For example, if your home is titled in the name of your trust, it will pass to your beneficiary probate-free. This can be quite an advantage. No matter what you may feel about probate, it appears to me that avoiding it is preferable to the cost and time delays.

Avoids multiple probates - If you own property in several states, you must go through probate in each of those states. Since a living trust avoids all probate (if the property is titled in the name of the trust), it can save significantly in probate expenses and time delays. Further, many times property will have to be probated at the death of each spouse.

> *Foster Markle owned 50 acres of land in his own name. Upon his death, it passed to his wife via his will. This was the first probate. Upon Mrs. Markle's death, the property will go through probate again.*

Leave your own instructions - A properly drawn trust will contain your own special instructions for your trustees. You have the opportunity to leave unlimited, detailed instructions concerning how you want to be cared for in the event of your disability and how you want your loved ones cared for upon your death. Since this is one of the primary advantages of a living trust, make sure that your attorney drafts the document to your specification and that it includes all the instructions you want.

Hard to contest - Unlike a will, which provides a forum for disgruntled heirs to contest, a living trust is very difficult to overturn. Remember our case from the chapter on wills:

*John and Elizabeth Benson had two sons, Chad and Randy.
While Chad had given them no problems, Randy was always in
trouble. In addition, he was extremely cruel to John and Elizabeth, to the point that they had ceased trying to continue a
relationship with him. In their wills, they left virtually all their
estate to Chad, with only 10% going to Randy. Upon their deaths,
Randy contested the will. He said that his parents were unduly
influenced by Chad and didn't understand what they were doing.
He told Chad that he would tie up the estate in court for years if
he didn't share a larger portion with him. Chad, not wanting to go
through the time and expense of fighting his brother, agreed to
give Randy 25% of the money.*

This scenario would have been difficult with a living trust
for three reasons.

- With a living trust, the assets are distributed to the
  beneficiaries almost immediately. It would have
  been of little or no value for Randy to threaten
  Chad, because Chad would have already received his
  share of the money. He would have had to sue
  Chad in court, and based on historical precedent,
  Randy would have lost.

- The living trust would have contained a "non-contest"
  clause. This would have stated that if any beneficiary
  were to contest the trust, he or she would receive
  nothing. Therefore, by contesting the trust, Randy
  would probably have lost even that amount to which
  he was entitled.

- With a living trust, the argument of incompetency or
  lapsed memory is difficult to use. John and Elizabeth would have worked with the trust constantly.
  Every bank and brokerage statement they received
  would have been sent to them as trustees. They
  would have received money and paid bills as trustees.
  They couldn't have been incompetent and done all
  that. Additionally, unlike a will which is usually filed
  away and never reviewed, they would have worked

with the trust constantly. John and Elizabeth would have been very much aware of the provisions of the trust.

Care for minor children - A trust provides a vehicle to take care of minor children. In the "pour-over" will, you name a guardian to care for the children. In your trust, you name a trustee (or trustees) to take care of the financial affairs of the children. Therefore, you can have two different people watching the children and watching each other for the benefit of the children. The kids and guardians stay out of probate court. They are provided for in the manner you desire. You can instruct the trustee, if you desire, to provide funds for special situations, such as private schooling, a wedding, special education, etc. You can provide instructions for distributing the money at the ages you desire. Chapter 11 provides a discussion of minor children.

A trust for minor children can also be part of your will. It is called a "testamentary" trust, and it is activated upon your death. If you feel more comfortable within the confines of the probate court, then this would be an option. If you would rather not involve the court, then a living trust would make more sense. Chapter 14 contains a comparison of both types of trusts.

Reduce estate taxes - Properly drawn, a trust can help reduce your estate taxes *if you are married* and if you have not previously utilized your $600,000 exemption. This is covered in detail in Chapter 10. This same savings can be realized through the use of a testamentary trust in a will, but it will go through probate. Additionally, it can be accomplished by leaving property outright to a person other than your spouse.

Avoid lawsuit problems - A properly drafted living trust, under the right circumstances, can be helpful in avoiding the problems of a lawsuit. This subject is covered in Chapter 26 by attorney Kelly Burke.

No time delays - Unlike a will, which must go through the probate process, the use of a living trust allows the beneficiaries to receive money and assets immediately. This is certainly an advantage in the case of families who have a need for immediate cash.

No additional or separate income tax returns - When a living trust is established, your income tax situation does not change. On trusts created after 1980, as long as you are trustee of your own trust, and as long as all the trust's assets are in the United States, you do **not** have to file a Form 1041. Instead, you report your income on your Form 1040 (or 1040A), just as you do now. There are no extra taxes to pay, no new forms to file, no separate taxpayer identification number. You are not beating the IRS out of any income taxes. Everything stays the same. Upon your death, depending upon the disposition of the assets, there can be additional tax forms. On trusts created prior to 1980, you have the option of reporting the income either way: on a 1040 or 1041.

Keep affairs private - A living trust keeps your personal finances private upon your death. Unlike a will, which is public record, your living trust is totally private - nobody will know your business unless your trustees choose to disclose it. There are times when a party with whom you are dealing, such as a stock brokerage firm, will want certain documentation concerning the trust. In these cases, it is not necessary to provide the entire document. Rather, an "Affidavit of Trust" can be provided, which will certify the trust's validity and contain copies of those portions of the trust of importance to the financial institution.

Can change the terms - You can easily change the terms of the trust during your lifetime. Remember, it is a **revocable** trust. That means that while you (the trustmaker) are alive, you can change the terms or can revoke the trust entirely.

Don't need to amend to change property - A question that always arises is, "Do I have to change my trust every time I buy or sell property?"   No, you do not. Your property is titled in the name of your trust. If you sell your home, you sell it as trustee of the trust. If you buy a new home, you title it in the name of the trust. It works like IBM. Every time they buy a new building, they don't change their corporate charter. The title is evidence of their ownership. Your trust works the same way. You can move your certificates of deposit, change your brokerage account, and buy and sell securities. None of these requires a change in your trust.

No ongoing fees - As long as you remain trustee of your own trust, there are no continuing fees. The only cost is to establish the trust. From then on, the only additional costs would be if you need to change the terms of the trust.   These changes usually take two forms: changing the trustees and changing the distribution provisions of the trust. The former can be avoided by naming sufficient successor trustees. Changing the distribution of property usually involves changing how children will receive the money upon the death of you and your spouse.

DISADVANTAGES OF A LIVING TRUST

Cost - Living trusts are **initially** more expensive than wills. We have all seen advertisements for will preparation for $50 or $100. Trusts, on the other hand, can cost anywhere from $500 to $2000 depending on the attorney and the work involved.

Cost, however, is a very difficult subject to quantify. How, for example, do you put a price on keeping affairs private, taking care of yourself and your family in the case of your disability or death, saving the time and cost of probate, whatever it may be, taking care of your minor children, etc? You can't. So you can't just compare the cost of wills and trusts. You are dealing with too many unknowns. You really have no idea what your heirs are going to need to handle your estate because *we don't think we have a problem until we have a problem.* You don't know how many dragons might pop up. Once again, it comes to planning. Are you planning for the best or planning for the worst? If it is the latter, then cost is not a significant factor.

One last factor concerning cost. If cost weren't a factor, most people (although probably not most attorneys) would agree that a living trust is more advantageous than a will. Therefore, the discussion is not necessarily whether a trust is better than a will; the question is whether or not a trust is worth the initial cost. This will be discussed in Chapter 15.

Lose court supervision - One of the disadvantages of a living trust is the opposite of one of the advantages - avoiding probate. While you avoid probate with a living trust, you also lose the court supervision of your estate. Since you are giving your trustee the power to do all these good things, it is possible that he or she might do something which is not in the best interest of the beneficiaries. With a trust, you lose some protection since the court is not overseeing the trustee. However, if you think this might be a problem, one way around it is to name co-trustees, such as a relative, friend, or trust department of a local bank.

Must transfer property into trust - As stated previously, if you are going to avoid probate with the living trust, your property must be titled in the name of the trust. Many people try to save attorney's fees by purchasing a book that includes all the forms necessary to do a trust. One of the many problems with doing this is that you may not follow through with the complete process, which includes transferring property into the trust. This is an integral part of the process and must be accomplished in order to realize full benefit. But if you think that transferring property is difficult when you are alive, think how much more difficult it will be after your death. Transferring property will be discussed in detail in Chapter 16.

No unique tax savings method - There are two types of taxes with which we concern ourselves in planning: income taxes and estate taxes. While a trust doesn't save any income taxes, it can be a big advantage when it comes to estate taxes - if you haven't previously used your $600,000 exemption. (Chapter 10 includes a full discussion of saving estate taxes with a trust.) It is important to note, however, that the same estate tax savings can be obtained whether you use a testamentary trust in a will or a revocable living trust. But remember our previous discussion of cost. Whereas a will is inexpensive and a living trust can run into higher dollars, a testamentary trust falls somewhere in between. Obviously, because of the additional work involved, the attorney must charge more than he would for the standard will. But, don't forget, the testamentary trust must go through probate, and that has some disadvantages.

Need a competent attorney - I hesitate to include this. It's the same as saying that one disadvantage of surgery is that you need a competent surgeon. While it seems obvious in medicine, it's not so obvious in law. There are some attorneys who attempt to practice in areas in which they are not totally qualified. The results of this can be disastrous for you. It is your duty to make sure that the attorney who does your estate planning work specializes in that area and can do good work.

Doesn't cut off time of creditors - A living trust, by avoiding the probate process, loses one of the advantages of probate: cutting the time in which creditors can attempt to get funds from the estate. Although this affects only a small number of people, it can be a concern to people who fear a lawsuit after their deaths. That is why, in planning with certain professionals, it is recommended that a small amount of property be left to go through probate with proper notification to the creditors. This can be done either by leaving some assets out of the trust to go through probate or by having the executor open a probate estate after your death.

Lack of understanding by advisors - One of the biggest problems in working with living trusts is the fact that most attorneys and advisors don't understand them or don't want to learn about them. There has been a pattern in many communities, when living trusts are first introduced, for certain advisors to denigrate their value. I know that has been my experience. There have even been "professionals" who have said that trusts are illegal! I have been truly shocked by the misinformation that is being spread as "truth". But as with many new concepts, many advisors don't like change - especially if the changes are introduced by another firm. They feel comfortable with the methods they understand and want to hold on to them. This reminds me of a sign on Ted Turner's desk: "Lead, Follow, or Get Out Of The Way." Don't let others get in the way of what's best for you.

Lack of understanding by institutions - In addition to the advisors who don't understand them, many of my clients also run into people who work for banks and brokerage firms who are not familiar with how to handle trust accounts. Although rare with brokerage firms who work with trust accounts daily, this occurs more often with banks. Many people go into a bank to change an account, and the person to whom they are talking has no idea what to do. One of the reasons for this is the natural turnover of people. Nevertheless, the manager should be familiar with trusts and be able to help.

COMPARING ADVANTAGES WITH DISADVANTAGES

Comparing advantages and disadvantages is never easy. Certainly, you can't make your decision based solely on the number of each. You must look at your particular situation and determine whether or not the advantages provided offset any of the disadvantages. That is why you need to work with a competent estate planning team. Everyone's situation is different. You must weigh the advantages and those factors that are important to you based upon your goals and priorities. The same is true with the disadvantages. You may look at the disadvantages and see no problems. On the other hand, there may be a few factors that concern you. Remember what I said earlier: this is **your** estate and **your** plan. You must ensure that the plan is designed for your needs and nobody else's.

Conclusion

I have seen the results of dying or becoming disabled with and without a living trust. Those distinct differences make me a believer in the benefits of the revocable living trust in the right situation. Again, I must emphasize the words **in the right situation.** Nevertheless, the living trust, more than the other planning methods, appears to fulfill the terms of our definition.

> *"During my life and after my death, I want to control and distribute my property in the manner I desire, minimizing all fees, taxes and court interference, preserving for myself, my family, and those I choose, the estate I have worked so hard to create."*

Does the living trust work during your life and after your death? **Yes.**

Does the living trust allow you to control and distribute your property in the manner you desire? **Yes.**

Does the living trust help you minimize all fees? Except for the initial cost, **yes.**

Does the living trust help you minimize taxes? **Yes.**

Does the living trust minimize court interference? **Yes.**

Does the living trust help you preserve your estate for yourself, your family, and those you choose? **Yes.**

That said, how do you know that you need a living trust? In Chapter 15 we will review the ways of determining if a living trust is for you and work to separate rhetoric from reality.

9

WHAT ARE THE WAYS OF STRUCTURING A LIVING TRUST?

The beauty of a living trust, or a testamentary trust, assuming your attorney has the flexibility, is that it can be structured to meet your specifications. In previous chapters, we spoke of the importance of molding your estate plan to your particular situation. Done properly, designing a living trust is like building a home. In the latter case, you hire an architect to draw up the plans, but you dictate the basics: number of levels, bedrooms, baths, pool, decks, etc. But no matter what you want, the architect must stay within certain guidelines. It will have a roof, walls, floor, electricity, running water, indoor plumbing, meet restrictive covenants, etc.

The same is true with your living trust. While it must also stay within certain legal guidelines, it will reflect your concern for your family and contain your instructions for caring for them.

While this is neither a do-it-yourself book nor a guide to structuring a living trust, it is important to get an overview of the process. We will look at how to live with a living trust in Chapter 16. At this point, we are only covering the basic decisions you need to make so you can receive maximum benefit from your trust.

DECISIONS THAT MUST BE MADE

There are four general decisions you must consider.

- Do you want **joint** or **separate** trusts?

- Who will be the **trustees**? These are the people who will carry forth your instructions both during your life and after your death.

- How will you provide for yourself and your spouse as **lifetime beneficiaries**?

- How do you want your money distributed to the **ultimate beneficiaries** upon the deaths of yourself and your spouse?

Let's go through each separately over the next few chapters. Remember there are three positions: trustmaker, trustee(s), and beneficiaries.

- The **trustmakers** are the people who set up the trust and transfer their property into it.

- The **trustees** are the people who will follow the instructions of the trustmakers for the benefit of the beneficiaries.

- The **beneficiaries** are the people who receive the benefit of the property in the trust. Again, you can hold all three positions in a revocable living trust.

SEPARATE OR JOINT TRUST

If you are single, you will obviously establish a separate trust. If you are married, you can either set up a joint trust for you and your spouse, or you can establish a separate trust for each of you. Which you choose depends upon your personal situation. Let's look at how this determination can be made.

Joint Trust

A joint trust is similar to joint tenancy. Both spouses are usually the joint trustees and together control the property. For most people, this is the most comfortable way of handling their assets because it is familiar. It is also convenient because there is only one trust document and one set of paperwork. A joint trust is used successfully in community property states as a means of holding property.

Separate Trusts

There are occasions when a married couple will use separate trusts.

- They have children by previous marriages and want to ensure that their respective children receive their just inheritance.

- A doctor or businessperson is concerned about the exposure of a lawsuit. The couple may put the bulk of their assets in the trust of the non-exposed spouse, thus protecting their wealth. For a detailed discussion of this aspect, see Chapter 26.

- They have entered into their marriage with separate property which they, for personal reasons, would like to keep that way. Second marriages are discussed in Chapter 30.

The ultimate decision you make will be dependent upon your particular situation. While I have reviewed each method, there are distinct advantages and disadvantages which you should discuss with your attorney.

CHOOSING TRUSTEES

Trustees

The next decision you need to make is selecting your trustees. As a rule, you will name trustees to serve in the following capacity.

- **Initial trustees** are those people who are the trustees the day the trust is established. If you are the trustmaker, you can name anyone you desire as the trustee. **Most likely you will name yourself and/or your spouse as initial trustees or co-trustees.** As trustees, you have the same control over the property as you do when it is in your own name. You can buy it, sell it, gift it, pledge it - anything you want to do - as long as it conforms to the rules of the trust and is for the welfare of the beneficiaries (most likely you and your spouse). If you are single, you can be the sole trustee. On the other hand, you can name any other person or financial institution as sole or co-trustee. For example, some older people name their children as trustees or co-trustees.

- **Disability trustees** are those people whom you appoint to take care of you in the event of your mental or physical incapacity. In a trust, disability is not a broken leg or a crushed hand. It is anything that will keep you from handling your own financial affairs. **While most people name their spouse as trustee,** the option is yours.

- **Death trustees** are those people whom you appoint to take care of the beneficiaries in the event of your death. **Again, the surviving spouse might be the sole trustee, or you may name co-trustees.** If there isn't a surviving spouse, then you can name any other person or persons as death trustees.

As you can see from the bold print, you and/or your spouse can hold all trustee positions, assuming you are able. This feature of control is what makes living trusts so popular today.

I like to see people list at least four successor trustees in the event one or more cannot serve. It is inevitable that circumstances could preclude a trustee from serving. By making necessary arrangements in advance, it will save time and expense down the road.

How to choose

Choosing your trustees can be one of the most difficult aspects of setting up your living trust. Trustees have a lot of power. They are going to be handling your money and following your instructions on how to care for you and your family. Therefore, you must have full confidence that they will do their jobs. You want trustees who think like you and share your values. You want people who care about you and will be concerned for the welfare of your family.

It goes without saying that your primary concern should be the trustworthiness of the trustees. One of the advantages of a living trust is its freedom from court supervision. That could quickly turn into a disadvantage with the wrong trustee.

It is possible that the trustee could defraud the beneficiaries of their money. Although you can require the trustee to furnish annual statements to the beneficiaries, if the latter are minors or handicapped, the reports will be of little value. If you have any concern that this might happen, then consider having joint trustees, such as two individuals, an individual and a bank, or just a bank.

Financial institutions as trustees

Speaking of banks, there are occasions when you might

desire a trustee with more experience and stability than a family member can provide. Some people feel uncomfortable naming a child as the sole-trustee, no matter what the age. Therefore, the use of a financial institution as a sole or co-trustee might make sense.

There are several advantages to using a trust department of a commercial bank as trustee. They are insured against illegal acts by employees - you don't have to worry about them running off with the money like Uncle Joe. They are experienced in handling trust affairs. They have the expertise to handle your investment dollars.

There are also several disadvantages. There is the cost of managing the trust, which usually averages one percent per year. Banks tend to be impersonal. They change personnel frequently. Many have run into financial problems themselves. And in some cases, their investment experience has been less than stellar.

However, nobody is perfect. Banks do make excellent co-trustees, and it can make sense to use them in this capacity. When coupled with a relative, a financial institution may serve your purposes well. If you feel the need for a commercial fiduciary, talk with a few trust officers and choose an institution with which you feel comfortable.

Obligation of the trustees

The obligation of your trustees is as strong as the law: they have the fiduciary duty of following your instructions as set forth in your trust. This is a responsibility that, when handled properly, can make life easier for you and your family.

John and Mary Richards set up a living trust naming themselves as initial trustees. They each listed their choice of successor trustees as follows:

John - Disability trustees	Mary - Disability Trustees
I. Mary, wife	1. John, husband
2. Sue and Bob, children	2. Sue and Bob, children
3. Jack, brother	3. Carole, sister
4. Kathy, sister	4. Janet, sister
5. First National Bank	5. First National Bank

John suffered a stroke and became partially paralyzed. Following the rules of their trust, Mary became sole trustee. She did not have to take John through "living probate", the process whereby she would be appointed guardian (discussed in Chapter 12). She didn't need the services of an attorney. She just followed the instructions contained in the trust.

If Mary becomes disabled, then their children, Sue and Bob, become co-trustees and will take care of their parents per the trust. If Sue and Bob cannot serve, then the successors listed in the trust will follow. In any case, no living probate is necessary.

John and Mary named the following trustees in the event of their deaths:

John - Death trustees	Mary - Death Trustees
I. Mary, wife	1. John, husband
2. Sue, Al and Bob	2. Sue, Al and Bob, children
3. Jack, brother	3. Carole, sister
4. Kathy, sister	4. Janet, sister
5. First National Bank	5. First National Bank

When John dies, Mary can take over without missing a beat. Because their property is titled in the trust, no probate will be necessary. There will be no expenses and no delays. Mary will be able to handle everything herself.

The disability and death trustees can be identical or different. In this case, the Richards felt most comfortable with Sue and Bob taking care of their affairs in the event of their disability but didn't want their youngest son, Al, involved in this aspect. However they did want all three working together upon their deaths. That way, none of the children would feel left out. Additionally, they each named different people as successors after their children. Their thinking was that if the spouse and children were not around, they would like their own relatives caring for them.

Conclusion

A primary advantage of a trust is that it allows you to choose those people whom you desire to handle your financial affairs. Whether those people are relatives, friends, or a financial institution, it takes some thought and planning.

10

HOW CAN I SAVE ESTATE TAXES AND CARE FOR MY FAMILY?

The next decision to be considered is how you want to use the trust to take care of your family upon your death. In addition, if you have an estate tax problem, you will want to consider how, at the same time, you can reduce the eventual estate tax liability of your heirs.

Previously we saw how to calculate estate taxes and looked at the case of Donald and Rebecca Purcell, whose children had to pay over $561,000 in estate taxes. One of the purposes of this book is to help you reduce the cost of your estate taxes. So let's take our first step toward that goal by examining the use of a living trust. **If you don't have an estate tax problem (you're married with an estate under $600,000 or you are single and can't use a trust to reduce your taxes), just concentrate on the structuring aspects and ignore the numbers.** While you can use either a testamentary trust (part of a will) or a revocable living trust to reduce estate taxes, we will concentrate on the living trust.

The $600,000 exemption

Remember from our previous discussion that most married people, at their deaths, leave all their property directly to their spouse. As a result, the heirs lose the advantage of the first-to-die's $600,000 exemption. One of the purposes of estate planning is to capture this.

It can be captured one of two ways: property can be left outright to another person or persons (totaling not more than $600,000), or property can be left directly to a "Family Trust" (also called Credit or Bypass Trust). In either case, the property is removed from the estate of both spouses, thus reducing future estate taxes on the death of the surviving spouse.

The problem with leaving it to another person (such as an adult child or other relative) is that the surviving spouse loses the benefit of the property. He or she will neither receive any income nor have the use of it since it belongs to somebody else. A solution to this, then, is to leave that amount directly to the Family Trust with the surviving spouse entitled to certain benefits.

The Family Trust

Upon the death of the first spouse, the trust will split into two sub-trusts: the Family Trust and the Marital Trust **(See Exhibit 2 on page 93)**. Some people refer to these as an "A-B" Trusts, the "A" referring to the Marital Trust and the "B" referring to the Family Trust. Up to $600,000 worth of property may pass into the Family Trust without adverse estate tax consequences. By doing so, not only do the heirs receive the benefit of an estate tax-savings tool, but the surviving spouse can receive the economic benefit of the funds in that trust.

The IRS allows the Family Trust to qualify for the first spouse's $600,000 exemption while providing funds for the surviving spouse....as long as the surviving spouse's access to this money is limited to certain "ascertainable standards", which include all of the following:

a. all the interest income from the Family Trust; and

b. principal as needed from the Family Trust for the

following:

1) health
2) maintenance
3) support
4) education; and

c. 5% of the value of the Family Trust or $5,000 per year, whichever is greater.

By providing no more than all of the above, you can keep the value of the trust out of the estate of the surviving spouse. If the surviving spouse has access to more than the ascertainable standards, then the IRS will consider it his or her property and include it in his or her estate.

I can't stress enough the importance of following these guidelines. The IRS has recently ruled in a case in which the rules of the Family Trust allowed the surviving spouse to receive money for "comfort" instead of "support". The IRS ruled that because of the use of the word "comfort", the value of the trust had to be included in the estate of the surviving spouse. Because of that error, the benefit of a vital estate-tax saving tool was lost. Even though the terms might mean the same thing, it is important to abide by IRS regulations.

However, even though there are restrictions, proper use of this trust can provide the surviving spouse with significant funds. On the other hand, the trust can be drawn to provide nothing for the surviving spouse but can, instead, provide for others, such as children.

There are several points to be aware of concerning the Family Trust:

- Once this trust is "funded" (after the first death), it becomes irrevocable. It cannot be changed. As such, it becomes a separate tax paying entity which receives its own federal identification number and files its own tax return.

- A "sprinkling" provision, if properly drawn, allows the trustee to "sprinkle" or direct funds from the trust to the children. This allows her to provide funds to her grown children without being limited by her $10,000 gift exclusion (discussed in Chapter 17).

- No matter how large the Family Trust becomes, the value is not subject to estate taxes when it passes to the heirs.

- While the **principal** in this trust can be free from the creditors of the surviving spouse, the **income** the spouse receives can be subject to the creditors.

- You can allow the surviving spouse a limited right to change the beneficiaries of this trust.

- Remarriage restrictions can be included in this trust whereby the surviving spouse would cease to receive any funds should he or she remarry.

Marital Trust

The second sub-trust is the "Marital Trust." It will consist of the surviving spouse's half of the joint trust property and, depending upon the size of your estate, it can also include the balance of the property that didn't go into the Family Trust. Exactly how it is structured will depend upon your circumstances. Since this goes to the surviving spouse estate-tax free, it is often called the "Marital Deduction Trust."

The major requirement, if you pass property to the surviving spouse under the unlimited marital deduction, is that, at a minimum, he or she must receive the income the trust generates, paid at least annually. Anything beyond that is dependent upon how you choose to structure the trust. The surviving spouse may receive: a maximum of everything, a minimum of interest only, or anything in between.

The Q-TIP trust

"Q-TIP" stands for Qualified Terminable Interest Property. This is a third sub-trust that can be used when you want the surviving spouse to have the benefit of the money but you still want to maintain some control over it. Use of this trust can still qualify for the marital deduction as long as the surviving spouse receives all the income. In addition to the income, the surviving spouse can be entitled to principal under certain conditions. Upon death of the surviving spouse, the property then passes according to the wishes of the first-to-die.

Although it might sound complicated, it really isn't. It is a way for the first-to-die to take advantage of the unlimited marital deduction by leaving property to the surviving spouse while still controlling access to that money and its ultimate destination.

There are several broad cases where this trust is used.

- A spouse wants to ensure that his/her children receive the money at the death of the surviving spouse but still allow the surviving spouse to receive income during his or her lifetime.

- The spouse wants to ensure that the funds aren't diverted to a new spouse in the event of remarriage.

- The spouse wants to make sure that there are controls so the money is not misused.

- A spouse wants to ensure that children from a previous marriage receive his/her rightful inheritance.

Let's look at two cases.

> *Louise and Mike Bowman (**Exhibit 2**) had been married thirty years when they set up their living trust. Their estate was $800,000. Mike, while concerned about saving estate taxes, wanted Louise to have access to virtually everything at his death, and vice versa. Neither was concerned about what the other would do with the money. They were joint trustees of the living trust with the other named as successor trustee. Louise died first. The first $400,000 went into the Family Trust. Mike will be entitled to all the income plus principal as needed for health, maintenance, support, and education. In addition, he can receive 5% or $5,000 per year, whichever is greater. This trust will provide significant estate tax savings for the children upon his death. Since the Bowmans wanted the surviving spouse to receive everything else, the balance went to Mike in the Marital Trust with no restrictions as to its use or disposition.*

●   ●   ●

> *Ralph and Barbara Stone (**Exhibit 3**) had been married six years. Each had grown children, and each brought assets into the marriage. At the time their trust was drawn, they had a joint estate of $2,000,000, with each owning approximately 50%. Both Ralph and Barbara wanted to make sure their respective children would receive their inheritance upon the death of the second spouse. Ralph set up his trust for the first $600,000 of his property to go into the Family Trust. He made his wife and his bank co-trustees with income-only going to Barbara. Upon her death, the funds in that trust will go to his children. The balance of his property (assuming today's value of $400,000) will be split. $200,000 will go into the Marital Trust for Barbara's use. She will be the trustee with full access and control over it. Because he wanted the balance of the property to go to his children, the remaining $200,000 will go in the Q-TIP Trust, with Barbara and the bank as co-trustees. Barbara will receive all the income plus principal for health needs only. At her death, the property will go to his children. Barbara's trust was set up to mirror his.*

Remember Donald and Rebecca Purcell? They saddled their children with $561,180 in estate taxes. Let's see what might have been had they planned differently.

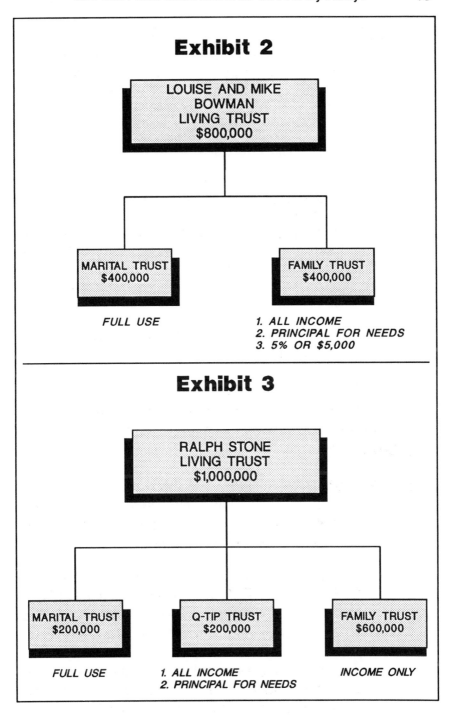

Exhibit 2

LOUISE AND MIKE BOWMAN LIVING TRUST $800,000

MARITAL TRUST $400,000

FULL USE

FAMILY TRUST $400,000

1. ALL INCOME
2. PRINCIPAL FOR NEEDS
3. 5% OR $5,000

Exhibit 3

RALPH STONE LIVING TRUST $1,000,000

MARITAL TRUST $200,000

FULL USE

Q-TIP TRUST $200,000

1. ALL INCOME
2. PRINCIPAL FOR NEEDS

FAMILY TRUST $600,000

INCOME ONLY

Donald Purcell was 48, his wife Rebecca was 46. They had three children, ages 21, 18, and 16. They had a total net estate of $2,000,000. This included the value of their home, stocks and bonds, retirement plans, personal property, his business, all life insurance, and the custodial accounts they had set up for their minor children. To avoid probate and to take care of themselves in the event of a disability, they had chosen to establish a joint revocable living trust. They died within weeks of each other as the result of an automobile accident.

The first $600,000 would have gone into the Family (bypass) Trust with the balance going to the Marital Trust for the benefit of Rebecca. (If they had wished, they could have included a Q-TIP Trust consisting of the balance of his property.) Upon Rebecca's death, all the money would have gone into a children's trust for the benefit of their children.

Calculating the tax

Let's calculate their estate tax had they taken advantage of a Family Trust (**Exhibit 4**).

- Mr. Purcell's share of the estate would have been the same as before, $1,000,000. Since he would have had a living trust, there would have been no probate expenses.

- His first $600,000 would have gone into the Family Trust, thereby avoiding any taxes. His remaining $400,000 balance would have gone into the Marital Trust and avoided taxes on that portion.

- Mrs. Purcell's adjusted gross estate would have been $1,400,000 (his $400,000 balance plus her $1,000,000 share). Remember, the $600,000 in the Family Trust wouldn't count against her estate.

- The gross estate tax on her $1,400,000 estate would have been $512,800, less the $192,800 credit, thus resulting in a net estate tax of $320,000.

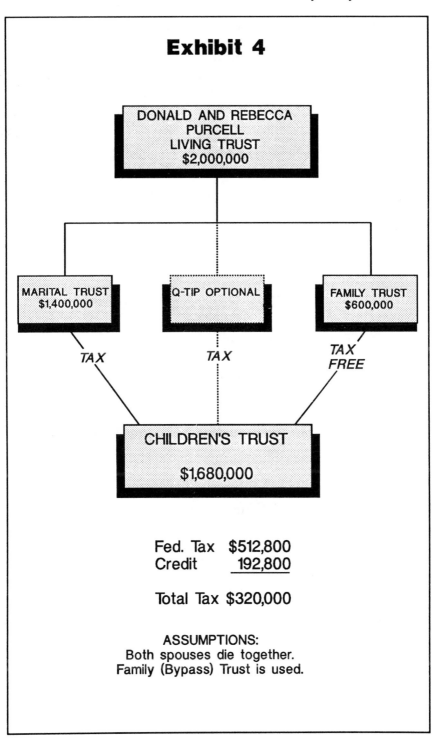

Exhibit 4

DONALD AND REBECCA PURCELL LIVING TRUST $2,000,000

MARITAL TRUST $1,400,000

Q-TIP OPTIONAL

FAMILY TRUST $600,000

TAX   *TAX*   *TAX FREE*

CHILDREN'S TRUST

$1,680,000

Fed. Tax $512,800
Credit   192,800

Total Tax $320,000

ASSUMPTIONS:
Both spouses die together.
Family (Bypass) Trust is used.

- Their children would have received $1,680,000.

As a result, the children would have received $300,780 more than they did under the previous scenario. Although the same effect could be realized if Mr. Purcell had left $600,000 directly to the children, there would be several problems. First, one of the children is a minor. We'll discuss this situation in the next chapter. Second, had Mrs. Purcell lived, she would not receive any economic benefit from that money. Third, the adult children would receive their share immediately, which might not be the Purcells' wishes. Finally, there would be no instructions whatsoever for the use of that money.

Now let's look at the same case but change two facts:

- Mrs. Purcell survives Mr. Purcell by **ten years.**

- The **estate grows** by 4% net per year.

Exhibit 5 shows the result with a **simple will.** The highlights:

- The value of the estate would be $2,872,266 at her death.

- The gross estate taxes would be $1,211,933, less her credit of $192,800, resulting in net estate taxes of $1,019,133.

- This would leave $1,853,133 for the children.

Compare this with **Exhibit 6,** which shows the result with a **Family Trust.** The highlights:

- Her taxable estate would be reduced to $2,072,342 because it would not include the $880,147 ($600,000 plus growth) in the Family Trust.

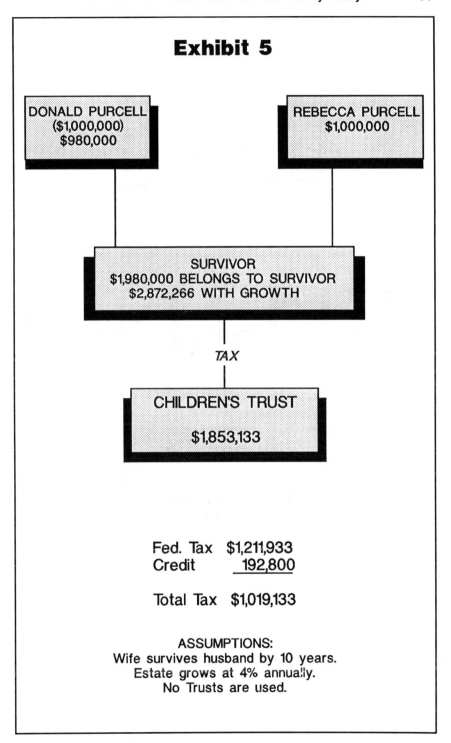

Exhibit 5

DONALD PURCELL
($1,000,000)
$980,000

REBECCA PURCELL
$1,000,000

SURVIVOR
$1,980,000 BELONGS TO SURVIVOR
$2,872,266 WITH GROWTH

TAX

CHILDREN'S TRUST

$1,853,133

Fed. Tax $1,211,933
Credit   192,800

Total Tax $1,019,133

ASSUMPTIONS:
Wife survives husband by 10 years.
Estate grows at 4% annually.
No Trusts are used.

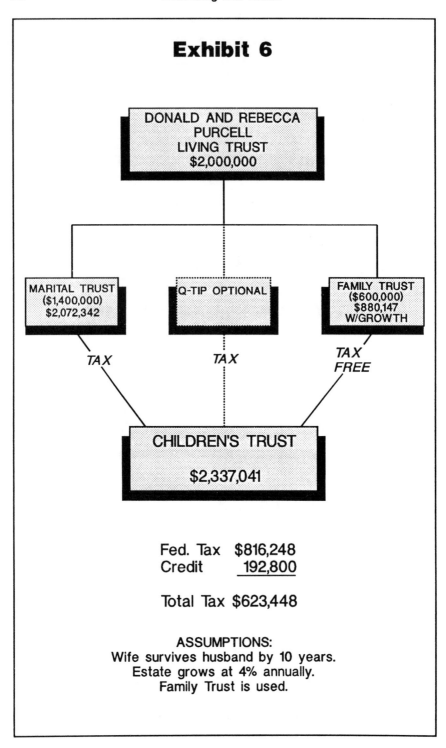

Exhibit 6

DONALD AND REBECCA
PURCELL
LIVING TRUST
$2,000,000

MARITAL TRUST
($1,400,000)
$2,072,342

Q-TIP OPTIONAL

FAMILY TRUST
($600,000)
$880,147
W/GROWTH

TAX

TAX

*TAX
FREE*

CHILDREN'S TRUST

$2,337,041

Fed. Tax $816,248
Credit   192,800

Total Tax $623,448

ASSUMPTIONS:
Wife survives husband by 10 years.
Estate grows at 4% annually.
Family Trust is used.

- The gross estate taxes would be $816,248, less her credit of $192,800, resulting in net taxes of $623,448.

- This would leave $2,337,041 to the children, an **increase of $483,908!**

Remember, no matter how large the Family Trust eventually becomes, it is not subject to estate tax at the death of the surviving spouse. In this example, the Family Trust grew to $880,147 and avoided estate tax. Even if it grew to three million dollars, there would be no estate tax at the second death, as long as it didn't violate any of the IRS regulations.

As you can see, the proper use of a trust to capture the $600,000 exemption of the first to die can save estate taxes. Although the illustrations show no estate taxes being paid at the first death, there are times when it might be wise to do so. For example, if you have property which is rapidly increasing in value, you may wish to pay estate taxes at the first death and remove that spiraling value from your estate.

Is this legal?

One question I get when discussing this estate tax savings aspect is "Is this legal?" Yes, it's legal. As stated earlier, everybody has a $600,000 exemption. You may leave $600,000 to any person estate-tax free. For example, upon your death, you can leave $600,000 to your child and the balance of your property to your spouse, free of federal estate taxes.

All we are doing in the trust is leaving your $600,000 to your children through your spouse, with some strings attached. As long as you abide by the "ascertainable standards", you can maximize your estate savings.

Tax savings by using your $600,000 exemption

The following table is provided to illustrate the tax

savings you might realize in your own situation. These are only generalized examples using various taxable estates and do not take into account any credits or special situations.

- Column 1 is the current value of your estate.

- Column 2 is your **net tax** (after the $192,800 credit) with a simple will (no Family Trust or other use of the unified credit). These figures assume probate and administrative expenses of a conservative 2%.

- Column 3 shows your **net tax** by capturing each spouse's $600,000 exemption. Whether this goes into a Family Trust or directly to the children, the results will be the same. Remember, we are assuming no probate or administration fees with the living trust.

For comparison purposes, I assumed the husband and wife died together.

CURRENT ESTATE SIZE	ESTATE TAXES WITHOUT FAMILY TRUST	ESTATE TAXES WITH THE FAMILY TRUST
$600,000	0	0
1,000,000	153,000	0
1,500,000	363,000	114,000
2,000,000	588,000	320,000
3,000,000	1,098,000	784,000
4,000,000	1,648,000	1,318,000
5,000,000	2,198,000	1,868,000
10,000,000	4,948,000	4,618,000

The figures above assume the husband and wife die together, which rarely occurs. Next, let's look at the **net taxes** if the first spouse were to die today and the surviving spouse

lived an additional ten years. Again, we will assume they owned the assets equally (or in a joint trust) and that the estate grew by 5% per year after the death of the first spouse.

CURRENT ESTATE SIZE	ESTATE SIZE IN TEN YEARS	ESTATE TAX WITHOUT FAMILY TRUST	ESTATE TAX WITH THE FAMILY TRUST
$600,000	$977,337	144,161	0
1,000,000	1,628,895	421,003	80,634
1,500,000	2,443,342	805,238	348,382
2,000,000	3,257,789	1,211,895	725,422
3,000,000	4,886,684	2,026,342	1,537,674
4,000,000	6,515,579	2,840,789	2,352,121
5,000,000	8,144,473	3,655,237	3,166,568
10,000,000	16,288,946	8,041,920	7,504,385

Let's further assume that the surviving spouse lives twenty five years, keeping the growth at 5% per year. The numbers are even more compelling.

CURRENT ESTATE SIZE	ESTATE SIZE IN TWENTY-FIVE YEARS	ESTATE TAXES WITHOUT FAMILY TRUST	ESTATE TAXES WITH THE FAMILY TRUST
$600,000	$2,031,813	603,588	159,522
1,000,000	3,386,355	1,276,177	449,930
1,500,000	5,079,532	2,122,766	1,106,860
2,000,000	6,772,710	2,969,355	1,953,448
3,000,000	10,159,065	4,670,486	3,646,626
4,000,000	13,545,420	6,532,981	5,415,484
5,000,000	16,931,775	8,395,476	7,277,979
10,000,000	33,863,549	16,931,775	15,915,860

Once again, you can see the significant estate tax savings by taking advantage of each spouse's $600,000 exemption.

Conclusion

As we have shown in this chapter, if you have an estate tax problem, capturing the $600,000 exemption of the first-to-die is very important. Unfortunately, it is a solution that is rarely used. That just means that Uncle Sam (and possibly your state) will get more of your estate than necessary.

While this strategy can be a big help in capturing the $600,000 exemption of both spouses, it is by no means the only one that can be used. In Chapter 17 we will begin looking at other techniques that can help reduce the cost of your estate taxes.

11

HOW CAN I PROVIDE FOR MY MINOR CHILDREN?

One of the saddest occurrences I see in my practice is the hardship inflicted on minor children when their parents die without the proper planning. It's analogous to visiting a children's hospital; it is most devastating when tragedies happen to innocent children. Unfortunately, there are too many situations where parents, either through misguided information, lack of knowledge, or procrastination, have structured their estates in such a manner that they totally ignore the present and future needs of their minor children.

When both parents die, the property has to go to someone. If the parents have failed to plan, then most, if not all, of their property will go to their children. Even if the parents have planned, they generally take one of two courses: (1) they leave property directly to the children; or (2) they leave it to the relative who is going to take care of the children. Let's look at each of these potentially disastrous scenarios.

LEAVING PROPERTY TO MINOR CHILDREN

The probate court

As you know by now, minors can't own property. So when you leave property to a minor, the probate court takes control. It appoints someone to take care of the children. In most cases, this is the person named in your will, known as the **guardian**. In addition, the court will appoint a guardian of the property. In some states, this person is also called a guardian, in others a **conservator**. This person may or may not be the same as the guardian of the child. Depending on your state of residence and the circumstances, he or she may have to post a bond. Among other things, it depends on who actually received the funds: did the children receive it directly (for example, as a beneficiary of a life insurance policy), or did it pass through the estate? In the latter case, through proper planning, you may be able to avoid the need for a bond.

The guardian/conservator will have to keep **accurate records** of how the money was used. Many states severely limit where the money can be invested and spent. If an extraordinary expense is desired (braces, etc.), then the guardian/conservator may have to go back to the court and ask permission. In many cases, this will require the services of an attorney, and that can get expensive. And then when the child reaches legal age, let's say 18, he or she receives the funds. What a comforting thought. My son getting all my money the day he turns 18!

In counselling clients, most are unaware of these problems. As a rule, clients don't want to tie the hands of those taking care of their children. I have yet to speak to anyone who wants to leave the future of his or her child in the hands of the probate court. And nobody wants his or her money wasted on bond premiums, attorney fees, court costs, etc. But it happens every day.

How minor children end up with property

The first question is, how and why do minor children end up with property? The answers are simple: they receive it as the result of improper advice given to their parents, lack of thought, or failure to properly plan. Let's explore.

A life insurance agent met with Lee Pike, who had just applied for a $500,000 policy.

Agent: *Mr. Pike, who do you want as beneficiary?*

Lee: *My wife, Judith Ann Pike.*

Agent: *If your wife doesn't survive you, who should then get the proceeds?*

Lee: *I guess my kids, Jeffrey, Brian, and David.*

Boy, wasn't that simple? In Mr. Pike's mind, his family is totally protected. His wife will have money to care for herself and the children. If they both should die, the children will have the money for their support. Perfect! Enter the dragon!

What really happened

Mr. & Mrs. Pike were on a trip to the Caribbean. They decided to take a day trip to a neighboring island aboard a small plane. A storm hit. The pilot was flying too low and crashed into the side of a mountain. Mr. and Mrs. Pike were killed.

At home, their family grieved. The children, still too young to comprehend the whole thing, were upset because their mommy and daddy weren't coming back. Luckily, however, Lee had taken care of his affairs. He and his wife had up-to-date wills and sufficient life insurance. Let's look at how their assets passed:

Home. Their home was owned jointly. Since they both were dead, the home went into their estate and passed in accordance with their wills.

Investments. They had some stocks and bonds in joint accounts. Since both joint tenants were deceased, the investments passed in accordance with their wills.

Retirement Benefits. Lee had a retirement plan at work. It passed in accordance with the beneficiary designation: first to his wife, if living; otherwise to his estate.

Insurance. Lee had life insurance. We know where that went.

His wife was deceased; his children got it.

His life insurance avoided probate because it went directly to the named contingent beneficiary: his children. Everything else went through probate. Remember, the house and investments went through probate because both joint tenants were dead. The retirement plan went through probate because the contingent beneficiary was his estate.

The wills were read:

> *His:*   *"I leave everything to my beloved wife, Judith Ann, if living, otherwise to my children, share and share alike."*

> *Hers:*   *"I leave everything to my beloved husband Lee, if living, otherwise to my children, share and share alike."*

Both named her sister, Cynthia, to be guardian of the children.

That was pretty simple, wasn't it? Everything was in order, and the kids got the money. Right? Wrong! That's not the way it actually turned out.

At the time, Jeffrey was 10; Brian was 9; David was 6. Since they were minors, they couldn't own property. What happened? The assets entered the jurisdiction of the probate court, and the dragon wasn't far behind!

Cynthia was nominated guardian of the children. Lee's brother, Alan, also wanted guardianship. Cynthia assumed that since she was named in the will, she would automatically be guardian. But remember, when you name a guardian in your will, you are only indicating your preference. It is not binding on the court.

But in this case, as in most cases, the judge went along with the Pikes' wishes and named Cynthia guardian of the children as well as guardian of the property (called the conservator in some states).

Without going into detail, it has turned out to be a difficult situation for all involved. Cynthia has had her hands full trying to raise her nephews along with her own children. Additionally, she has had to worry about handling her nephews' money. By the law of her jurisdiction, she has been limited as to where she can invest the money. In addition, she is required to file periodic reports with the court. Because her house is too small for all the children (she has three of her own), everybody is constantly bickering. Ideally, she would like to add two rooms to her home or purchase another. But she can't afford it. Every time there is an extraordinary expense for the children, she has to receive the permission of the probate court. This requires the assistance of an attorney, which is running into money. The entire process is putting a lot of pressure on her, and that affects the children. Alan has offered to take two of the children off her hands, but she knows that wasn't what her sister and brother-in-law really wanted. So she continues to struggle and does the best she can. I doubt this was what Mr. and Mrs. Pike had in mind.

Mercifully, this will end someday. When Jeffrey turns 18, he will get a check for what is left from his 33%. When Brian turns 18 he will get a check for his 33%. And when David turns 18, he will receive his 33%. But what happens if David, due to medical, emotional, or other problems, needs more money? What if medical bills are running so high that his 33% is eaten up? Can he get part of Jeffrey and Brian's? No way. He is out of luck.

It is doubtful that you would deny one of your own children medical care because it would take from the others. Yet, when the probate court has control over funds for several children, it considers each child's share separate and distinct.

Why do people put their children in that situation? Two reasons. First, they don't believe they are going to die (remember the Ostrich Syndrome). And second, they believe that even if they do die, some miracle will cause everything to work out (the Ostrich Syndrome, Part II).

When I relate a case such as the Pikes, there are those who criticize me for looking at what they think is an atypical situation. They tell me I shouldn't worry people needlessly because things usually turn out okay. I respond in two ways. First, in my experience, these situations are not that unusual. They happen every day. But second, what sense does it make to plan only for the best? That's like a physician not worrying about prescribing a certain medication because most people don't die when they take it.

Remember, *we don't think we have a problem until we have a problem.* In my opinion, **hoping for the best is malpractice.** I owe it to my clients and to you, the reader, to properly outline the problems you might be facing as a result of your current planning. Let the others try to shield their clients from potential obstacles. That's neither my style nor intent.

LEAVING THE MONEY TO A RELATIVE

Okay. You agree that the above situation wasn't satisfactory. But you think you have the solution. Why couldn't the Pikes have left the money directly to Cynthia? That way she could have raised the kids the way she wanted, without court interference.

Just as there are potential problems when you hold property in joint tenancy with a non-spouse, there are potential problems here. They stem from the fact that as soon as Cynthia received the money, it would have been hers, not the children's. After all, she was the named beneficiary. So let's look at a few of the potential dragons.

Let's first assume the best.

Cynthia received the money and carefully spent it on the children as needed. She didn't waste a penny, but neither did the children have to do without. They made it through high school. She paid for their college. The day David graduated from college, she was finished with her obligation. There was money left over. So she brought the boys into her den, sat them down, and gave them each 1/3 of the money, explaining that this was what was left of the money their parents left her to take care of them.

Gift consequences - Had she done this, she would have made a **gift**! That's right. Remember, it was her money. The minute she gave it to the boys, she made what might be a taxable gift, as we will see in Chapter 17. And that's the best that could have happened. Let's look at the consequences of other scenarios.

Divorce - What would have happened had Cynthia gotten **divorced**? Whose money would it have been, anyway? It would have been hers! And her husband could have made a valid case for going after it. He could have claimed that it was part of the marital estate, accumulated during their marriage. Even if he couldn't get any of it, it could have affected the final settlement.

Lawsuit - What would have happened had Cynthia been **sued**? The money would have been her asset - all of it would have been at risk.

Death - What would have happened had Cynthia **died**? That money probably would have ended up with her husband. What if they had both died? The money would probably have gone to Cynthia's children, unless other arrangements had been made. It is doubtful that Jeffrey, Brian, or David would have received anything.

All kinds of things could have happened, and they're all bad. Remember the dragons. Why take chances when there are better alternatives?

There are two things Mr. and Mrs. Pike could have done, and they both involve trusts. First, they could have included a testamentary trust as part of their will. Second, they could have created a living trust. Let's look at both.

USING A TRUST

A **testamentary trust** is a trust created by the will. Upon the death of Mr. & Mrs. Pike, their assets would pass into the trust rather than directly to the children. They could have named Cynthia as guardian of the children and could have named Alan, or anyone else they wanted, as trustee of the property. They could have left instructions in the trust as to how the money was to be invested, how it was to be spent, and how it would eventually pass to the children.

While this type of trust provides definite advantages over a simple will, the problems with it are essentially the same as those of wills. First, the will must be probated. Therefore, a testamentary trust won't avoid the time delays and costs related to probate. In addition, it will be under the jurisdiction of the probate court and possibly result in some of the problems discussed earlier. And, of course, a contest of the will by other heirs (such as children by a previous marriage) can cause the entire will to be thrown out, and it's anyone's guess what might happen then.

If having the probate court oversee the trust is important to you, then consider the testamentary trust. If you would prefer to keep the court out of the process, then you can consider a living trust. The differences between the two trusts are covered in Chapter 14.

With a **revocable living trust**, the trust will contain language that establishes a special sub-trust for your children. All your assets, if that is your desire, will flow directly into that trust. No muss, no fuss, no probate. At that point, your trustees will take over and follow your instructions.

No matter which type of trust you choose, there are some basic decisions that need to be made. Let's look at a few of them.

Guardians

One of the most difficult decisions is who will be the

person or persons to rear your children? Who will be the person to give the love, affection, and guidance once you are not around? This alone is the single reason that most people don't plan: they can't decide or agree on a guardian. As a result, they do nothing, and leave that decision up to the court.

The guardian should be someone who shares your values and be a person you feel would do a good job rearing your children. But realize that nobody can do as good a job as you can - nobody will care about your children as much as you do. But that is not a valid excuse for avoiding your obligation to name someone. However difficult the decision, it is still better than leaving your children's future up to the court.

The guardian is not named in the trust; he or she is named in the will. If you have a testamentary trust, then the will which contains the trust names the guardian. If you have a living trust, the documents should include a "pour-over" will which, among other things, names a guardian for your children.

It is important to realize that your nomination of a guardian does not guarantee that choice by the court. While the court will try to honor your wishes, there may be extenuating circumstances which prevent that. For example, a natural parent will usually have the first opportunity to become the legal guardian of your common children, no matter how much you might abhor the thought.

Trustees

Once you have named someone to rear the children, you should choose a different person to take care of the financial responsibilities. That person is known as the trustee. Although the trustee and guardian can be the same person, it is preferable to have different parties occupying each position.

The trustee's first job is to handle the funds and to invest them carefully. Unlike the probate court, which in many jurisdictions allows the money to be invested only in federally-insured banks, you can give the trustee as much or as little leeway as you see fit.

The second job of the trustee is to assist the guardian financially. It is the trustee who provides the guardian with the funds for your children.

What we have done is taken the two elements of rearing children, caring for them and supporting them financially, and divided it between two different parties. While parents normally handle both aspects, this is extremely difficult for a guardian who is rearing your children in addition to his or her own. It makes more sense for the guardian to care for the children and the trustee to handle the finances.

Instructions

When it comes right down to it, one of the major advantages of a trust is that it can contain your special instructions to the trustees on how to care for your loved ones. Think of your trustees as your baby sitter. Just as you leave instructions for your baby sitter when you go out for a night on the town, so you will leave instructions for your trustees in your trust.

Let's give the Pikes what they never received: a second chance. We'll see how things might have been with different planning.

> *Mr. and Mrs. Pike set up a revocable living trust. They titled all their property in the trust. The trust was the beneficiary of Lee's life insurance and the contingent beneficiary of his retirement plan. Upon Lee's death, the trust split into the family and marital trust. Upon Mrs. Pike's death, all the property flowed into the "children's trust." They wanted both sides of the family involved in rearing their children. In their "pour-over" will, they named Cynthia as guardian of the children. In their trust, they named Alan as trustee. Additionally, they set forth their instructions to*

Alan covering many different occurrences, for example:

- *The trustee was instructed to provide the necessary principal and interest for the benefit of the children.*

- *He should distribute money on the basis of need, rather than equality. For example, if David needs money for special education, it should be provided, without concern about spending an equal amount for the other children.*

- *The trustee should assist Cynthia in any manner he feels will make the environment better for the children. For example, if she needs an addition to her home and there is, in his opinion, sufficient funds without financially harming the children, then it should be done.*

- *The trustee may advance money for a business or practice when the children get older, assuming it doesn't harm the remaining children. The eventual inheritance of that child will be reduced by this amount.*

- *When the youngest child is 25 or completes college, which-ever occurs first, 25% of the funds will be distributed equally among the boys. They will receive the remaining 75% in three equal installments every five years. In the meantime, the trustee should provide funds for medical assistance should the need arise.*

- *He was instructed to hold the funds in trust should any of the boys become mentally incapacitated, using it for that child's needs for as long as he remains in that condition.*

The trust contained many more instructions for different eventualities. It was full of the Pike's instructions for the care of their children.

Upon the deaths of their parents, the boys' futures would be assured. Cynthia, as guardian, would be able to rear the boys to the best of her ability. Alan, as trustee, would follow all his brother's instructions. The court would not be involved. There would be no delays whatsoever. When Cynthia needed money, she would contact Alan. In the meantime, the money would be invested conservatively for growth. When Cynthia gets cramped in her home, there should be sufficient funds in the trust to pay for adding two bedrooms to her home. While there will be problems from time to time, there are no circumstances that Cynthia and Alan should not be able to handle. The boys would receive their inheritance when mandated by their parent's trust.

Unfortunately, in real life, this "second-chance" scenario never happened.

Conclusion

I relate the Pikes' case with the hope that their disaster will serve to show you how things can be handled with the proper planning. So many bad things can happen when dealing with minor children. Instead of releasing control of your estate to the dragons, keep it yourself. It will be much better for all involved.

12

WHAT OTHER TYPES OF TRUSTS ARE AVAILABLE FOR MINORS?

Most of my clients have a desire to reduce their taxes, whether they be estate or income taxes. Many have considered shifting income to their children in order to take advantage of the child's lower tax bracket. But the federal government has severely reduced many of the options. Nevertheless, a few are still available.

UGMA/UGTA

Definition

UGMA, which stands for **Uniform Gifts to Minors Act,** allows adults to invest in certain assets as custodians for their children. The types of property invested are limited to banks, securities (stocks, bonds, mutual funds), life insurance, and annuities.

UTMA, which stands for **Uniform Transfer to Minors Act,** is an expanded form of UGMA. Basically, it removes most of the restrictions concerning allowable investments and transfers between trusts and estates. Fewer states allow the UTMA than the UGMA.

Process

The property is held in the name of an adult, usually a parent, as custodian for the child. It reads "John Smith, Custodian for Randy Smith, under the (your state) UGMA". The property constitutes a gift to the child. Since it is a "present interest" gift, it qualifies for the $10,000 annual exclusion.

Taxes

If a parent makes the gift, serves as custodian, and dies, the property is included in his or her **estate**. However, if another party is the custodian, it is included in the estate of the child.

Income earned in the account is taxed to the minor. The party responsible for the tax depends on the age of the child.

- If the child is under the age of 14, there is no tax on the first $1,000 of investment income. Income above $1,000 is taxed to the parents at their income tax bracket.

- If the child is 14 or older, all investment income will be taxed to the child at his or her tax bracket.

Distribution of the property

The child receives the property at the age of majority, which is governed by state law. You have no choice in this matter; it is automatic by operation of law.

Advantages

- Depending on the application of the tax laws explained above, it serves to get income taxed to the child instead of the parent.

- It serves to get assets out of the estate of the parent and into the child's, unless the parent is also the custodian.

- Unlike the typical trust, it is a no-cost way to put assets in the name of the child.

- It removes future appreciation of the assets from the estate of the parent.

- Trust assets can be used for health, maintenance, support, and education of the child, at the custodian's discretion.

Disadvantages

- The property goes to the child at the age of majority, no matter what the parent may desire.

- The gift is irrevocable - the parent cannot get it back if a financial emergency arises.

- Upon reaching the age of majority, the child may demand a formal audit of the account.

- The value of the account is included in your estate if you die while acting as custodian, and your child is still a minor.

SECTION 2503(b) TRUST

Definition

This trust, named after the IRS code section 2503(b), can provide continuous income to the child during the period he or she is a minor.

Process

A trust is established for the benefit of the child. The gifts are "present interest" gifts and qualify for the $10,000 annual exclusion. However, since the gift results in a stream of income, only the present value is included in the calculation.

Taxes

The **income** is taxable to the child under the same rules as above. If the child is under the age of 14, investment income in excess of $1,000 is taxed to parents at their tax bracket. If the child is age 14 or older, the income is taxed to the child at the child's bracket.

Distribution

While there is no requirement as to the distribution of the principal, income can last a lifetime or be directed to any person.

Advantages

- It does not require distribution of the principal to the child.

- The trust qualifies under the $10,000 gift exclusion.

- The income is taxed to the child subject to above limitations.

- There is a great deal of flexibility over distribution of principal.

Disadvantages

- Specified income must be distributed to the child at least annually.

- All income earned by the trust must be distributed to the child.

- Any income not paid during the years the child was a minor must be paid out at the age of majority.

SECTION 2503(c) TRUST

Definition

The Section 2503(c) trust allows a person to make a gift to the child but still maintain control of the property. Unlike the Section 2503(b) trust, this trust does not require mandatory distributions of income.

Process

The property is gifted into the trust for the benefit of the child. Since it is a gift of "present interest", it falls within the $10,000 annual exclusion. Income need not be paid until the child reaches age 21. At that point, the trust must be distributed to the child. However, the child can choose not to take it.

Taxes

If the donor is the trustee and dies before the child is 21, the value is included in the **estate** of the donor.

Income, if distributed, will be taxed to the child beneficiary. If the income is left to accumulate in the trust, it will be taxed to the trust itself.

Distribution

The property can be distributed to the child at age 21. However, the child can choose to leave the property in the trust while retaining the right to remove it anytime he or she desires.

Advantages

- It removes the property, and the eventual appreciation, from the estate of the donor.

- It can shift income from higher bracket of donor to lower bracket of child. Since the child under 14 is in the same income tax bracket as the parent (after the first $1,000 of income), this is only effective if the child is over the age of 14.

- The child can choose to leave property in trust beyond the age of 21.

- There is no requirement for income distribution while the child is a minor.

Disadvantages

- It is an irrevocable gift to the child to which the child is entitled anytime after the age of 21.

- The trust assets must be available to child at age 21.

- Upon the death of the donor, the value of the trust is included in his or her estate if the child is under the age of 21.

- If the child dies before the age of 21, the trust goes to the child's estate.

Conclusion

By taking advantage of the difference in tax brackets between you and your children (and/or grandchildren), you can reduce not only your income taxes but your estate taxes as well. Combining this with sensible estate planning should be an integral part of your overall plan.

13

HOW CAN I PROVIDE FOR MY ADULT CHILDREN?

If you have adult children, you will want to determine how they will eventually receive your estate. While this is an area that doesn't receive much thought ("We'll just leave everything equally to our children"), there are some thought processes you might want to entertain.

Every child is different, and whether we care to admit it or not, we treat each child differently. Some children are responsible; others are not. Some handle money well; with others it goes through their hands like water through a sieve. Some can hold a job; others jump from one to another. While they were young, we were able to work around these differences to help them function within their limitations. Now that it's time for them to receive their inheritance, doesn't it just make sense to continue to work within their strengths and weaknesses?

Some people say, "I don't care what happens to the money after it goes to my kids. If they waste it all, that's their problem." If that's your preference, you can leave it to them outright and not worry about it.

But a great number of the people I counsel are concerned about what happens to their money. They are making a great effort to ensure that the government doesn't get it because they think it will be wasted. Having their children fritter it away isn't much better. So they choose to specify how their children will receive the money.

While we are going to discuss leaving money to adult children, the information applies no matter who the person is, as long as he or she is an adult.

Let's take a look at some of the basic decisions you might want to consider:

- **Do you want your children to receive equal shares or do you want the shares divided unequally?**

Gary and Beverly Smith have three children. The youngest, Margie, has received a lot of help from Gary and Beverly over the years. She decided to go to medical school, which required a substantial sum of money. After her residency, she opted for private practice. Gary and Beverly helped finance this, also. Their other children, however, have not been so lucky. Both have scraped by on modest incomes. Although Gary and Bev have been able to help out occasionally, their funds have been generally limited because of the assistance they have given Margie. Upon drafting their trust, they decided that the bulk of their estate should go to the other two children, since Margie had already received the benefit of their money.

• • •

Randy Forrest has two children, Robert and Darrell. Robert has been a responsible citizen, is married with children, and holds a good job. Darrell, however, has been a mess. He has been in and out of jail and has had continual problems with drugs and alcohol. He has cost his father heartache and money over the years. Randy has not heard from him in the past five years. His original plan was to leave all his money to Robert. His attorney recommended a living trust because it would be harder to contest. Randy knows Darrell well enough to know what would happen when he discovered he was cut out. He would clean up, put on a suit, go down to the court and make a great impression. And if he did end up with any money, it would just go to purchase more drugs. Randy knew of no other solution, and felt relatively comfortable with it.

Between the time Randy gave his attorney instructions and the trust was actually drafted, Randy had the thought that at some point, Darrell might straighten out, as many children eventually do. Darrell is, after all, still his son, and despite everything, his father still loves him. He decided to leave Robert 75% of his estate in a lump sum. The balance would be put into a trust for Darrell with a bank as trustee. He didn't want to make Robert trustee because that might put him under too much pressure from his brother. The trust contains a special set of instructions. The money is to be invested with all interest accumulating. If Darrell gets a job within two years, and remains employed by the same firm for twelve months without getting into any kind of trouble, he can start receiving the interest from the trust. If he then continues to stay out of trouble (which means never being found guilty of an offense and staying out of jail), he can receive one-fourth of the principal every five years. In the meantime, he would continue to receive interest. Should he ever get into trouble (as defined above), the trust would terminate, and all the money would be paid to Robert.

- **Do you want the money to go to your children in one lump sum or do you want it spread out over a period of years?**

Daniel and Donna Smith have what they consider to be irresponsible children. Daniel constantly complains that the only time he hears from the children is when they want money. While talking with his attorney, he decided that it would be a total waste to leave his estate to the children in one lump sum. He knows them well enough to realize that the money would be gone in a matter of weeks. He decided, instead, that the funds would be held in trust until they reach the age of 60. He knows they aren't saving anything for retirement, so he decided that he would be their retirement plan. His trust provides that they will receive 10% a year for 10 years, starting when they reach 60.

• • •

Robert and Suzanne Templeton have three children: Kathy, Jackie, and Ted. Kathy and Ted are responsible adults. Jackie has never met a dollar she didn't spend. Robert and Suzanne realized that if they leave Jackie's share to her in a lump sum, it would be gone immediately. But they didn't want to penalize their responsible children. So, they structured their trust in such a manner to allow Kathy and Ted to receive their one-third shares in a lump sum. Jackie, on the other hand, will receive her share 1/4 upon the death of her parents, 1/4 five years later, 1/4 five years later, and the balance five years after that. Robert and Suzanne hoped that at some point, after blowing the earlier money, Jackie will settle down and be more responsible.

Many people are reluctant to treat their children as the Templetons did. They think that if they do, the children will be angry with them. They don't want that as the last memory. And that is a valid concern.

However, if you are a loving parent, don't you want to do what is best for your children? Isn't that the real reason you're doing this planning in the first place?

I present these cases for illustration purposes only. You need to do whatever makes you comfortable. After all, it is your estate to do with as you please.

Of course, you don't have to leave your estate to your children. Unless you run up against state laws dealing with minor children, you can do any type of planning you wish. You can leave your money to other relatives, friends, a charity, or any combination thereof.

Conclusion

Planning for adult children is an area that receives very little thought because most people don't realize how easy it can actually be. This is just another case where it can make sense to take advantage of the planning opportunities available to help control and preserve your estate.

14

HOW DO TESTAMENTARY AND LIVING TRUSTS COMPARE?

There has been some criticism of living trusts by attorneys and others who believe that it is not as valuable a planning vehicle as people are being led to believe. To a point, they are correct. A living trust is not for everyone, no matter what some might say. There are other types of planning methods that might be used, depending upon your particular situation. For the most part, however, the living trust has some very strong arguments in its favor.

In their condemnation of living trusts, these detractors compare them with wills. And they always come up with the same few arguments: the cost of a living trust is too high; you have to transfer your property into a living trust; and probate isn't so bad. Those may or may not be valid points. But many of these same people say if you do need a trust, then you should do a testamentary trust, which is part of your will. At that point, the issue is not between a living trust and a will. It is instead between a testamentary trust containing a family trust and a living trust containing a family trust. To help clear up this conflict, it is important to look objectively at the two types of trusts.

There is a basic difference between the two trusts:

- A **testamentary** trust is part of your will and takes

effect at your death.

- A **living** trust is in force during your lifetime **and** after your death.

Let's look at the issues:

- **Cost** - The cost of a testamentary trust will fall somewhere between a will and a living trust. As a result, a testamentary trust should initially cost less than a living trust. Consider, however, that the testamentary trust must be probated. Therefore, no matter how easy probate may be, the total cost for a testamentary trust should be greater than that of the living trust.

  There are some who say that for the attorney, the testamentary trust is the best of all worlds: not only can he charge more for drafting a will containing a testamentary trust, he also gets to probate the will. In some businesses, that would be considered "double-dipping". Personally, when I was faced with the choice between a testamentary trust and a living trust, I chose to spend a little more initially for a living trust. That way, I could enjoy the living benefits of the trust and keep my family out of probate.

  One last point concerning cost. Considering inflation, the cost of probate most certainly will go up. If you do a living trust now, you have frozen your cost at the price of the trust today.

- **Probate** - As long as your property is titled in your revocable trust, it avoids probate. A testamentary trust, being part of a will, guarantees probate and all its problems.

- **Disability** - A revocable trust will contain your

instructions for taking care of you and your family in the event of mental incapacity. A testamentary trust doesn't take effect until your death and does nothing for your disability.

- **Save estate taxes** - Both a living trust and a testamentary trust can save estate taxes for married couples.

- **Contestation** - While it is extremely difficult to successfully contest a living trust, it is easy to contest a will containing a trust.

- **Ongoing fees during life** - Since a testamentary trust is not valid during life, no ongoing fees are required. Neither are any ongoing fees required, under normal circumstances, with a living trust.

- **Tax forms** - Neither trust requires any special tax forms until after the death of the first spouse. No special forms are required during life.

- **Transferring property** - For a living trust to avoid probate, the trustmaker must transfer his property to the trust prior to his death. Nothing is transferred into a testamentary trust until death. But if you think that it is hard for you to transfer your property into the trust now, think about what your family will have to go through when you're not around!

However, there is one vital point that most people seem to miss concerning the testamentary trust: **most of the property of the first-to-die normally bypasses the will and never makes it into the testamentary trust in the first place.** Most couples own the bulk of their assets jointly. With the average testamentary trust I have seen, property titles have never been changed. What this means is most of the property passes according to its own rules, bypassing the will, and thus bypassing the testamentary trust. As a result, the testamentary trust holds virtually no property, totally defeating its purpose.

Ann and Chris Tanner had an estate valued at $1,500,000. Their planner suggested setting up a testamentary trust to save estate taxes. They met with their attorney, and he drafted the trust. They went home thinking they would save a significant amount of taxes. Their property was owned as follows:

Home	Jointly owned	$	500,000
Brokerage Account	In Chris's name	$	100,000
Retirement Plan	Payable to Ann	$	550,000
Life Insurance	Payable to Ann	$	200,000
Bank Account #1	In Ann's name	$	125,000
Bank Account #2	In Chris's name	$	25,000

Chris died. Unfortunately, things didn't quite work out the way they had planned. In spite of the fact that they had a testamentary trust, not much of the property actually made it into the trust, as the following reveals.

Home	Directly to Ann		
Brokerage Account	**Into the trust**	**$**	**100,000**
Retirement Plan	Directly to Ann		
Life Insurance	Directly to Ann		
Bank Account #1	Stayed in Ann's name		
Bank Account #2	**Into the trust**	**$**	**25,000**

Of all their property, only the brokerage account ($100,000) and Chris' bank account ($25,000) went into the family trust. The rest of the assets went directly to Ann by operation of law. The result was that instead of taking advantage of the $600,000 exemption upon Chris' death by passing that much into a family trust, only $125,000 passed into the trust. This may end up costing them potentially hundreds of thousands of dollars in estate taxes.

As you can see, they received little value from the testamentary trust. What could they have done to make the testamentary trust more valuable?

Let's look first at what Chris could have done.

• He could have changed the beneficiary on his life

insurance from Ann to the trust. That would have increased the amount flowing into the family trust from $125,000 to $325,000. But that still would have been well short of the $600,000 he would have needed in order to receive maximum benefit.

- He could have changed the beneficiary designation on his retirement plan from Ann to the trust. The problem with doing that is a rule that affects retirement accounts: if the surviving spouse receives the benefits upon the death of the account holder, he or she can roll it into an IRA and defer the income taxes until she starts making withdrawals. If anybody else (such as a trust) receives those benefits, it is subject to income taxes immediately. In this case, although the $550,000 could have gone into the family trust, doing so would have made the entire amount immediately subject to income taxes. (We're not going to even discuss the effect of the "success tax" covered earlier.)

- The only remaining viable alternative would have been to change the ownership on their home from "Joint Tenants With Rights of Survivorship" to "Tenants in Common." That would effectively split the ownership of the home in two, allowing Chris' half to flow into the family trust upon his death. Beside the fact that he would still be short of the $600,000, the real problem with doing that is his half of the house would have had to go through probate. It is bad enough that jointly owned property must go through probate at the second death. Not too many people are excited about the idea of taking property that would have been probate-free at the first death and forcing it through probate.

Let's look at Ann's alternatives.

- The only thing that would have helped in the event that Ann died first would have been to change the ownership of the home as discussed above. Even then, only $400,000 ($275,000 from half the house and the $125,000 bank account) would have gone into the family trust. This would have left her still short of the optimum $600,000. The only way she would have had enough property to hit the $600,000 figure would have been to put the home totally in Ann's name. But that would have put Chris well short of the $600,000. And again, potentially pro- bate-free property would have been forced through the probate process.

A joint living trust, on the other hand, would have allowed the first $600,000 to go into the family trust, no matter which spouse died first. They could have taken advantage of his $600,000 exemption and avoided probate. To me, it makes no sense to force property through probate when that can easily be avoided with a living trust.

Equalization

One other factor that needs to be considered in structur- ing estates has to do with a concept known as "equalization."

*Robert and Michelle McMahon's estate was valued at $2,400,000, the bulk of which consisted of a home ($500,000), his business ($1,200,000) and his life insurance ($400,000). The balance of the property consisted of bank accounts and personal belong- ings. The home, business, and insurance were owned by Robert. The balance was equally owned. The problem was that if **Michelle** were to die first, only $150,000 (half of the other property) would be available to take advantage of the $600,000 exemption. This could result in unnecessary estate taxes at Robert's death.*

It was recommended that the McMahons "equalize" their estates by putting sufficient property into Michelle's name to bring her up to $600,000. This could have been done one of three ways: retitling the home in Michelle's name; splitting ownership of the business between Robert and Michelle; or placing their assets in a joint living trust.

The attorney recommended the living trust because it would allow Bob to maintain partial control over all the assets while saving probate costs and estate taxes. Although there were other methods that could have been used, the attorney felt this was the best.

Conclusion

Let's compare a testamentary trust and a living trust using our definition of estate planning.

"During my life and after my death, I want to control and distribute my property in the manner I desire, minimizing all fees, taxes and court interference, preserving for myself, my family, and those I choose, the estate I have worked so hard to create."

	Testamentary Trust	Living Trust
• Effective during your life	No	Yes
• Effective after your death	Yes	Yes
• Control property as you desire	Yes	Yes
• Distribute it as you desire	Yes	Yes
• Minimize fees (other than set-up)	No	Yes
• Minimize taxes	Yes	Yes
• Minimize court interference	No	Yes

To review, a living trust can do all that a testamentary trust can do, but the reverse isn't necessarily true. A testamentary trust has limits. And back to my old argument: if you are going to spend additional money to have a trust drawn, why not consider a living trust which will avoid probate and a possible contest, keep your affairs private, cost less in the long run, hold all your property, care for your family following your death, **and** care for you upon your disability?

15

HOW DO I KNOW IF I
NEED A LIVING TRUST?

To this point, we have discussed a variety of planning issues, with many more to come. Much of our discussion has revolved around, and will continue to revolve around, the revocable living trust. Nevertheless, there is still the determination of whether a living trust is for you. To help sort out the issues, let's review some of the areas where it might be helpful.

WHICH IS BETTER FOR YOU - A TRUST OR A WILL?

First, understand that I make no money from wills or trusts. I am unbiased with no axe to grind other than to help you make the best decisions **for you.** Even though I prefer a living trust for my own situation, it's not for everybody. So let's look at some of the questions you need to consider.

Are you married with an estate larger than $600,000?

If the answer to this question is "yes", you have an estate tax problem. You learned from our earlier discussion that each person can pass the equivalent of $600,000 upon his or her death. Anything greater than that is subject to estate taxes. If you wish to reduce your estate taxes, you will want to capture the $600,000 exemption of each spouse. Remember, under traditional planning, the exemption of the first-to-die is usually lost. So let's again review the ways to capture it.

- Leave the property outright to a person other than your spouse. Doing this has its own disadvantages. Mainly, the property would be gone, and the surviving spouse would receive no further benefit from it. But if the surviving spouse has no need for that money, then this is an option.

- Give it away. During your life you may gift money as you desire. Any gifts over your annual $10,000 exclusion will count against your $600,000 lifetime exemption, as discussed in Chapter 17.

- Use a trust. If you want to keep control of the property, if you don't want to give it away during your life, and if the surviving spouse needs the income from the property, then a trust is undoubtedly the best alternative. You know by now that my preference in this case would be a living trust rather than a testamentary trust.

Do you have minor children?

If you do, the only decision you need to make is whether you want to write the rules for their care, or you want the court to write the rules. If it is the former, then, in my opinion, the most effective way to care for your children is through the use of a trust. You name a guardian for the children in your will; you name trustees for the property in your trust. In addition, you can specify how you want them cared for and when they should receive their inheritance. Once again, the choice is between a living trust and a testamentary trust.

Do you wish to avoid probate?

Although probate may not be as bad as some people make it out to be, it is an issue that must be considered. Your state laws, the composition of your assets, and the way your assets are owned are but a few factors that will affect the probate process. It is possible that you might feel more comfortable under the supervision of the probate court. And while it possibly might be advantageous to go through probate, those situations are rare. Remember, property owned by a living trust avoids probate. While that alone may not be the only reason to do a living trust, it does enter into the equation.

Are you concerned about your mental disability?

If you're not, you should be. We never know when we are going to become incapable of handling our own financial affairs. There are really only two ways to resolve this. One way is a power of attorney, which is discussed in Chapter 22. The other way is through a living trust, which names successor trustees and contains instructions in case of your disability. Remember, a testamentary trust (part of a will) is of no benefit during a disability.

Are you concerned about a contest of your estate?

As discussed earlier, the probate court is a forum for contesting a will. While a living trust doesn't guarantee protection, contesting it is much more difficult.

Do you own property in different states?

Wills are interpreted under different rules in different states. In addition, if you own property in other states, you must go through probate in each of those locales. A living trust avoids this.

Are you married and wish to protect assets?

Many professionals and business people face liability threats. Normally, they place their assets in the name of the non-exposed spouse. Chapter 26 covers a way you can utilize a living trust to protect your assets. While living trusts are not designed to be a protection mechanism, they can be useful in this area.

Are you concerned about your spouse's ability to manage funds?

In many marriages, one person totally handles the financial affairs. In these cases, the surviving spouse is often left substantial funds but no training in handling them. The use of a trust allows you to name trustees or co-trustees to make sure the surviving spouse is cared for and the money is not wasted.

Do you want to guarantee your children's inheritance?

Many people are concerned about what will happen to their assets upon their deaths. They are especially concerned if they have children. How can they be sure the children will, in fact, end up with the money? What happens if the surviving spouse remarries and loses that money to his or her new spouse? A properly drawn trust can take care of this potential problem.

Are you concerned about the initial cost?

Probably the answer is "yes". But before making up your mind, let me ask you a few questions. Are the points made previously of concern to you? If so, do you think the living trust can solve them? If the answers to these questions are yes, then the living trust could prove advantageous to you.

If you are concerned about the cost, let me ask you one more question. **If a living trust were to cost the same as a will, which would you choose?** If your answer is a living trust, then the question is not between the will and the trust. Rather, it is whether it is worth the extra initial cost to do a trust. That's a decision only you can make.

LIVING TRUSTS VS. WILLS

In the previous chapters, we discussed the differences between living trusts, testamentary trusts, and simple wills. I pointed out my preference for the living trust due to the many advantages I believe it offers.

Understand the major difference between a will and a trust: a simple will is a simple document in which you specify how you want your property to pass upon your death. A living trust is a document that becomes effective immediately and can solve many of the planning problems that we discussed. Most people with whom I speak agree that the living trust, more so than a will, fulfills our definition of estate planning.

If that is true, if the living trust has all these advantages, why is there so much controversy? Why are so many attorneys against the living trust? Why do they continue to favor wills?

There are several possible answers: tradition, honest belief, ignorance, or money. Either they feel comfortable with wills because that is what they know, or they honestly don't believe that the probate system is so bad, or they haven't been adequately trained in trusts, or they like the money they make from probate. In any case, it is a situation not likely to change.

It is the Hatfields and the McCoys....the Democrats and the Republicans....the Giants and the Dodgers. It will never be resolved to everyone's satisfaction. There will always be two sides, each disagreeing with the other.

So now it's up to you to decide. After all, it has been the public who has picked up the living trust ball and decided to run with it. If we, as Americans, didn't see probate as a problem, we wouldn't be concerned. If we hadn't experienced delays, we wouldn't care. If it didn't cost us money, we wouldn't be upset. But we are. Unfortunately, most attorneys have yet to accept this.

Greyhound vs. Delta

I liken this controversy to transportation. If you have to get from Denver to Dallas, you have several choices. Among them, you can go by bus or plane. To me, the bus is like traditional will planning. The plane is like the modern living trust planning. Both will eventually get you where you want to go. The bus will be cheaper initially. But if you are in business, you might lose time, which translates into money. The bus ride might be slower. It will have a lot of stops, delays, and turns. You might get tired, bored, or upset. But you will get there. The plane will cost more initially. However, the ride will be smoother, much more pleasant, and save considerable time.

Now, if you talk to the bus driver, he doesn't think anything is wrong with traveling by bus. He thinks it is enjoyable. He figures "what's the rush?" As they say, relax and enjoy the ride. And if someone asks him about flying, he will try to talk him or her into taking the bus. Besides, he isn't qualified to pilot a plane. His career is at stake.

The Delta pilot can't understand that. While he could probably drive a bus, he can't understand why everyone doesn't want to fly and arrive at their destination more efficiently and pleasantly.

This may be a little farfetched, but to me it is a good analogy. Trusts are the modern way to plan. They are more expensive initially, but probably less expensive in the long run. Yet, to try to get one side to agree that the other is better is impossible. And that's our problem. We are face to face, guns drawn, neither side willing to flinch. It becomes necessary for you to decide for yourself.

More acceptance

Earlier I indicated that one of the more difficult problems working with living trusts is the number of advisors and attorneys who are not willing to accept the merits. This is especially true when living trusts are first introduced into a community. Nevertheless, I am truly amazed, when addressing groups of people from across the country, by the number of people who have living trusts. This shows the national level of acceptance, no matter what local detractors may say.

THINGS TO WATCH OUT FOR

As you entertain the use of a living trust, here are some factors with which to concern yourself.

Make sure the attorney is knowledgeable

Estate planning is a very specialized area. Only a relatively small number of attorneys are properly trained in this field. Make sure that the attorney you choose knows what he or she is doing. Interview more than one, if necessary. Talk to friends and various professionals. If the attorney isn't familiar with this type of planning, move on to another one. Keep searching until you can find one who will do what you want. Remember, this is your plan.

Beware of "do-it-yourself" books

There are many people who try to save money by buying a book of forms (or computer software package) with which to do their own living trust. They skim through to find the forms they think apply to their situation, and complete them. Who knows what will happen from that point forward? Those forms may or may not work. Most of them are difficult to understand. They may not be valid in your state. They may not fit your needs. Why spend a lifetime accumulating an estate and then destroy it because you want to save a few bucks? If you are going to do it at all, do it right. Work with an experienced estate planning attorney. It will be money well spent.

Watch out for the living trust "businesses"

These are the folks "selling" living trusts. They are not attorneys. They are just ordinary folks holding seminars and using other methods to get you to buy a living trust. Possibly they will have you complete a set of forms and mail it to an attorney somewhere to do the legal work. You may never meet face to face with an attorney. Or you might not meet with the attorney until he or she delivers the trust. Possibly they will supply you with a completed trust and suggest that you take it and review it with your own attorney. You may be asked to write two checks: one to the attorney and one to the living trust salesperson. In any case, I am concerned. You need to meet with a knowledgeable attorney **before** taking any action. You are paying for an attorney - you deserve to have his or her advice before proceeding. You deserve the best. Again, don't try to short cut.

Conclusion

Estate planning is serious business. You need an unbiased opinion as to the best course for you. Obviously, this is difficult because everyone seems to have an axe to grind. That's why I am presenting all sides in this book and letting you see for yourself the advantages and disadvantages of various planning methods. Once you decide to take action, please work with a professional. It's one thing to buy a book on how to fix a leaky faucet. It's another thing to fix your own leaky estate. Leave it to a professional.

16

HOW DO I LIVE
WITH MY LIVING TRUST?

If you and your attorney have decided that a living trust is for you, then you will do things a little differently than you have in the past. Let's go through some of those, starting with the way your property is titled.

TITLING YOUR TRUST

Like a corporation, a trust has its own name. The title of your trust will include these important elements: trustees, trustmakers, and trust date. Earlier, we saw how Mr. and Mrs. Jones titled their trust:

> "Robert C. Jones and Mary F. Jones, trustees, or their successors in trust, under the Robert C. and Mary F. Jones Living Trust, dated April 4, 1991, and any amendments thereto."

YOUR DOCUMENTS

The living trust

Obviously, the centerpiece of your planning will be the trust itself. As we have discussed, this will be where you name your trustees and beneficiaries and include your instructions for the care of those beneficiaries.

Pour-over will

The Jones' living trust should also include a separate "pour-over" will, which does two things:

- it names a guardian for their minor children; and

- it puts (pours-over) into the trust any property that is not in the trust at their deaths.

This last point is very important. Ideally, the Jones' property will be titled in the name of their trust. However, it is possible that, for one reason or another, some of their property might still be titled in their names when they die. If that happens, that property will pass according to their will, not in accordance with their trust.

With a pour-over will, any property not titled in the Jones' trust at their death will automatically go (pour-over) into the trust, thus following the instructions contained therein. Although this property will go through probate, it will at least get into the trust.

Affidavit of trust

One of the cumbersome aspects of a living trust is proving to various institutions that you are, in fact, a trustee of a trust. One way to do this is to carry the trust with you and show it to the institutions. However, one of the advantages of a trust is that it is a private document, and there is no reason to carry it around and show it to everyone. One way to avoid this, and ensure your privacy, is with an affidavit of trust.

The affidavit of trust is a notarized form in which the trustees (1) certify that the trust is in effect; (2) indicate the title of the trust; and (3) list the current trustee(s). This form, when attached to the sections of the trust which are applicable to the institution (the title page, statement of revocability, successor trustees, the powers, the signature pages, etc.), will give the institution the information they need and eliminate the need to provide the entire document.

TRANSFERRING PROPERTY INTO THE TRUST

Your trust need not include a list of your assets, anymore than IBM's corporate charter lists the property they own. Instead, you will merely title your assets in the name of the trust, thereby indicating ownership.

Once your attorney has drafted your living trust, the first thing you need to do is transfer your property into the trust. Remember, you don't *have to* transfer all your property into the trust, but whatever you don't transfer will have to go through probate.

One problem we face is that many attorneys and planners are interested in nothing more than selling living trusts. But drafting the trust is just part of the process - the property needs to be transferred into the trust as well, otherwise many of the advantages of the trust will be lost. Although many critics of trusts consider transferring property a problem, in my experience, it isn't.

As a matter of practice, my firm helps our trust clients transfer their property. Once the attorney has completed the trust documents, he or she prepares new deeds for the real estate. My assistants then help our clients transfer all their other assets by preparing the necessary letters and paperwork. At this point let's look at the various types of property and how the transfer can be accomplished.

Real estate

You indicate ownership of real estate by a deed. That deed contains the name of the owner. Therefore, to transfer the ownership of real estate from yourself to the trust, you need a new deed. This is usually done by an attorney, although you can do it yourself. Normally, a new warranty deed is prepared whereby the old owners (you and your spouse) convey the property to the new "owners", your living trust. In the Jones case above, the new owners of the property will be:

> "Robert C. Jones and Mary F. Jones, trustees, or their successors in trust, under the Robert C. and Mary F. Jones Living Trust, dated April 4, 1991, and any amendments thereto."

Because you are transferring your property from yourself to yourself, this transfer does not activate the "due on sale" clause of a mortgage. You are not changing the terms of the mortgage. You are still responsible for it. You can still qualify for the homestead exemption. You are just changing the title of the property being held as collateral.

Bank accounts

How you change the name on your bank accounts depends on the type of account.

- You can change your **checking account** by changing the name on the bank's records. Even with all the computers, most banks still use a card that indicates the name on the account and contains your signatures. Most banks that I have worked with don't require that the trust name be reflected on the checks themselves. You can imagine the confusion of a cashier at your local supermarket if you present a check drawn on a trust account.

- You can change the name on your **savings account** by informing the bank that you wish to change the account into your trust.

- Some banks allow you to change the name on your **certificates of deposit** without penalty. Other banks want to charge you a penalty, as if you are redeeming it prematurely. If this occurs, you might want to wait until renewal to make the change, or threaten to change banks.

Your bank will want proof that the trust exists, the names of the trustees, and the powers of the trustees. The affidavit of trust should handle this. Otherwise, just take the trust to the bank and let them make copies of the sections they need.

Automobiles, boats, campers, etc.

This is one area where you run into differing state laws. In some states, you need to transfer the titles into the name of the trust if you wish to avoid probate. In some states, these items can be transferred after death without probate. In some states, there might be a transfer tax required. Check with your local authorities to determine your state's rules.

Brokerage accounts

While the title of bank accounts can usually be changed, that is not the case with brokerage accounts. Once an account has been established, the name on that account cannot be changed. Instead, an entirely new account with a new number is established. Then the assets are transferred from the old account to the new one.

The new account should be titled in the name of the trust. The old account owners (again, presumably you and/or your spouse), will provide a letter of authorization to the brokerage firm to transfer the assets from your old account into the trust account.

As in the case of the bank, the affidavit of trust with the applicable powers is all they need. They do not need the entire trust, and don't give it to them.

Mutual funds

Although each mutual fund has its own procedures, they are pretty standardized. They require a letter from the old account holder (you and/or your spouse) instructing the fund to change the name of the account to the trust name. You will have to get your "signature guaranteed" (not notarized) by a bank or brokerage firm.

Stocks and bonds

If you have the stock and bond certificates yourself (as opposed to having them held in a brokerage account), then you will have to send a letter to each transfer agent along with the old certificate containing the instructions on how you want the certificate re-registered. Again, you will have to get your signature guaranteed. Be sure you make the certificates "non-negotiable" (a broker can tell you how), and send the certificates "registered mail - return receipt requested."

Life insurance

This one is easy. The owner of the policy writes a letter to the insurance company instructing them to change the beneficiary to the name of the trust. Some companies require that you use their own forms. In that case, they will mail them to you.

Since life insurance goes to a named beneficiary, or named contingent beneficiary, thus avoiding probate, some people question the necessity for making any changes, especially if there are no minors involved. But there are several reasons for doing this.

First, if you are married and have an estate tax problem, you will want to get money into the Family Trust. If the proceeds pass directly to the spouse, this won't happen.

Second, if you are concerned about how the money will be used if it goes directly to a beneficiary, the trust can contain your instructions and limitations.

Third, if one of the beneficiaries is disabled and not able to handle his or her own affairs, then having the proceeds payable to the trust can avoid the "living probate" problems discussed in Chapter 22.

Fourth, if one of the beneficiaries or contingent beneficiaries is deceased, the trust will indicate the ultimate distribution of the funds.

Finally, if all of the primary and contingent beneficiaries are deceased, it will keep the proceeds out of your estate, thus avoiding probate.

Retirement accounts

This is the trickiest area of all because of the unique rules involving retirement plans.

Barry McLean works for a major corporation. He has been contributing to a 401(k) for the past ten years. In addition, he has some Individual Retirement Accounts which he started in the early 1980's. The beneficiary on all these accounts is his wife, Marie; the contingent beneficiaries are his adult children, equally.

Here is the problem. With retirement accounts, if the beneficiary is a spouse, he or she can roll it into an IRA (regardless of the amount) without any income taxes due. There will be income taxes, however, on any amount the spouse eventually receives from the rollover account. On the other hand, if the benefits are received by anyone other than the spouse, the entire benefit is subject to current income taxes. So if you make the living trust the beneficiary of a retirement account, the benefits become income taxable immediately, even if the beneficiary of the living trust is the spouse.

Therefore, what we usually do is leave the spouse as primary beneficiary of the retirement account but make the trust the contingent (secondary) beneficiary. In the above case, if Marie is alive when Barry dies, she can receive the benefits and roll them into an IRA herself. She can then make the trust the beneficiary of her rollover account. If she is not alive when Barry dies, then the trust will receive the benefits, and they will be distributed according to its instructions. As another alternative, she can disclaim the asset, and it will go into the trust.

If you are not married, then you can just change the primary beneficiary to the trust. In either case, make sure you check with your professional advisors to determine the best way to handle it.

Tax-deferred annuity

A tax-deferred annuity works similarly to the IRA. If the spouse receives the benefits, that money is not income taxable to him or her until the interest is withdrawn. However, if those benefits are received by anybody other than the surviving spouse, the growth in the account is subject to income taxes.

Therefore, if you are married, make your surviving spouse the beneficiary of the annuity and the trust the contingent beneficiary. If you are not married, make the living trust the primary beneficiary.

Savings Bonds

Department of the Treasury Form PD 1851 is used to change the registration on savings bonds from your name to your trust. The form states that you do not have to report any deferred income at that time as long as you meet the "grantor trust provisions of the Internal Revenue Code and you are treated as the owner of that portion of the trust represented by any tax-deferred accumulated interest on the reissued bonds."

Untitled property

What about your personal affects: jewelry, household goods, etc? Those items aren't titled. How are they handled? One of two ways.

- Usually, the trust will indicate that all other property will be considered part of the trust and will pass according to the instructions contained therein. So if you have split your property equally between your children, then all your other "stuff" will be included in that formula.

- Many trusts will provide a separate mechanism for transferring special items. For example, you want your wedding ring to go to your daughter, your gun collection to your son, and your coin collection to go to your granddaughter. The trust can provide a special form that allows you to indicate specific distribution of items to individuals. These personal items will pass according to your written instructions rather than the general instructions of the trust.

Buying and selling property

Many people question the difficulty of buying and selling property in the trust. Actually, it's quite simple. When you buy a piece of real estate, you merely instruct the closing attorney to title it in the name of the trust. When you sell property owned by the trust, you merely sell it as trustee of the trust. Nothing has to be done with the trust. Remember, the trust doesn't list your property. Ownership is indicated by the title.

Special bequests

A trust, like a will, allows you to provide special bequests for those you wish to remember. The best way to do this, other than the untitled property discussed above, is to indicate in your trust the person(s) to whom you want the property to pass. This might be a specific amount of money you want to leave to a certain party. It might be a certain piece of property. You can handle it however you desire. On the other hand, instead of tieing your trustee's hands by assigning certain property to each beneficiary, you might find it easier to specify the percentage to each, and let the trustees divide it to the mutual benefit of everyone involved.

One other point concerning percentages and dollar figures: there is a tendency to specify dollar figures when leaving money to non-children beneficiaries, such as grandchildren, nieces, nephews, charities, etc. The problem with doing that is (1) inflation might make the dollars worth a mere fraction of what you thought; or (2) your estate might dwindle due to unforseen circumstances, and the amount they end up receiving could be a larger percentage than you had intended. Therefore, many people choose instead to use percentages to keep all the numbers relative.

Where to keep your trust

The question always arises as to where the trust should be kept: in the home or in a safe deposit box. I recommend that the attorney draft and execute two sets of the trust. The original can be kept at home and the duplicate original given to a relative, successor trustee, or put in the box at the bank.

The problem of keeping your only copy at the bank is that if the safe deposit box is sealed at your death, it will be difficult for your successor trustee to get in. The problem with keeping the only copy at home is in the event of a fire, it could be destroyed. With two original sets, you are better protected.

In addition, your trust is a "living" document. You will want to refer to it. You will want to ensure that it constantly meets your desires. Keeping it handy makes that easier.

Special instructions

You should also leave instructions pertaining to the following:

- Special instructions for burial.

- A list of your key advisors (attorney, CPA, etc.).

- Location list of your important papers.

- A list of benefits to which you may be entitled.

- Any anatomical gift instructions.

- Safe deposit box instructions.

You can see the importance of letting people know any special instructions and locations of key items. This is true whether or not you have a trust. These items are important and can make the task of those you leave behind easier.

These instructions should be included with your living trust documents. While not part of the trust, file them together so your successor trustees can find them. While most of the above are pretty simple, anatomical gift instructions must follow your state's laws.

Asset list

It is important that you leave a complete list of your assets and the location of specific documents. You probably have bank accounts at different institutions. You may have several brokerage accounts. You probably have many different insurance policies. Many heirs come across certificates or insurance policies from their parent's estates. They have no idea if the policies have any value. They may have been policies that were canceled years ago. There may be stock certificates that became worthless in 1962. They just don't know. That causes a lot of grief, because it isn't easy to track those things down.

As with the special instructions discussed above, providing your heirs with a complete list of what you have and letting them know where it is can make settling your estate so much easier. Believe me, they will appreciate your efforts.

Caution

I have said this before, and I'll say it again. One of the disadvantages in buying a book that just has living trust forms is that you don't get proper advice. You don't know the proper way to set up your trust. You don't know what provisions to include. And you don't know what to do when the trust is finally established. I don't believe that these important decisions should be left to chance and inexperience. Please, consult a professional and make sure everything is handled properly.

Conclusion

Although what we have discussed in this chapter might sound complicated, it really isn't. Hopefully, those who have helped you with the trust will assist you in this process. The job of planning isn't worth starting if it is not properly completed. Make sure you obtain proper assistance and advice in transferring your assets.

PART III

REDUCING YOUR ESTATE TAXES

17

HOW CAN GIFTING
REDUCE ESTATE TAXES?

One of the estate-reduction techniques planners often recommend when working with large estates is a planned gifting program. It is important to familiarize yourself with the rules because gifting affects so many different areas of estate planning. Earlier chapters covered transferring property into joint tenancy, giving assets to children, and calculating estate taxes, all of which have gift-tax implications. Future chapters examine removing life insurance from your estate and other advanced techniques, many of which involve gifting.

Proper use of gifting is ignored by most people. The reason for this is a lack of understanding of its advantages and uses. Additionally, there is a lot of misunderstanding concerning this area due to the number of law changes over the years.

The definition of a gift

While you and I know what we consider to be a gift, all that really matters is the Internal Revenue Service's definition. It is relatively simple: *anytime you transfer property to another party for less than its fair market value, you have made a gift.*

The rules

- Each year, **you may gift $10,000** (in cash or property)

to each and every person you wish, free of gift taxes.

- You may **transfer to your spouse unlimited** amounts of cash or property with no gift tax implications.

- If you are married, **you and your spouse may agree to make a joint gift (called "gift splitting") of $20,000** free of gift taxes, to each and every person you desire in any year. Even if you make that gift with your money, it will be considered a joint gift if your spouse consents.

- If you make a gift in excess of $10,000, or you and your spouse make a split gift (as defined above), you are required to **file a gift tax return.** For gifting and other issues involving individuals who are not citizens of the United States, see Chapter 29.

- If the gift results in a tax obligation (as discussed below), **the giver, not the receiver,** is responsible for any gift taxes.

- There are **no income taxes** due either in giving or receiving a gift.

- To qualify under the annual exclusion, **the gift must be a "present interest."** That means that the recipient must have full and immediate access and use of the property. You cannot make a gift with "strings attached." For example, if you give your son 100 shares of IBM but say, "You can't sell this for five years," it won't qualify under the annual exclusion.

- There are no gift tax implications if you pay another person's **medical costs or education expenses.** As long as you actually pay the bill, as opposed to giving that person the money and letting him or her pay, you don't have to worry about gift taxes. Additionally, there's no dollar limit on the money that can be spent, and no restriction on who that person can be.

- Any amount you gift in **excess of $10,000 effectively** reduces your $600,000 combined gift and estate credit equivalent, which we have been referring to as your $600,000 exemption.

- If you **guarantee a loan** for another person, that guarantee is considered a gift at the time you make it, even if it is never needed.

Unified gift and estate tax

Our tax code provides for a unified gift and estate tax calculation. You remember from previous discussions that upon your death, you can pass an unlimited amount of property to your spouse estate-tax free and can pass the equivalent of $600,000 to other persons as a group. Upon your spouse's death, he or she can pass another $600,000 free of estate taxes.

If during your lifetime, you make a gift in excess of $10,000, then you must file a gift tax return, and the amount of the gift in excess of $10,000 reduces your $600,000 exemption. Remember, you really have a $192,800 tax credit, but for illustrative purposes, we use the value of that credit, $600,000.

In 1990, Ralph and Martha Jenkins gave their daughter $20,000. They agreed to make it a joint gift and thus were required to file a gift tax return. However, since it fell within the exclusion ($10,000 each), there was no gift tax due.

In 1991, Mr. and Mrs. Jenkins gifted another $60,000 to their daughter. Again, they make it a joint gift, effectively meaning that each made a gift of $30,000. But this time there was an additional factor: what to do about the $40,000 overage? Since they each were considered to have made a gift of $30,000, they each exceeded their $10,000 exclusion by $20,000. As a result, they filed a gift tax return, and had to reduce each of their $600,000 exemptions by $20,000, making it $580,000. Upon Mr. and Mrs.

Jenkins' death, they will be able to pass only $580,000 estate tax free instead of $600,000.

There are, of course, ways to take maximum advantage of gifting. For example, had Mr. and Mrs. Jenkins each made a gift to their daughter and son-in-law, they could have made joint gifts totalling $40,000 before encroaching into their lifetime maximum of $600,000. They could have also made gifts to each of their grandchildren, although, as discussed previously, there are special considerations with minor children.

Estate under $600,000

If your estate isn't valued at more than $600,000, and you haven't used any of your $600,000 exemption, then the amount of a gift will have no affect at all.

Mr. Jenkins' mother was elderly and could no longer live alone. Mr. Jenkins decided to have her move in with them. She had an estate of $250,000. After she moved in, she decided to sign everything over to him. Her gift was $240,000 after subtracting her $10,000 exclusion, resulting in the requirement that she file a gift tax return. However, no taxes were due. All the gift did was reduce her $600,000 exemption to $360,000. Since she had no more property, this reduction will have no effect.

● ● ●

Sarah Jefferson had an estate worth $185,000. She was concerned about the cost of a prolonged nursing home stay and decided to give her assets to her four children. Because her estate was under $600,000, and she hadn't used any of her $600,000 exemption previously, there were no gift tax implications. Additionally, this money was not taxable to her children when they received it. However, there were nursing care implications which are discussed in Chapters 23 and 24.

Estate reduction

Gifting is a very important part of estate planning, although it tends to be underutilized and misused. There are not many ways to reduce the value of your estate, but planned gifting is one. Used properly, gifting can be a valuable tax-reduction method.

> *Richard and Margaret Greene have an estate worth $8,000,000. They have sufficient income from their current investments and retirement plan and would like to reduce the size of their estate as much as possible. Since the Greenes have four children and 14 grandchildren, they are able to give $10,000 to each. Therefore, a continuing program of gifting will allow them to give a combined $360,000 per year. After ten years, they will have reduced their estate by $3,600,000 plus all the future growth in those assets.*

You might consider giving away rapidly appreciating property. For example, if you have a piece of real estate that you feel will increase in value, you might gift it to a child to remove it from your estate. Upon your death, it will not be included in your estate for estate tax calculations. However, there are other considerations.

Cost basis

One involves the "cost basis", which is your cost of your property. Assume you bought a piece of real estate for $10,000. Upon sale, a capital gain, the difference between the sales price and the cost basis of $10,000, must be realized. There are two rules that apply to cost basis.

- If you give property away, the cost basis remains the same and is transferred to the recipient. Therefore, the recipient, upon sale of the property, will have income taxes on the difference between the sales price and the $10,000 cost basis.

- If you die and that property is inherited, the heir receives a "stepped-up basis". That means that the cost basis is not your cost basis of $10,000, but it "steps-up" to the value at your death.

Let's compare these two scenarios.

Leon Farnsworth purchased land on the outskirts of town for $10,000. Over the years the property increased in value to $80,000. He gave it to his son, Tommy. As you know by now, he made a gift of $70,000 (the $80,000 market value of the property less his $10,000 annual exemption). This had the effect of reducing his $600,000 exemption to $530,000. Tommy held it for a number of years and then sold it for $150,000. Tommy paid tax on the capital gain, which was the difference between the sales price and his cost basis. Since he received the property as a gift, his cost basis was the same as his father's, $10,000. That resulted in income tax on $140,000. On the other hand, Mr. Farnsworth was able to remove the appreciation of the property from his estate.

Now, let's look at what might have happened had Mr. Farnsworth instead chosen to hold the property. In this situation, we'll assume that it was worth $150,000 on the day Mr. Farnsworth died.

*The property would have passed to Tommy, and he immediately could have sold it for $150,000. While there is normally capital gains tax on the difference between the sales price and the purchase price, in this case, there would have been none. Even though Tommy would have sold it for $150,000, that figure would have been his cost basis. When Mr. Farnsworth died, the cost basis of the property would have "stepped-up" from the original cost to the **market value on the date of his death**. As a result, there would have been no income tax due. However, the entire $150,000 would have been included in Mr. Farnsworth's estate for estate tax purposes.*

Estate taxes versus income taxes

These scenarios point out the difficulty in the decision making process. Estate taxes currently are higher than income taxes. In our planning, the relative value of income taxes vs. estate taxes must be taken into consideration. Would it have been better for Tommy to pay income taxes upon sale of the property while allowing his father to remove a substantial sum from his estate? Or should Mr. Farnsworth's estate have paid estate taxes on the entire amount but given Tommy a "stepped-up" basis? While there are too many variables to answer here, it is a factor that must be considered.

Notice also that you get the worst of all possible tax worlds with gifts. While the value of the gift is the value of the property on the day the gift is made ($80,000 in the above case), the cost basis for the recipient remains at the basis of the donor ($10,000). The IRS gets you coming and going in this case.

Using your annual gift to create wealth

Many people use their $10,000 annual exclusion to reduce their estate, as reflected by the previous case. But all that will do in the Greene's case is reduce their estate by $360,000 annually and create that amount for their children and grandchildren. As noted in the example, after ten years, they will have reduced their estate by $3,600,000 and created $3,600,000 worth of wealth for their heirs.

But there is a better alternative.

Richard and Margaret Greene could have used that $360,000 per year to purchase a second-to-die insurance policy that is covered in the following chapters. Even if they had used only half of their exclusions, or $180,000 per year, they could have purchased a $9,332,000 policy, using current projections! In ten years, based on today's assumptions, the death benefit on that policy would have grown to $11,666,450. Therefore, not only would they have reduced their estate by $1,800,000 over ten years, they would have created $11,666,450 worth of wealth for their children and grandchildren! And this is using only half their annual gift exclusions. To make it even better, if properly established, this amount would have been income tax-free and estate tax-free! If they lived another twenty years, they would have been able to create $15,000,000 tax-free for their heirs! And, don't forget, if they die in the first year, the entire $9,332,000 would be paid.

Of course, the children and grandchildren would have lost the benefit of half of the annual gifts. But they would have substantially increased their inheritance. Let's look at another case.

Ben and Nora Adams have an estate valued at $1,100,000. They are close to the $1,200,000 combined cut-off ($600,000 each), so they have decided to start gifting some assets. They have three children, so together they could gift $60,000 per year. As long as their estate doesn't grow much, they should be in good shape from an estate-tax standpoint. But they don't like the idea of giving up control of their assets to the children. And they know if they give them cash, the money will probably be wasted.

In the Adams' case, they could purchase a $2,400,000 second-to-die policy for $60,000 payable for fifteen years. In ten years, the death benefit would be over $3,000,000! You can see the leverage available by using life insurance.

If your goal is to make the fullest use of estate planning, doesn't it make sense to maximize your gift exemption? The wealth you can create is enormous. And by using the techniques covered in the following chapters, this money can be free of all taxes! What better legacy to leave?

Loan guarantees can result in taxable gifts

Here's a shocker: if you guarantee a loan for another person, it is subject to gift taxes.

Joan Malone wanted to help her son begin a new business. That business required $50,000 in operating capital. Unfortunately, her son didn't have that available, nor could he qualify for a loan. However, Joan could qualify. Therefore, she went with him to the bank and guaranteed the loan. That innocent step resulted in a gift to her son of $40,000 (the amount in excess of her annual $10,000 exclusion).

The IRS has recently ruled that guaranteeing a loan for the benefit of another results in a gift. This requires that a gift tax return be filed, thereby reducing the donor's $600,000 lifetime exemption by the amounts in excess of the $10,000 annual exclusion. This is true even if the guarantee is never exercised.

Loan guarantees can also result in additional estate taxes

Additionally, for married couples utilizing the unlimited marital deduction discussed earlier, it causes even more potential problems. Normally, we just concern ourselves with the rule that for property to qualify for the unlimited marital deduction, the surviving spouse must receive income from that property annually. But there are a few other conditions. Among them: there must be nothing that will cause his or her interest in that property to end.

However, a loan guarantee represents a contingent liability. We don't know if it will ever be exercised. Upon the death of the guarantor, that guarantee doesn't end. It is passed on to the estate. Therefore, any money passed under the unlimited marital deduction may be needed to meet those guarantees. As a result, that property will be disqualified for the marital deduction and instead will be counted against the guarantor's $600,000 lifetime exemption.

This ruling can have dramatic effects on estate taxes. It can even disqualify a Q-TIP trust for the unlimited marital deduction. The ramifications are enormous, and there are no attractive solutions, other than providing sufficient liquidity in the estate and some careful, creative planning.

Putting property into joint tenancy

One problem that frequently occurs is the result of property being placed into joint tenancy with a non-spouse. We talked about the potential problems with joint tenancy earlier in the book. Remember, if you place property (stocks, bonds, real estate, etc.) into a joint account with a child, you are technically making a gift to the child. To make matters worse, the entire value of the property is included in your estate at your death. Talk about a no-win situation!

Conclusion

Gifting, while an important part of estate planning, is not the solution to all your problems. You still must give up control of the property, and when push comes to shove, many people don't want to do that. Nevertheless, if one of your goals is to reduce your estate taxes, and you have taken into consideration the income tax consequences for your recipients, then proper gifting can prove very valuable in the long run. Be sure to obtain qualified legal and financial advice.

18

HOW CAN I AVOID PAYING ESTATE TAXES ON MY LIFE INSURANCE?

If you are like the majority of my clients, you will probably be surprised to learn that, under most circumstances, life insurance proceeds are included in your estate when you die. Most people assume that since the proceeds are payable to someone else, they aren't included. Not true. Let's once again look at the Purcells.

They had a $2,000,000 estate which included $750,000 of life insurance. Upon Mr. Purcell's death, $600,000 went into a Family Trust, while the balance went into the marital trust for Mrs. Purcell. Upon her death, all her property passed to their children with the amount over her $600,000 exemption being subject to estate taxes. Because their estate included $750,000 worth of life insurance, they missed out on yet another tax-saving opportunity.

CURRENT RULES

Ownership of life insurance

First, understand that there are two taxation issues when it comes to life insurance: income taxes and estate taxes. While life insurance proceeds are, under normal circumstances, **income tax free**, they can be subject to **estate taxes**, depending on the size of your estate. It's all based on something known as "incidents of ownership."

According to the IRS, you have **incidents of ownership** in a policy if you maintain certain rights, such as changing the beneficiary or owner, pledging the policy as collateral, borrowing against or surrendering the policy, etc. The result of these "rights" is that the policy proceeds are included in your estate at your death.

In order to keep life insurance proceeds out of your estate at your death, you must either:

- never have incidents of ownership in the policy, or

- live at least three years after transferring the ownership to another party.

Ownership is the primary determination as to where the value of the death benefit falls.

Robert Marks borrowed $500,000 from Brittingham Bank and Trust to build an office. The bank required that Mr. Marks purchase a life insurance policy to cover the loan in the event of his death. When he died, the $500,000 death benefit was included in the value of his estate, even though it didn't go to a family member. Of course, the value of his estate was increased by the elimination of the debt he owed the bank. Nevertheless, because he owned the policy, it was included in his estate.

An important point to remember is that if your estate is subject to estate taxes, and you are, for example, carrying a $500,000 insurance policy, your family might not realize the full benefit of the $500,000. They may only keep the amount that is left after estate taxes have been paid. The only way to receive full benefit from that policy is to make sure that neither you nor your spouse have any incidents of ownership.

Cross-ownership no longer an advantage

Before talking about how to do that, let's talk about what no longer works. For years, life insurance agents have told their clients that the husband should own the insurance carried by the wife, and the wife should own the insurance carried by the husband. The reason for this was, prior to the Economic Recovery Act of 1981, there were potential estate taxes at the death of the first spouse. Therefore, it made sense to get the proceeds of the life insurance out of the estate of the first to die. The result was a strategy that involved what was called "cross-ownership" of policies.

However, that strategy no longer saves estate taxes because there is no tax due at the first death if you take advantage of the unlimited marital deduction. Unfortunately, there are still many so-called "professionals" telling people that cross-ownership should be used to save estate taxes. So be aware of advisors who are still operating under old laws.

THIRD PARTY OWNERSHIP

Under current law, the most effective way to remove life insurance proceeds from the estate is to have the policy owned by someone other than the husband or wife. As long as neither the husband nor the wife have any "incidents of ownership", the proceeds will not be subject to estate taxes. For a single person, the same rules apply. As long as he or she doesn't own the policy, it will be excluded from his or her estate for tax purposes, subject to the three year rule discussed below.

Transferring an existing policy

After hearing this, the first thought of many people is to transfer the ownership of their policy to another party. After all, given the choice between purchasing a new life insurance policy in which he has no incidents of ownership, and transferring the ownership of an existing policy, most people will choose the latter. Unfortunately, there is a problem with this tactic.

The previous tax laws included a special provision for gifts made "in contemplation of death." In a nutshell, it meant that any gift made within three years of the death of the donor was pulled back and included in his or her estate for tax purposes. The thinking of the Internal Revenue Service, rightly or wrongly, was that this gift was being made in order to allow the donor to reduce his or her estate-tax liability. The Economic Recovery Tax Act of 1981 repealed this provision except in a few cases, one of which happens to be life insurance.

As a result, **the three year rule still applies for life insurance.** If you transfer ownership of a life insurance contract within three years of your death, the death proceeds will be included in your estate for estate tax purposes. To put it another way, the only way to exempt a transferred policy from your estate is to retain no "incidents of ownership" for a period of three years prior to your death.

> *In 1987, Dr. William Bartels purchased, and was the owner of, a $500,000 policy. On January 10, 1989 he removed it from his estate by gifting it to his son, John. (There would have been gift tax problems had the policy contained cash value.) He died March 21, 1990. Since that was within three years of the transfer, the $500,000 was included in his estate.*

This rule makes planning with existing life insurance very difficult. Though it would be great to transfer an existing life insurance policy, it is ludicrous to plan that you are not going to die within three years. If you know when you are going to die, then planning is easy. In my opinion, it is too risky to face the exposure of dying within three years and then having a substantial amount of estate taxes due.

Children as owners of your life insurance

To avoid the three-year rule, the prudent way to plan is

to have some other party own your policy from the beginning. One option that a number of my clients choose is to make their adult child or children owners of the life insurance.

As far as the IRS is concerned (at least today) if your children own your life insurance policy, and you never possessed any "incidents of ownership", then it will not be included in your estate for estate tax purposes, even if you die within three years. However, the IRS is always attempting to pull life insurance proceeds into the estate, so it is imperative to keep on top of recent rulings.

There are some **potential pitfalls** to having a child own your life insurance:

- The insurance becomes an asset of the child, and just as jointly owned property with a child causes problems, so does this. As his or her asset, any values can be attached in the event of a lawsuit, divorce, judgement, etc.

- If you want to provide income for your spouse from the proceeds of your insurance, then he or she would have to receive that money from the owner, which is the child. This, in turn, will create other problems. First, there is no guarantee the child will give the money to the parent, since it legally belongs to the child. Second, if he or she does give the money to his parent, he is making a gift. Making your spouse the beneficiary won't work because then the money will be included in his or her estate at death, and that is what you were trying to avoid in the first place.

- If a child is an owner, there is no guarantee that he or she won't cash the policy in early.

- If you pay the premiums directly on a policy owned

by others, there can be gift tax implications on the payments over your $10,000 annual exclusion.

A trust as owner of your insurance

Because of the problems stated above, the solution in many cases is to have your life insurance owned by an **Irrevocable Life Insurance Trust.** If handled properly, you should not run into any of the problems we have discussed.

Although the use of an irrevocable trust is more cumbersome and involves more steps than any other method, I believe it is the prudent fashion for owning life insurance. It complies with the IRS regulation that states that a life insurance policy not owned or paid for by an individual will not be included in his estate. Let's go through this process step by step.

- An attorney drafts an irrevocable trust. For safety's sake, it is recommended that you not even call it a life insurance trust.

- A trustee and successor trustees are named. These people should definitely not be either you or your spouse. Many attorneys recommend that you not name one of the beneficiaries as a trustee, either. The safest course of action is to have a disinterested third party - a financial institution, your CPA, etc. - as trustee.

- You gift an amount slightly larger than the life insurance premium to the trust. This gift is made under your $10,000 gift exclusion. This gift will be considered a "present interest" gift if you utilize the "Crummey Provisions" (from Crummey vs. IRS, 1968), which are described shortly. These payments may be made annually or in one single payment.

- Upon your death (or the deaths of you and your

spouse if it is a joint trust), the proceeds are paid to the beneficiaries estate-tax free, assuming everything has been handled properly.

There are some **disadvantages** with the use of the trust.

- The trust is irrevocable. Once you have made the gift, you cannot get it back. The values that build in the policy belong to the trust, not you.

- It is complicated and involves specific steps under the "Crummey Provisions" described on the following page.

- It must be drafted by an estate planning attorney who understands the intricacies.

- There can be some gift tax implications between the beneficiaries based on the gift made to the trust.

- This trust has a separate federal identification number and, if it shows taxable earnings, must file an income tax return.

There are some basic decisions you must make in structuring your insurance trust.

- Is it going to be a single or joint trust? A single trust is used when (1) you are not married or (2) the surviving spouse is going to have a need for the insurance benefits. A joint trust is used when the primary purpose of the proceeds is to pay estate taxes.

- If your purpose is to provide for your spouse without having the proceeds included in either of your estates, there are very strict rules that must be followed. These parallel the rules governing the family trust discussed earlier.

- Who will be the ultimate beneficiaries, and what will be their rights? As a rule, the terms of this trust follow the terms of the living trust for continuity.

The Crummey provisions

Discussing the Crummey provisions might fall under the category of "telling you more than you want to know," but it is a vital part of the irrevocable insurance trust. As discussed in the previous chapter, in order for a gift to qualify under the $10,000 annual exclusion, it must be a "present interest." That means that the recipient must have full and unrestricted use of that gift today, with no strings attached.

The problem with life insurance is the nature of the trust. In an irrevocable trust, the interests of the beneficiaries are **future interests.** That is because they have no current rights in the policy. All the "incidents of ownership" are vested in the trustee. That means that the gift will not qualify as a "present interest" gift.

Therefore, to make it "present interest", specific steps must be taken. Those steps fall under the Crummey Provision, aptly named after the landmark case, Crummey vs. IRS (1968). Without getting technical, it involves the following steps (see **Exhibit 7**).

1. You gift the premiums to the trustee of the trust.

2. The trustee then notifies the beneficiaries (presumably your children) in writing of the gift and gives them a limited time (usually 30 days) to withdraw the premiums.

3. The beneficiaries then sign a waiver declining the money.

Exhibit 7

Irrevocable Life Insurance Trust

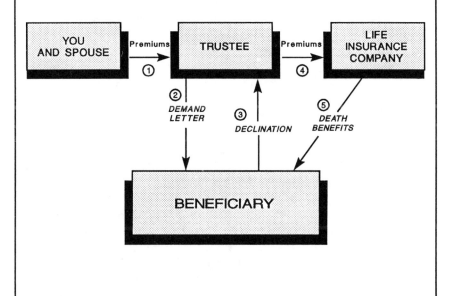

4. Once the trustee has received this waver, he or she then pays the premiums to the insurance company.

According to the IRS, that withdrawal privilege given to the beneficiaries is sufficient to allow the money to qualify for a "no strings" gift.

Keep in mind, however, that the IRS is constantly challenging estates to bring the life insurance proceeds into the estate. Nevertheless, they haven't won a case where the trust was properly established and the necessary procedures followed. So it is imperative that you only work with qualified professionals who stay abreast of the constant changes in IRS regulations. Otherwise, it could cost your estate hundreds of thousands, or millions, in estate taxes.

Benefits of the insurance trust

Let's assume we can bring the Purcells back from the grave and pretend they planned differently.

> *Their estate, valued at $2,000,000, included a $750,000 life insurance policy on the life of Mr. Purcell, owned from the beginning by an irrevocable trust. This resulted in the $750,000 being excluded from their estate. This had the effect of reducing their taxable estate to $1,250,000. Upon Mr. Purcell's death, $600,000 of his property went into a Family Trust, the balance went into the marital trust for Mrs. Purcell. When she died, she passed $650,000 to her children, with only $50,000 subject to estate taxes. The balance of the estate, ($1,981,500) passed estate-tax free! The resulting taxes were only $18,500.*

This $18,500 is a far cry from the $320,000 their children had to pay when their life insurance was included in their estate. **Exhibit 8** shows a diagram of this amazing tax savings.

Let's recap the financial results of our planning for Mr. and Mrs. Purcell. **We have reduced their estate taxes from $561,180 under the simple will, to $18,500 using various**

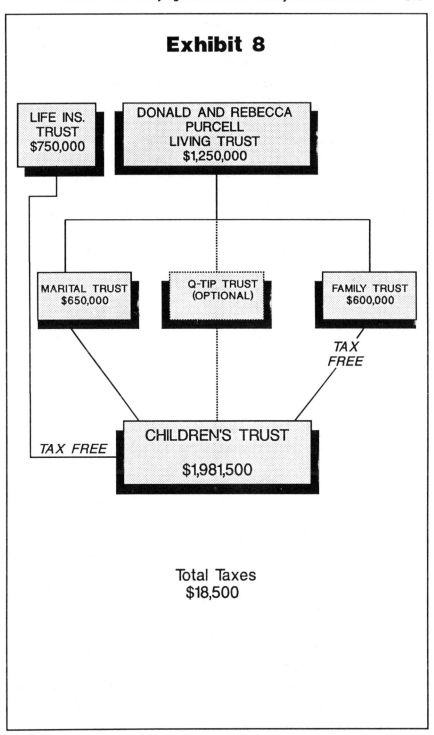

Exhibit 8

LIFE INS. TRUST $750,000

DONALD AND REBECCA PURCELL LIVING TRUST $1,250,000

MARITAL TRUST $650,000

Q-TIP TRUST (OPTIONAL)

FAMILY TRUST $600,000

TAX FREE

CHILDREN'S TRUST $1,981,500

TAX FREE

Total Taxes $18,500

planning methods. As a result, we have increased the amount of their children's inheritance from $1,379,220 to $1,981,500. Not bad for a day's work! Can you see now why I feel so good about my profession? Where else is it possible to help people save so much money so easily?

Tax savings with a life insurance trust

The following table shows the net estate taxes for various scenarios. Column one is the estate size; column two the net estate taxes without use of the credit equivalent; column three the net estate taxes with the Family Trust (or other use of the exemption of the first-to-die); and column four the net estate taxes using the irrevocable trust.

CURRENT ESTATE SIZE	ESTATE TAXES WITHOUT FAMILY TRUST	ESTATE TAXES WITH FAMILY TRUST	ESTATE TAX WITH INSURANCE TRUST
1,000,000	153,000	0	0
1,500,000	363,000	114,000	0
2,000,000	588,000	320,000	18,500
3,000,000	1,098,000	784,000	430,500
4,000,000	1,648,000	1,318,000	912,500
5,000,000	2,198,000	1,868,000	1,455,500
10,000,000	4,948,000	4,618,000	4,205,500

Since it is rare that both spouses die simultaneously, the following table assumes the husband dies today and the wife in ten years. The first column represents the estate today; the second represents the value in 10 years assuming 5% annual growth; the third is the net estate tax assuming no family trust (or other use of the exemption) and no insurance trust; the fourth is the net estate tax assuming a Family Trust but no insurance trust; and the fifth is the net estate tax assuming the family trust plus an insurance trust containing $750,000 coverage on the husband (first to die).

CURRENT ESTATE SIZE	ESTATE SIZE IN TEN YEARS	TAXES WITHOUT FAMILY TRUST	TAXES WITH FAMILY TRUST	TAXES WITH INSURANCE TRUST
$1,000,000	$1,628,895	421,003	80,634	0
1,500,000	2,443,342	805,238	348,382	4,009
2,000,000	3,257,789	1,211,895	725,422	177,100
3,000,000	4,886,684	2,026,342	1,537,674	926,838
4,000,000	6,515,579	2,840,789	2,342,121	1,741,285
5,000,000	8,144,473	3,655,237	3,166,568	2,555,733
10,000,000	16,288,946	8,041,920	7,504,385	6,832,466

Let's assume, instead, that the surviving spouse lives an additional twenty-five years. Again, we are assuming that the estate includes a $750,000 life insurance policy. As you can see, this becomes less significant as the estate becomes larger. However, it can also be assumed that the larger estates would include larger amounts of life insurance, which are not reflected here.

CURRENT ESTATE SIZE	ESTATE SIZE IN 25 YEARS	TAXES WITHOUT FAMILY TRUST	TAXES WITH FAMILY TRUST	TAXES WITH INSURANCE TRUST
$1,000,000	$3,386,355	1,276,177	449,930	0
1,500,000	5,079,532	2,122,766	1,106,860	264,050
2,000,000	6,772,710	2,969,355	1,953,448	686,554
3,000,000	10,159,065	4,670,486	3,646,626	2,376,743
4,000,000	13,545,420	6,532,981	5,415,484	4,069,920
5,000,000	16,931,775	8,395,476	7,277,979	5,881,108
10,000,000	33,863,549	16,931,775	15,915,860	14,645,985

Incredible leverage with life insurance

One of the primary advantages of an irrevocable trust is

that it gives you the opportunity to create a tremendous dollar pool that is **federal income tax-free, state income tax-free, federal estate tax-free, and state inheritance tax-free.** Although we talk about the $10,000 annual exclusion, you are not limited to that figure. By exceeding it, you can multiply the value of your $600,000 exemption.

> *Richard and Juanita Mason had an estate valued at $1,800,000. Richard's retirement income was such that he didn't need any of the principal to provide for himself and his family. As a matter of fact, he was reinvesting all the interest from his investments, which was causing his estate to grow. Richard was an astute businessman, very much aware of estate tax consequences. He was intrigued by the leverage of the life insurance trust, but didn't want to commit himself to annual payments. He said he would feel more comfortable just investing a lump sum of $100,000.*

The following table shows the Mason's alternatives using current projections. They could have left the $100,000 in tax-free bonds earning 7% and continued to reinvest the interest at that rate, or they could have transferred $100,000 into a life insurance contract providing a $600,000 initial death benefit. The death benefit could then grow annually as the cash values inside the policy grew. Both sets of figures assume the investment is in an irrevocable trust.

Year of Death	Value of Tax-Free Bonds In a Trust	Value of Life Insurance In a Trust
5	140,255	700,575
10	196,718	757,653
15	275,903	831,227
20	386,968	941,882
25	542,743	1,003,845

As you can see, the $100,000 created tremendous

leverage when used for life insurance. And, don't forget, we don't know when they are going to die. One thing about the insurance, it is guaranteed to pay the death benefit, even if they die immediately. Their other investments won't do that.

One note about the single deposit. Since the Masons used the Crummey provisions described earlier, they were each able to gift $10,000 to each of their two sons. Nevertheless, there was still a $60,000 ($30,000 each) overage that came off each of their $600,000 lifetime exemptions. But the use of that $60,000 created an unbelievable return-on-investment that is both income-tax and estate-tax free for their sons. Nothing can do it better.

Generation skipping

I work with a great number of older citizens who want to provide for their grandchildren. By doing so, they can accomplish three things. First, they can help secure the financial future of their grandchildren. Second, by giving away assets, they can reduce their own estates. Third, if their children are going to have an estate tax problem, by skipping them and going directly to the grandchildren, they can save estate taxes at their children's death. Otherwise, by the time the grandchildren receive it, it could be whittled down to a fraction of its former value. As a result, the incentive for skipping generations is great. Unfortunately, the effectiveness of generation skipping has been reduced by the current rules.

- A generation skipping tax is charged on all transfers to a person or persons two or more generations below (younger) than the transferor.

- This tax is **in addition** to any estate or gift taxes that are incurred.

- The generation skipping tax rate is the maximum estate tax rate in effect at the time (currently 55%).

- Every person may exempt $1 million for generation skipping tax purposes.

- The transfers may occur one of three ways: as a distribution (such as from a trust); upon death; or as a gift.

- The transferor may exempt transfers under his $10,000 annual exclusion except, as a rule, for transfers into a trust.

The above rules have drastically reduced the effectiveness of generation skipping. The fact that, if you want to distribute more than one million dollars to your grandchildren at your death, you can actually pay more in taxes (caused by the combination of the generation skipping tax and the estate tax) than the gift itself reduces your incentive to generation skip, which is exactly what the government wants. But the reason that this subject has been included in this chapter is that, once again, life insurance can do more for you in this area than any other type of strategy.

Creating wealth with generation skipping

Since a $1,000,000 exemption can ordinarily only shelter a $1,000,000 transfer, those individuals with large estates who would like to leave more property to their grandchildren and great-grandchildren are limited. If they do take advantage of the exemption, the balance of their estate will still be heavily taxed. However, there is one way to maximize that exemption, and that is through the use of life insurance in an irrevocable trust.

With life insurance, instead of creating only $1,000,000 for your grandchildren, you can create many times that. In the Mason's example, we saw how they could create $600,000 from a $100,000 investment. Imagine what they could have done if they had a larger estate and used their $1,000,000 exemption to purchase an insurance policy for the benefit of their grandchildren! They could have created over **$6,000,000 estate and income-tax free** in addition to substantially reducing the size of their estate. The possibilities are endless, and the dollars created enormous.

Insurability

We have spoken about some of the ways life insurance can benefit your heirs. In the course of the book, we will cover more. However, what if you are not in the best of health? This might cause you to doubt your ability to qualify for life insurance. You may be surprised to find that you might, in fact, get coverage. Many companies specialize in higher-risk individuals. By working with an insurance professional that represents different companies, you may still be able to obtain coverage.

Additionally, it is much easier to obtain a second-to-die insurance policy (discussed in the following chapter) since it covers two people. The insurance company uses the combined mortality of both parties to arrive at a premium. This is a tremendous advantage in the event of health problems.

Of course, if you do have a medical problem but still qualify, the premiums may be higher than would otherwise be the case. At that point, then, you must determine the merit of the insurance. But at least give it a try. You may be pleasantly surprised.

Caution

One word of caution here. As they say on television, "Don't try this at home, kids." The techniques described in this chapter are not the kinds of procedures you should do on your own without professional advice. Make sure you are working with both a competent estate planning attorney and a life insurance professional who understand the intricacies of insurance trusts and generation skipping. The laws concerning irrevocable trusts and Crummey powers are very strict and complete. If this isn't handled properly, the IRS dragon will jump all over you and pull the entire proceeds of the life insurance into your estate...which is exactly what they would like to do.

19

HOW CAN I SUBSTANTIALLY
REDUCE MY ESTATE TAX COST?

In previous chapters, we have discussed various ways to reduce estate taxes: the use of trusts; gifting money out of your estate; the life insurance trust; and generation skipping. Nevertheless, even after these steps have been taken, additional estate taxes may be due. How will they be paid?

Remember, in most cases, estate taxes are due at the death of the second spouse. Your CPA calculates the gross estate, reduces it by any liabilities and credits, and arrives at the tax. **That tax must be paid within nine months.**

Paying estate taxes

> *Charles and Ruth Webster have an estate that is projected to be nearly $4 million at the second death. Of that value, approximately $1 million consists of a business owned by Charles. Even after taking advantage of each of their $600,000 exemptions, their children will still have an estate tax bill of $1,318,000.*

That is a lot of money to send to Uncle Sam! Mr. Webster's business needs to gross $19 million to **net** $1.3 million. Where will the tax money come from? Let's look at the alternatives.

1. Use **Cash** - Their children could send the IRS $1,318,000 in cash from their inheritance (if they

have it). If not, they could have to liquidate assets.

2. **Borrow** the money - The heirs might be able to go to a bank and borrow $1,318,000.

3. Pay in **Installments** - Since the Webster's estate meets the qualifications of Internal Revenue Codes Section 6166, the heirs could pay the IRS in installments.

4. Pay with **Discounted Dollars** - Instead of forcing his children to pay $1,318,000, Mr. Webster could pay 10% of that amount, in advance, over a period of years. This technique, which involves life insurance, can reduce the cost of his estate taxes by 90%!

Let's take a look at the each of the alternatives in detail, exploring the advantages and disadvantages of each.

CASH

Most estates are able to pay the taxes with available cash. The Websters' estate should have sufficient liquidity, either in cash or assets, with which to pay the taxes. However, there are several disadvantages to this.

- They will have to pay 100 cents on the dollar. While this might not sound so bad now, I believe it will be less attractive as you continue this chapter. I will show you a way to reduce the cost of your estate taxes to the point that it could cost only **ten or twenty cents on the dollar!**

- If they have to liquidate assets (sell stock, bonds, real estate, business property, etc.), there is no guarantee that they won't have to sell more than $1,318,000 worth of property to raise that much cash. Forcing a quick sale usually means accepting less than full value. Additionally, the stock or real estate markets may be down or the country may be in a recession. Any number of things could make this extremely difficult or displeasing. In this case, it could easily cost more than 100 cents on the dollar.

BORROW

It amazes me at the number of people who assume their heirs will be able to go a bank and borrow the money with which to pay their estate taxes. They presume that since the estate has assets, a financial institution will jump at the chance to lend them the money.

It goes without saying how financial institutions feel about lending money today. It's not easy to borrow, under the best of circumstances. While it is possible that there may be sufficient assets to use as collateral, you would need a very friendly banker. And even if the money could be borrowed, it would result in substantial interest.

We don't know what the banking situation will be when the Websters' children are faced with estate taxes. But we do know that we can't depend on the banks to finance their estate taxes. And we will see shortly that borrowing is, in fact, the most expensive of the various alternatives.

INSTALLMENT PLAN

The IRS, being the kind organization that it is, allows for an installment plan to be used in two situations.

Section 6161

In rare cases, the IRS may grant the heirs an extension

of up to ten years if they can be convinced that there are sufficient reasons for not paying the taxes. For its part, the IRS has certain guidelines that must be met. In addition to the interest, a bond may be required. Although this sounds good, we will see how costly it can be.

Section 6166

This section is used when the value of a closely held business or farm exceeds thirty-five percent of the adjusted gross estate. If the Websters still qualify at their death, their estate taxes could be paid over a period of up to 14-years, with the first four being interest only. Interest at a rate of four percent would be added, which could double the cost. In addition to the heavy interest charges, there are a few other disadvantages. First, the IRS can hold a lien on their property. This can result in some obvious problems. Second, the reduced interest rate applies only to the first $1,000,000 of business value. Third, any gifts made within three years of death can be pulled back into the estate for calculation purposes. Fourth, a bond may be required. Fifth, since only a portion of the estate taxes can usually qualify, cash is still required. Finally, there are a myriad of rules and regulations that make this plan difficult.

While the IRS has made a valid attempt at helping people allow their heirs to keep their businesses, it is still an expensive alternative. There is still a much better way, and that involves the use of **discounting** the cost of your estate taxes with life insurance.

LIFE INSURANCE

Some of my clients hate to talk about life insurance. They don't like insurance agents; they don't like the premiums. That's okay with me. I hate doctor bills, too. But that doesn't mean I am going to avoid doctors, especially if I want to enjoy a long and healthy life. Life insurance, too, is necessary if you want to maximize your assets and provide for your family.

The truth is that life insurance companies provide a benefit nobody else can match. They accept relatively small amounts of dollars from you (premiums) and guarantee to pay large amounts of dollars (death proceeds) to your beneficiaries. That doesn't sound so bad to me.

The problem with life insurance is not the product, but the way it has been sold. Historically, the industry has attracted some poorly qualified men and women. With the enormous number of agents and so many companies, it is difficult to ensure that each salesperson is properly trained and qualified. After all, you don't have to be a rocket scientist to get an insurance license. As a result, most agents are unaware of the intricacies of the estate planning market.

On the other hand, there are some unbelievably qualified agents representing fantastic insurance companies. The job, therefore, is to separate the wheat from the chaff, and that's not always easy. But don't condemn an entire industry for the actions of a few. Life insurance is too important for that.

Over the years, many of my clients have passed away. And do you know what? Not one widow refused the life insurance check. Not one advisor told his client's family that they really didn't need all that insurance money. Not one child told me to send the money back. Life insurance is the consummate unselfish act. You are providing a special benefit for your loved ones, and that's very generous.

Massive dollars when needed

Life insurance can do for your family what no other product can do: guarantee substantial dollars when they are needed most. Can your investment in Xerox do that? Can your real estate investments do that? Can your retirement plan do that? Can your certificates of deposit do that? No. None of these investments can **guarantee** massive dollars when they are needed......unless you invest massive dollars. But life insurance can provide the big bucks when they are needed most. That is why it is such an invaluable planning tool.

Life insurance to pay estate taxes

Referring to the Webster case, the children will need $1.3 million with which to pay estate taxes. We have looked at the alternatives, none of which involves paying less than $1.3 million. But my job is to help you reduce your outlay for estate taxes. So let's look closely at the last alternative, life insurance.

- Mr. Webster could purchase a $1,000,000 policy that, using current projections, would have a death benefit that increases each year until it reaches $1,318,000 in the twentieth year, the projected date of the second death. The annual premium for that amount of insurance would be approximately $12,000 for twenty years, or $240,000 if he lives that long.

But there is an even better way to fill the need. It is a relatively new type of coverage called a **"second-to-die"** policy. Since estate taxes aren't due until the second spouse dies, prudent planning would suggest buying a policy that won't pay until that occurrence. By insuring both parties with a policy that pays at the second death, you take advantage of joint mortality for a reduced premium.

- In the Webster's case, a premium of under **$6,000** per year for 20 years would fund a policy that, using current projections, would also have a death benefit of $1,318,000 in 20 years. This is less than half of the cost of the policy on Mr. Webster alone. An investment of $120,000 over 20 years, assuming the Websters live that long, can provide over $1.3 million, **estate and income tax free!**

Choices in paying taxes

Let's review the alternatives by looking at actual dollars (See **Exhibit 9**).

1. Pay cash of **$1,318,000.**

2. Borrow the money - at 8% per year for 10 years, for a total cost of **$1,964,210.**

3. Use Section 6166 - paying interest only for four years and then amortizing the balance over 10 more years, for a total cost of **$1,636,257.**

4. Purchase insurance - with an initial premium of $6,000 for twenty years (present dollars) for a maximum of **$120,000**, using current projections.

For me the choice is easy. Paying $120,000 beats $1,318,000, $1,964,210, or $1,636,257 any day of the week. Why would anyone choose any of the other alternatives?

THE SKEPTICS ASK.......

The insurance doubters among you have all kinds of reasons why you shouldn't use life insurance. Let's answer some of those questions.

How about the net present value of the money?

Good question. Although premiums will have to be paid starting today, death benefits won't be paid until some time in the future. Therefore, you can't compare paying $120,000 starting today with $1,318,000 paid in maybe twenty years.

That may be correct. That's why I provided the lower part of Exhibit 9. While the top half of the page reflects the total cost of paying $1,318,000, the bottom half shows the net

Exhibit 9
A Comparison of Funding Alternatives

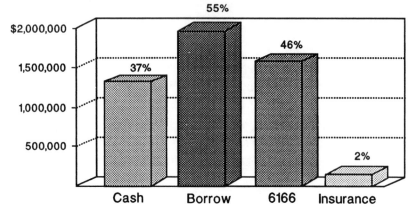

Cash: $1,318,000

Borrow: At 8% ten annual payments of $196,421
               would total $1,964,210.

IRC   Immediate cash need at death of $938,173
Section   plus interest payments of $31,071 each
6166:   year for four years, then principal and
               interest payments of $57,380 for ten
               years for a total of $1,636,257.

Insurance: Initial premiums of $6,000 for twenty
               years for a total of $120,000.

NET PRESENT VALUE*		
	Total	Cost of One Dollar
Cash	$340,596	$1.00
Borrow	356,509	1.05
IRC 6166	349,092	1.02
Insurance	68,014	0.20

* Calculated at 7.00% over 20 years

present value.   And, as you can see, insurance is still the cheapest source of dollars.

Can't we just invest the money ourselves and receive a higher rate?

Although it is possible, there are two reasons why this is highly unlikely.

- If the Websters want that same return in another type of investment, they will need to earn **28.63% after taxes** on that same $6,000 investment for 20 years.   In their tax bracket, that would be an earnings rate of 43% before taxes, which is virtually impossible.   Don't forget, there are no income taxes on the growth of the cash value in a life insurance policy.   Additionally, they would have had to put this fantastic investment in an irrevocable trust, like the life insurance, to remove it from their estate.

- Even if they could find such an investment, will that investment **guarantee them a million dollars if they die the first year?**   Of course not.   Life insurance is unique because it is the only investment that can guarantee a large amount of money from day one. Since our date of death is unknown, nothing else can possibly work as well.

Since I am not as old as Mr. Webster, why should I worry? After all, I've got a lot of years to go.

You hope you do.   But let's be realistic.   What's to guarantee that you won't die tomorrow?   Everybody is in good health until the day comes that he or she is no longer in good health.   How can you possibly know what that day is for you? No one plans to be killed in an accident.   Maybe it's tomorrow; maybe it's 40 years from now.   Maybe you want to take that chance, but I don't.   Proper planning should not be a game of

Russian Roulette. You are going to die. That's guaranteed. Why not also guarantee that no matter when that day comes, your family will not suffer financially?

Why not just pay my estate taxes in cash? I have the money.

What if the Websters have that money sitting in the bank or in liquid assets? Why should they bother with life insurance since the children will have sufficient cash with which to pay the estate taxes?

That philosophy totally misses the point. Whether or not they have the cash is irrelevant. They are going to lose nearly 33% of their estate in taxes! What difference does it make whether or not they have that 33% sitting in the bank? Don't you think they would like to pay those taxes with the cheapest dollars possible? The Websters have spent a lifetime building that estate. Why should they throw one-third of it away needlessly? Using the methods in this chapter, they are able to **reduce the cost of their estate taxes from 33% of their estate to 3%!** Why in the world wouldn't they want to do that?

Why can't I just buy term insurance?

This is another excellent question. After all, over a 20 year period, isn't term insurance usually less expensive than ordinary insurance? Well, yes and no. While over a twenty year period term insurance might be less expensive than a policy on Mr. Webster's life only, it will likely be more expensive than a second-to-die policy. But cost isn't the only factor. There are two other considerations.

- We don't know when the Websters are going to die. If the purpose of this insurance is to pay estate taxes, which it is, and Mr. Webster purchases a term policy, what happens if the insurance expires before he does? If you look at insurance industry statistics, most term insurance never results in a death claim;

it usually lapses before the insured dies.

- Term insurance has a nasty habit of getting increasingly expensive. While term insurance is cheap at younger ages, it gets prohibitive at older ages. And, remember, our purpose is to pay the estate taxes. What happens if Mr. or Mrs. Webster lives to age 80? They will no longer be able to afford term insurance. If the insurance is no longer in force, how will their heirs pay the estate taxes? We're back to square one because term insurance is only a temporary solution to a permanent problem.

What happens if the annual premium is over my gift tax exclusion?

*Bobby Anderson has one primary goal: to leave his entire $5,000,000 estate to his children, estate tax-free. He has worked hard for the past thirty years and wants his children to receive every penny from his efforts. It sickened him when he was told that if he were to die today, **almost 45% of his hard work would go to the government** in the form of estate taxes. To resolve this, his estate planning team recommended that Mr. Anderson purchase a $2,200,000 life insurance policy and place it in an irrevocable trust. To fund the policy, he would transfer $40,000 per year for ten years from his assets to the irrevocable trust. However, he has only 2 children. That means he will exceed his $10,000 annual exclusion by $20,000 per year for 10 years.*

But that's not much of a problem. His children will receive a much greater benefit from his using the additional $20,000 to buy insurance than they would if they inherited that much. The only consequence will be a reduction of his $600,000 exclusion by the overage. Nevertheless, his children will get the death benefit - $5,000,000, or 100% of his estate, free of taxes! As a result, he will have turned $200,000 of his $600,000 exclusion into $2,200,000, estate and income tax-free! In other words, $200,000 will do the work of $2,200,000.

The only logical solution

Looking at this logically, not emotionally, there's no other choice. It's a pure business decision. No matter what your bias, life insurance is the best solution to this problem.

> *Roger Borders hated life insurance. He hated agents. He hated premiums. But he realized he needed to do some planning. He warned me, "Lots of insurance agents are bugging me. While I want to do some planning, I don't want to buy any life insurance. The only reason I'm willing to talk to you is because of your reputation and the fact that you're not just an insurance agent." I said, "No problem. I won't mention life insurance."*

> *At our first meeting, we discussed his particular problems. At the time, he owned a business, some real estate and had an estate of approximately $1.3 million. Again, he indicated that he wasn't interested in any life insurance. We held another meeting, this time with his wife and attorney. I presented a computer analysis of their potential tax liability. The analysis showed a future estate tax liability of approximately $300,000, based on conservative assumptions of growth, inflation, and life expectancy. He said, "Where in the world are my kids going to get that kind of money without selling our assets? Nothing we have is liquid." I replied, "I could tell you, but I agreed not to, because it involves the 'L' word, and you don't want to hear it."*

> *His wife jumped in, "Oh, yes, we do." I told them that at their ages, for $4,000 a year for approximately ten years (based on then-current projections), they could invest in a second-to-die policy that would provide the needed $300,000 cash for their kids. But we also looked at all the alternatives as outlined previously. I showed him the cost breakdown of each method of payment. Being a successful businessman and realizing that there were no acceptable options, he chose to pay his taxes with the discounted dollars provided by insurance.*

The attraction of life insurance is not that it is such a great investment. The enticement is a result of the fact that the life insurance industry operates under favorable tax laws. Used properly, life insurance has four primary advantages.

- Cash values, unlike most investments, grow **tax deferred.** No income taxes have to be paid on the earnings.

- Death Benefits are paid **income tax free,** under most circumstances.

- If properly established in an irrevocable life insurance trust, or with third-party ownership, the growth and death benefits will also be **estate tax free.**

- The proceeds, if paid to a named beneficiary, are generally **free from the creditors** of the insured.

Conclusion

I don't want to sound like an insurance salesman trying to shove life insurance down your throat, because that's not the intention. Believe me, if there existed a real estate or stock market investment in which you could invest $4,000 and be guaranteed $300,000 immediately, income and estate-tax free, I would recommend it. But there isn't. There is no other investment, when used properly, like life insurance. The key is to work with a professional who can show you how to use insurance to **your** advantage.

Remember our definition:

> *"During my life and after my death, I want to control and distribute my property in the manner I desire, minimizing all fees, taxes and court interference, preserving for myself, my family, and those I choose, the estate I have worked so hard to create."*

If you truly want to minimize all taxes and preserve the estate you have worked so hard to create, then properly structured life insurance may be part of the solution. So forget how you feel about it - look at the benefits.

20

WHAT SHOULD BE MY CONCERNS WHEN BUYING LIFE INSURANCE?

The insurance industry has undergone substantial changes in recent years. Because of the importance life insurance plays in estate planning, it is critical that we review the areas that can cause financial problems.

Twenty-two years ago, when I first entered the financial industry, this discussion would not have been as vital as it is today. In those years, there were few concerns about the safety of life insurance companies......everybody just assumed they were secure. However, all that has changed. With the recent failures in the insurance industry, it is imperative that we evaluate each and every life insurance company we are considering and choose only those that are conservative and stable.

There are approximately 1,800 life insurance companies and seemingly 18 million agents, most of whom seem to be calling or sending you information daily. You obviously don't have the time, or inclination, to talk to all these people. If you did, you wouldn't have time to work or run your business. On the other hand, it is vital to work with a competent life insurance professional, whether it be a life insurance agent or a financial planner.

QUALITY OF THE COMPANY

Even though there are over 1,800 life insurance companies, only a relative handful are what I consider worthy of recommending to my clients. You have seen and heard the stories about the companies that have been seized by their state insurance commissioners or forced into bankruptcy. We can assume there will be more problems in the future. This is precisely what you want to **avoid** when buying a life insurance policy. Safety must be your primary concern!

Rating Services

Unless you are a financial analyst and familiar with the insurance industry, you have to depend on the various rating services to do your work for you. At present, there are five major services.

- **A. M. Best and Company** is the oldest insurance company rating service. They rate approximately 1380 insurance companies as follows: A+ (Superior), A and A- (Excellent), B+ (Very Good), B and B- (Good), C+ (Fairly Good), C and C- (Fair). Of the 774 companies rated in those categories, 544, or 70%, are rated A- and above. As a result, many people are of the opinion that A. M. Best may not be as reliable as once thought. Insurance companies are charged $500 a year for these ratings.

- **Standard and Poor's** rates the claims-paying ability for approximately 150 companies and provides solvency ratings for about 1600 companies. In my opinion, the solvency ratings don't have much value. However, the claims-paying ability ratings are valid and important. Those ratings are: AAA (Superior), AA+, AA and AA- (Excellent), A+, A and A- (Good), BBB+, BBB and BBB- (Adequate) and as low as D. Because Standard and Poor's charges anywhere from $15,000 to $28,000 per year, only the higher quality companies tend to get rated. As a result, approximately 95% of the companies are rated A- or better.

- **Moody's Investor Service** rates approximately 80 companies for financial strength. The ratings are Aaa (Exceptional), Aa (Excellent), A (Good), Baa (Adequate), Ba (Questionable), and as low as C. Moody's charges $25,000 per year for this services. Again, since only the higher quality companies are willing to pay for this rating, most get rated A or better.

- **Duff and Phelps Inc.** is another company that rates the claims paying ability of approximately 60 life insurance companies. Their rating grades parallel Standard & Poor's. Their service costs the insurance company $17,000, and again, virtually every company is A- or better.

- **Weiss Research** is a relatively new service that rates approximately 1750 insurance companies and sells those ratings to the general public. Their ratings are A+, A and A- (Excellent), B+, B and B- (Good), C+, C and C- (Fair), D+, D and D- (Weak), E (Very Weak) and F (Failed). Unlike the other services, Weiss comes down hard on the insurance industry, placing 70% of the rated companies in the "C+" to "D-" range. The reason for this is that these ratings are predicated on a worst-case (depression) scenario. Because this service is so new, it doesn't yet have a long track record. Most industry professionals scoff at Weiss because of his lack of insurance industry background or established credibility. Yet, because of the publicity he has received from marketing his service, Mr. Weiss has a constituency that is willing to pay to hear what he has to say.

Although the insurance industry has gone through difficult times over the past several years, there are people who are trying to take advantage of this in a way that is not beneficial to the policyholder. You need to take what you read with a grain of salt. Although there have been a few failures, they represent a minor portion of the industry. As a rule, the industry is strong. Nevertheless, you still must take care in choosing your companies. What you want is an insurance company that has conservative management, stability, and superior strength.

In my practice, I feel comfortable working only with those companies that have an "A+" rating from A. M. Best **in addition** to a top-level rating from one or more of the other services. Since all major companies are rated by A.M. Best, you can easily find that rating. On the other hand, because of the cost, only a limited number choose to be rated by the other services. However, more and more companies are feeling pressure from agents and policyholders to spend the money to be rated in order to allay the fears of consumers.

I recommend that when purchasing large amounts of insurance, you diversify between different companies. The reason for this is twofold. First, for safety reasons, it makes sense to spread the risk. But, even more important, you don't know which companies will perform best over the years. They all differ in their investment policy. As a result, the amount of interest they credit to their policyholders will vary. By using different companies, you aren't placing all your eggs in one insurance basket.

KNOWLEDGE OF THE AGENT

Picking an agent is difficult, especially since most people aren't aware of an agent's competency until it's too late. While most agents are honest, hard working people who want to do what is best for their clients, the majority are not familiar with complex estate planning concepts.

Picking an agent is like picking a business partner. You frequently don't know if there is a problem until one occurs. As a result, you need to interview an agent to see if he really knows what he's talking about. One of the purposes of this book is to present the necessary concepts so you'll have a basic idea as to what you want and need. Then you can find the professionals to help you.

Scrutinize the agent. Are you compatible? Does he or she share your values? Does he ask the right questions? Does he listen to your answers? Does he want to help you solve your problems first or just try to get you to buy a policy? Does he know the insurance business enough to help you, or do you have to educate him? Does he want to work with other professionals (attorneys, CPA's) or do it all alone? Be careful here, because we are talking about large sums of dollars being saved or lost on the basis of advice.

COMMON MISTAKES TO AVOID

Historically, many of the choices regarding insurance have been left to chance. There has been a lack of good advice and information for the insurance-buying public. This has resulted in a plethora of needless mistakes. Let's look at a few.

Proceeds payable to minors - We have previously discussed the problems with making a minor the beneficiary of your life insurance policy. I think it goes without saying at this point that it should be avoided. Instead, consider using a trust as beneficiary of your insurance proceeds.

Proceeds payable to your estate - It is amazing how many policies I review where the insured's estate has been designated as the beneficiary. In my opinion, this is one of the worst mistakes that can be made. There is virtually no advantage in naming the estate as beneficiary, other than it is simple and requires no thought. However, there are significant expensive disadvantages.

- The insurance proceeds, which are, as a rule, creditor-free when paid to a named beneficiary, become subject to the creditors of the insured when paid to his or her estate.

- The proceeds, which avoid probate when paid to a named beneficiary, must go through probate when paid to the estate of the insured.

- The proceeds will be included in the estate of the insured for estate tax purposes, regardless of who owns the policy.

- The proceeds will pass according to the insured's will, and that raises the various problems that were covered earlier.

Ownership by the wrong party - The owner, not the insured, controls the policy. While you might want to designate another party as owner for financial reasons, understand the ramifications. It takes complete control out of your hands. However there is a very good reason for removing the insurance proceeds from your estate: saving your heirs potentially hundreds of thousands of dollars in estate taxes.

Don't forget what was mentioned earlier about cross ownership of policies. It is no longer advantageous for the wife to own the husband's insurance, and vice versa. To remove it from both of your estates, it must be owned by an independent third party, such as an irrevocable trust or a child.

Indiscriminate changing of ownership - Changing the ownership of a policy, while easy to do, brings in all the dragons, with income, gift, and estate-tax ramifications.

When Bernard Madison went into business, his life insurance agent suggested having his corporation purchase and own a policy on his life. Over the years, the policy built up substantial cash values. One day, on the advice of his agent, he transferred ownership of the policy from the corporation to himself. As soon as he did that, the cash value in the policy became income to him personally and resulted in a significant tax liability.

● ● ●

Chris Boyd owned a $250,000 life insurance policy on himself that had $50,000 in cash value. To remove it from his estate, he transferred the ownership to his son, Rudy. That immediately created a gift of the cash value. Additionally, when Chris died two years later, the entire $250,000 was included in his estate because he died within three years of transferring the ownership.

Relying on inflated projections

As you review insurance proposals, remember they are based on current interest rate and mortality assumptions (as are the figures used throughout this book). Both of these can and will change over the years.

One caution about interest rates. We saw what happened in the savings and loan industry: those institutions that took the highest risks and desperately needed money offered the highest rates. Of course, the consumer didn't care since the deposits were insured. Well, you don't have that luxury with life insurance. Be skeptical of unusually high rates. Don't get caught in the trap of "rate chasing."

State guarantee funds

There is currently concern about the financial stability of a few companies. Even with the current problems, the insurance industry has a very enviable record of protecting policyholders assets. One mechanism in place to provide additional protection are the state guarantee funds. While not government-backed bank insurance, these funds do guarantee deposits with insurance companies. They are funded by the companies who sell insurance in each state and are designed to protect the policyholders residing in that state. The funds have the power to assess the companies if large claims arise. The benefits paid, however, are limited and vary from state to state. The majority of the funds provide coverage up to $300,000 in death benefits, $100,000 in cash values, and $100,000 for annuities.

One reason you don't hear much about these funds is that insurance agents aren't allowed to tell you about them. The states don't want to be in a position where agents, and policy purchasers, don't worry about the safety of a company because they know that there is insurance. They know what happened in the savings and loan industry, and they don't want agents to use that guarantee as a sales tool. As a result, most people don't hear about these until there is an insurance company failure.

I can see that point and personally agree with it. If it weren't for FSLIC insurance, we wouldn't have had such a big problem with the savings and loans. But depositors didn't care about the bank because they knew it was insured.

When it comes to insurance, it is important you make your choice as if there were no protection from outside forces. Make sure the company is highly rated based on the services discussed earlier. Then, hopefully, you will never find yourself in a position of relying on a guarantee fund.

Conclusion

The insurance industry provides a needed service to us all. Unfortunately, unscrupulous sales practices by some agents has given it a bad name. But insurance can still do things that other financial vehicles cannot. By exercising care and caution, you will be able to enjoy its benefits without experiencing its pitfalls.

21

HOW CAN CHARITABLE GIVING REDUCE MY TAXES AND INCREASE MY INCOME?

Over the years, Americans have been generous with charitable donations. We have given unselfishly to churches, synagogues, health organizations, medical foundations, hospitals, colleges, and other charitable organizations. This has provided us with tax deductions as well as good feelings from helping others.

Recently, a new light has been shed on charitable giving, one that provides even greater benefits to both the charities as well as the givers. As a result, charitable giving is a planning field unto itself. It is an integral part of estate planning that creates all kinds of opportunities for everybody involved.

Charitable giving is a legitimate practice when handled responsibly. If you are going to get involved in charitable giving, remember there are many IRS rules which are just waiting to trip you. Nevertheless, the opportunities are endless. You will be amazed by the benefits.

Legitimate charities

Over the years, many groups have passed themselves off as genuine charities, of which many were frauds. While we are usually familiar with what is a legitimate charity, the IRS has made it easy for us by publishing a list of qualified charities.

Types of Giving Programs

There are a number of techniques that can be used for charitable giving. Four of the primary methods are:

- **Charitable Remainder Annuity Trust,** which provides a fixed income stream to a noncharitable beneficiary (for example the donor and his spouse) for a period of time, after which the property creating the income goes to the charity.

- **Pooled Income Fund,** in which a donor's gift is combined with the gifts of others and provides a stream of income to the donor.

- **Charitable Lead Trust,** which provides a flow of income to a charity for a certain number of years, after which the trust ends, and the property reverts to a noncharitable beneficiary.

- **Charitable Remainder Unitrust,** the discussion of which follows.

CHARITABLE REMAINDER UNITRUST

The charitable remainder unitrust (CRUT) is the most flexible of the various charitable trusts. The type of CRUT that I think is best suited to the individual needs of most people is the "net income unitrust with a make-up provision", which we affectionately refer to as NIMCRUT. Let's look at this form of CRUT and see how it might be used.

A NIMCRUT is a type of charitable remainder unitrust into which you gift property that will go to a charity upon the death of you and your spouse. In the meantime, you have the opportunity to receive the income from that trust in addition to a number of other benefits outlined below. The CRUT has become extremely popular with people because it offers flexibility and a variety of benefits that cannot be achieved elsewhere.

- The NIMCRUT can be used as a supplement for a qualified retirement plan.

- It can permit you to sell appreciated assets without having to pay capital gains taxes.

- It can protect assets from lawsuits.

- With the NIMCRUT, you can receive benefits now while leaving money to a qualified charity later.

- You can reduce estate taxes by moving assets into a NIMCRUT.

Parties to the trust

A NIMCRUT is irrevocable, which means you can't change the terms (although there are a few things you can change, as we'll see later). Like all trusts, it has a **trustmaker** (you), a **trustee** (can be you or another person), an **administrator** (a professional third-party), and a **beneficiary** (a charity). It also has an **income beneficiary**, which can be you, your spouse, etc.

Funding the trust

Once you establish the trust, you "fund" it with "property." After the initial contribution, you can continue to add to it anytime you desire. You can even leave property through your will or trust. The trust can be funded with property in the form of appreciated assets, such as real estate or stock.

Benefits of the trust

First, for your contribution, you receive a **federal income tax deduction.** The amount of that deduction is based on the "present value" of the interest income you will receive from the trust. (Present value refers to the economic value today of the stream of income you will receive in the future.) The write-off also takes into consideration such factors as the age of the income beneficiaries (to determine how long you might receive the income), current interest rates (to calculate present value of the income stream), your adjusted gross income (to determine the amount of charitable write-off to which you are entitled), type of property (cash and real estate, for example, are treated differently), and the interest rate you will be receiving over the years. It is a complicated calculation for which I use a sophisticated computer program.

The second benefit occurs if you contribute appreciated property (stock, real estate, business interest, etc.). Since the trust is a tax-exempt entity, trust property in most cases can be sold with **no capital gains tax.**

Be aware that a charitable contribution of appreciated property is a tax preference item that can create an Alternative Minimum Tax (AMT) liability in a limited number of situations. Check with your CPA to determine any AMT ramifications.

Third, if you serve as your own trustee, **you control** how the money is invested. Generally speaking, you can choose between stocks, bonds, mutual funds, or annuities. As with any investment, it should be consistent with your financial goals, risk tolerance, years to retirement and the interest of the charitable beneficiary.

Fourth, you will **receive income** from the trust.

- To the extent that it is available, you may receive a fixed percentage of the trust assets. You have a choice in how you want to receive it - annually, semi-annually, quarterly, or in some cases monthly.

- The amount of income you receive is a function of the size of the trust in addition to how you've invested your assets.

- Depending on the type of trust, you can receive only income (no principal), or a payout of both interest and principal to the extent principal is needed to reach the income rate (percentage) that you have chosen.

Fifth, upon the death of the last income beneficiary (usually you and your spouse), the **proceeds go to the charity** or charities of your choice. But they must be legitimate charities. In addition, many people choose to set up a **family foundation**. This permits their children to dispense the funds to charities over the years.

Protection for your children

The one concern I always hear is, "If I receive the income until both my wife (husband) and I die, and then the principal goes to a charity, then what's in it for my kids?" That's no problem. All we need to do is establish what we call a "wealth replacement trust". You'll recognize it as a variation of the irrevocable life insurance trust discussed earlier.

You take some of the tax benefits (remember you get a write-off for the contribution) and/or some of the cash flow and gift it to the insurance trust. The trustee will then purchase a life insurance policy (such as a second-to-die) in the trust for the benefit of the children. If structured properly, this does several things: (1) it removes the proceeds of your life insurance from your estate, (2) it ensures your children will receive their rightful inheritance; and (3) it protects those values from a lawsuit.

The trust in action

So the bottom line is this: you can contribute as much or as little as you desire; the money is protected from lawsuits; it is free from estate taxes; you can include and exclude anyone you desire; you can turn the income stream on and off as you desire; and you receive a tax deduction for the contribution.

Helen and Larry Peterson, ages 62 and 61 respectively, owned real estate which they purchased years ago for $120,000. The value had appreciated to $1,000,000. Mr. Peterson was planning to retire within two years. He wanted to sell the real estate and invest the proceeds in something that would provide some income. The problem was that he and his heirs would have had to pay significant taxes on that money: income tax at sale; estate tax at death.

Sales Price	$1,000,000
Cost Basis	120,000
Gross Profit	$ 880,000
Income Taxes	334,400
Net Profit	$ 665,600
Estate Taxes	366,080
Net to Heirs	$ 299,520

Over 70% of the value of the property would have been lost to income and estate taxes! (This calculation assumes current federal and average state income tax rates.) This means if the Petersons had **sold** the property, **paid** the capital gains tax, reinvested the money, **spent** the income, and then **died,** their heirs would have received only $299,520 of the $1,000,000!

This really concerned Mr. Peterson. He had visions of leaving a large sum to his children, not to Uncle Sam. He was already getting hit badly enough by taxes and didn't want to make it worse. So let's take a look at how he improved his situation.

Instead of selling the property outright, the Petersons established a Charitable Remainder Unitrust and donated the property to it. **Exhibit 10** illustrates how this worked. Let's go through it step by step. Because your situation will be different from the Petersons, we are not going to include any AMT ramifications in our calculations.

Step 1. The Petersons contributed their $1,000,000 piece of property to their charitable remainder trust which then sold it.

Step 2. They received a tax deduction of $229,200 which resulted in an income tax savings of $87,906.

Step 3. They took $34,782 and funded the first year's life insurance premium in a wealth replacement trust.

Step 4. The $1 million from the sale of the property was invested in bonds that averaged 9% per year income. After income taxes, they should receive a total of $1,284,034 over their life expectancy.

Step 5. They are taking part of that income each year for the next nine years to fund the life insurance trust. That amount should total $340,038, based on current projections.

Step 6. Upon their deaths, their family foundation should receive $1,590,752, based on their current life expectancy and current projections.

Step 7. Additionally, their heirs (children) will receive $2,644,366 from the insurance trust, estate and income tax free.

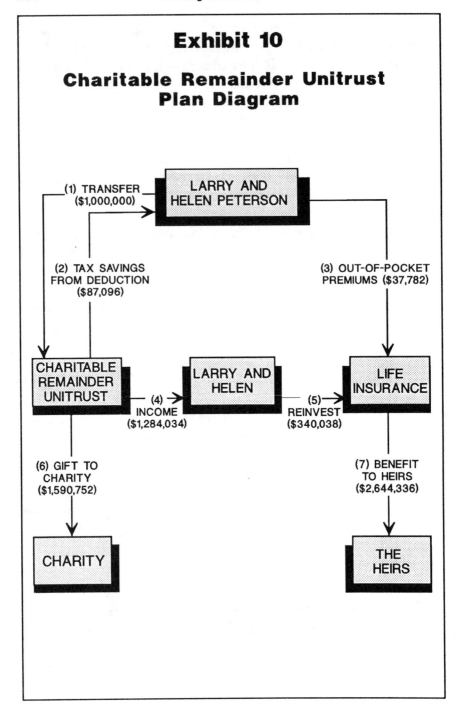

Exhibit 10

Charitable Remainder Unitrust Plan Diagram

LARRY AND HELEN PETERSON

(1) TRANSFER ($1,000,000)

(2) TAX SAVINGS FROM DEDUCTION ($87,096)

(3) OUT-OF-POCKET PREMIUMS ($37,782)

CHARITABLE REMAINDER UNITRUST

LARRY AND HELEN

LIFE INSURANCE

(4) INCOME ($1,284,034)

(5) REINVEST ($340,038)

(6) GIFT TO CHARITY ($1,590,752)

(7) BENEFIT TO HEIRS ($2,644,336)

CHARITY

THE HEIRS

Let's compare two alternatives:

Alternative #1. The Petersons **sell the property** as they would normally. They pay the capital gains taxes, and reinvest it at 9%. At their deaths, the money, after estate taxes, goes to their kids.

Alternative #2. The Petersons **contribute the property** to their Charitable Remainder Unitrust which sells it and reinvests the proceeds at 9%. They receive the income and use a portion of that to purchase a life insurance policy in a wealth replacement trust. At the second death, the insurance proceeds go to their children, while the balance of the CRT goes to their family foundation.

	1. Without CRUT	2. Using CRUT
CONTRIBUTIONS		
Market Value	$1,000,000	$1,000,000
Savings from Tax Deduction	0	87,096
Capital Gains Tax on Sale	334,400	0
Net to Invest	$ 665,600	$1,087,096
CASH FLOW		
Income During Life	$1,093,944	$1,371,130
Less: Insurance Premiums	0	377,820
Net Spendable Income	$1,093,944	$ 993,310
ESTATE FOR HEIRS		
Gross Value of Estate	$ 665,600	0
Plus: Life Insurance	0	$2,644,336
Less: Estate Taxes	366,080	0
Net Estate for Heirs	$ 299,520	2,644,336
SUMMARY OF BENEFITS		
Net Income	$1,093,944	$ 993,310
Estate for Heirs	299,520	2,644,336
Amount to Charity	0	1,590,752
TOTAL BENEFIT	**$1,393,464**	**$5,228,398**

You can see the leverage the Petersons were able to achieve with a properly structured charitable unitrust. If they had needed more income, they could have just reduced the amount of life insurance. If they didn't need all the income, they could have increased the life insurance. Whatever their needs, the flexibility is tremendous. It provides income for them, a substantial estate (free from income and estate taxes) for their children, and a considerable benefit for their favorite charities. Why wouldn't they make that choice?

There are many other instances where a charitable trust can be used to reduce capital gains exposure. You might have a business you wish to sell in which you have a very low cost basis. Possibly you have a tremendous profit in a stock but don't want to sell it because of the capital gains. There are various situations where the proper use of a charitable remainder unitrust can be extremely beneficial to all the parties. Selling your business/farm/professional practice is covered in Chapter 27.

CHARITABLE TRUSTS AS RETIREMENT PLANS

Many of my professional and business clients complain about their retirement plans. As a rule, there are three problems. First, the pension plan is overfunded, meaning that no additional contributions can be made. Second, so much has to be contributed for the employees that the owner receives little actual benefit. And third, they get penalized with the "success tax" discussed earlier in the book.

Benefits

One of the alternatives you might consider is the use of a NIMCRUT as a retirement plan, which offers many benefits.

- You can make contributions for yourself and not include any other person.

• There are no mandated contributions; you can contribute as much or as little as you wish.

• There are no penalties for early withdrawal or requirements that you start receiving income.

• You can choose among a number of investment options that could allow you to receive tax-free income upon your retirement.

• You can provide a lifetime income for yourself and your spouse.

• As a general rule, you receive a partial tax deduction for your contribution.

• You can leave money to your children, estate tax free, through a wealth replacement trust.

• You can leave substantial dollars to your favorite charity or charities.

• The funds in the trust are protected from lawsuits. Of course, when you start receiving income, that portion is not protected.

• There is no "success" penalty for excess accumulations or distributions.

Dr. and Mrs. Charles Adams were unhappy with their retirement plan. It had reached the point where it was of little benefit to them relative to the amount of money they had to contribute for the employees. They expressed this concern to their planner and emphasized that they were interested in doing something that would benefit them. The planner recommended they fund a charitable remainder unitrust. They began contributing $25,000 per year into the trust. That contribution provided a deduction, based on various factors, of approximately $3,611 in the first year, which would increase to $7,451 in the fourteenth year. The money will grow in a guaranteed fund earning a current rate of

8%. Upon retirement in 15 years, Dr. and Mrs. Adams can begin to draw income. In this case, based on current rates, they will receive annual income of $53,870. However, since the value of the trust will go to a charity upon their deaths, their daughters would forfeit part of their inheritance. Therefore, the Adams' attorney drafted a wealth replacement trust into which Adams will transfer $3100 per year for 15 years toward a joint and survivor insurance policy. This policy should have a death benefit of $677,000 at their deaths, based on current life expectancy. By placing it in an irrevocable life insurance trust, it will provide estate tax-free benefits for their daughters at their deaths and replace the lost inheritance. Best of all, their favorite charities will receive approximately $694,383 at their deaths. Everybody wins!

The plan

Exhibit 11 illustrates the plan. The numbers are based on today's interest rates, today's tax schedule, and today's life insurance rates. Obviously, this will change over the years, but here is a step by step description.

Step 1.   Over 15 years they will transfer $350,000 to the trust.

Step 2.   This will result in a total tax savings of $25,312.

Step 3.   They will pay premiums of $46,500 to the life insurance trust.

Step 4.   They should receive annual income of $36,000 **after tax** or a total of $721,180 based on their life expectancies, payable as long as one of them is still alive.

Step 5.   While making the contributions, the tax savings of $25,080 will be reinvested.

Step 6.   At their deaths, the charity should receive $694,383.

Exhibit 11

Charitable Remainder Unitrust Plan Diagram

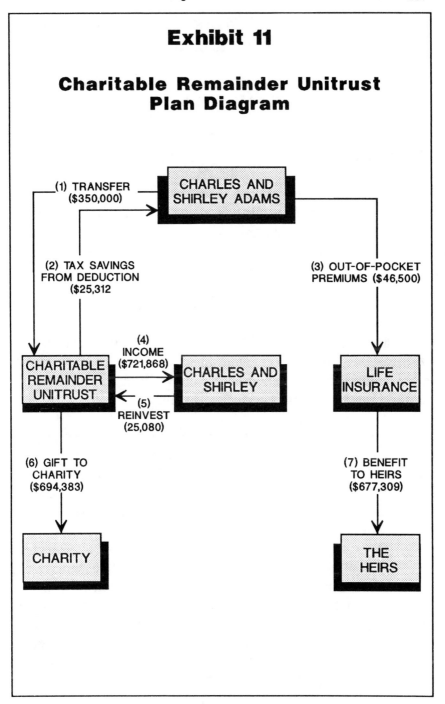

(1) TRANSFER ($350,000)

CHARLES AND SHIRLEY ADAMS

(2) TAX SAVINGS FROM DEDUCTION ($25,312

(3) OUT-OF-POCKET PREMIUMS ($46,500)

CHARITABLE REMAINDER UNITRUST

(4) INCOME ($721,868)

CHARLES AND SHIRLEY

LIFE INSURANCE

(5) REINVEST (25,080)

(6) GIFT TO CHARITY ($694,383)

(7) BENEFIT TO HEIRS ($677,309)

CHARITY

THE HEIRS

Step 7. At their deaths, the children should receive $677,309, based on current projections.

The Adams will have invested a total of $350,000 and created a total value of $2,093,791 for themselves, their heirs, and their favorite charities.

Conclusion

This example is not designed to be an in-depth comparison of the benefits of a NIMCRUT and a qualified retirement plan. With the latter, there are many factors involved. However, many physicians and executives are using NIMCRUTs to supplement their qualified plan.

While in some respects, a qualified retirement plan makes sense because of the 100% write-off, there is a trade-off. You are subject to early withdrawal penalties and forced distributions; you must include all employees; you have outrageous administrative expenses; you have little control; and you can get penalized for superior performance.

With the NIMCRUT, while the write-off is smaller, you can leave more to your favorite charities, you can maintain control over the trust, you can receive all the benefits yourself, you can include whomever you desire, and, properly structured, your heirs will receive their inheritance estate tax-free.

More and more of my clients agree that the charitable remainder unitrust should play an important part in their overall planning.   They feel that in conjunction with the wealth replacement trust, the benefits are immense. And slowly but surely, the more knowledgeable accountants and attorneys are beginning to see that it's not a tax-avoidance scheme, but a legitimate plan that provides unique benefits for their clients. Once they understand what a great planning tool it is, they appreciate it even more.

PART IV

PROTECTION DURING YOUR LIFETIME

22

HOW CAN I PROTECT MYSELF IF I BECOME DISABLED?

"Disability" is a word that scares many people. And it should. Because, believe it or not, at most ages, your chances of becoming disabled are many times greater than your chances of dying. Yet while many people have made some type of plan in case of their premature death, few have taken action to protect themselves and their families in the event of their disability.

This chapter addresses both aspects of disability: the disability that keeps you from working and earning a living, and the disability that keeps you from making financial decisions.

DISABILITY FROM WORK

If you became disabled today, could you support yourself and your family? Would you have sufficient income to meet your everyday expenses. Could you make your mortgage, car, and credit card payments? Could you buy food, clothing, and medical supplies? If not, then you need to look carefully at disability insurance.

A disability occurs as the result of an accident or sickness that keeps you from earning an income. If you work for the government, or a corporation, or a generous employer, then you probably have insurance to cover you in this event. If you don't, you may want to give it a look.

Disability insurance pays you a monthly income when you are unable to work. When talking about disability insurance, there are some decisions you need to make and some factors you need to consider.

- **Waiting period** - is the number of days until your disability benefits begin. Obviously, the shorter the waiting period, the higher the premium.

- **Benefit period** - is the number of years for which you will receive benefits. It can range anywhere from two years to your lifetime. The longer the benefit period, the higher the premium.

- **Benefit amount** - is the monthly income you will be paid by the insurance company. This is a percentage of your income, usually limited to 60%.

- **Premium payor** - is the party paying the premium. If you have a corporation, then that entity can pay and deduct the premium. However, the benefits are taxable when you receive them. On the other hand, if you pay the benefits yourself, they are not tax-deductible, but neither are the benefits income taxable when you receive them.

- **Your job description** - will have a large bearing on the premium. Obviously, if you work at a hazardous waste site, your premiums will be higher than if you work in an office.

- The **definition of disability** - determines when the insurance company considers you disabled. Much of this is a function of your job. A professional (such as a physician), can receive benefits if he is unable to continue the duties of his particular specialty. An unskilled worker, on the other hand, will receive benefits as long as he is unable to perform any job for which he is suited.

- **Continuation of coverage** - is your right to maintain the coverage and current premium. You should look for a policy that is guaranteed renewable and non-cancelable.

MENTAL INCAPACITY

Beyond what we just covered, there is also another category of disability. It is the type that will not only render you incapable of working but will also make you incapable of making financial decisions. This is the area that relates to estate planning.

Jack Johnson and his wife, Ruth, had a difficult life. They had overcome numerous financial and medical problems. To make matters worse, one day Jack was hit by a car while jogging and ended up in a coma. The bulk of their property was in joint tenancy. Ruth, shaken by the entire experience, was nevertheless ready to carry on with the family's finances. However, she ran into some problems.

- *Jack began receiving a monthly disability check. Ruth didn't know how she should handle depositing the checks since they were payable to her husband.*

- *The Johnsons had a brokerage account with a local firm. One day, Ruth needed money and called the broker to sell some stock. If the broker had known that Jack was mentally disabled, he would not have executed the trade, because joint accounts need the authority of both parties. Even if he had done what she wanted, the check would have been payable to Mr. and Mrs. Johnson. She was not sure whether to tell the broker the truth.*

- *She wanted to sell their home, which was owned jointly. She knew she couldn't do this without his signature.*

Now we all realize that people sign their spouse's names on checks every day of the week. But we also know it is against the law. Banks can't accept forgeries, even by a spouse. And I know stockbrokers transact business in joint accounts after speaking to only one party. But that's not supposed to happen either. The fact is that Mrs. Johnson's hands were tied financially. She ran into a roadblock at every turn.

What we have is a string of problems for which most people don't plan, but more than a few experience. In fact, *we don't think we have a problem until we have a problem.* And as long as both Mr. and Mrs. Johnson were functioning normally, they didn't have a problem. But Jack became disabled, so all of a sudden, they did have a problem, and a big one at that.

LIVING PROBATE

We talked about death probate earlier. Living probate, on the other hand, is a process in which a person is declared mentally incompetent and a guardian is appointed. Basically, it entails the embarrassing situation of having to lay before the probate court the details concerning the person claimed to be incapacitated. Then, after the necessary doctor's statements, testimony, etc., the court appoints a guardian.

Groucho Marx

We all know who Groucho Marx was - a great comedian. As Groucho got older, he become more and more unable to make decisions. His health, like that of many older people, was deteriorating. At the time, he had a live-in girl friend, Erin Fleming. Erin felt that Groucho could no longer make his own decisions and petitioned the court to have him declared mentally incompetent. In order to do this, she had to go through living probate.

In this case, the court appointed Erin as guardian and the Bank of America as custodian of the funds. This went on for a while, but Erin didn't like it; she didn't want the bank involved. So she petitioned the court again, this time to be named sole custodian. There was, however, considerable negative reaction. The bank trustees didn't like it and thought that their bank should be named sole custodian. Groucho's family came out of the woodwork and decided that one of them should be named custodian.

You probably remember what happened next. It was in all the newspapers and on television. Groucho went through a long, humiliating proceeding during which witnesses, friends, enemies, and anyone else who had anything to say took the stand and testified. All kinds of bad stuff came out. Groucho just sat in his wheelchair the entire time and listened, tears rolling down his cheeks, unable to contribute. It was a sad situation.

After a lengthy proceeding, Groucho's grandson was named custodian. Shortly thereafter, Groucho Marx died. A sad ending to a great life. But it wasn't over, because then Groucho's estate had to go through more - they had to probate his will!

Who made all the money from this fiasco? Three guesses, and the first two don't count. We all know the answer to that one. Even with all the legal advice that Groucho could, and should have received, he wasn't spared this humiliation and expense.

The Groucho Marx story is a famous case because of his status as a celebrity. After hearing that story, many people say, "I'm not rich and famous like Groucho; this could never happen to me." It certainly could. Read on.

Blanche Hardy's husband, Franklin, was a logger for a timber company. While cutting timber one day, a tree "kicked-back" and knocked Franklin out. In fact, the doctors didn't expect him to live. After a week, however, the doctor said to Blanche, "The good news is your husband is going to live; the bad news is he will have the mind of a three-year old." She was devastated. But she loved him and wanted to spend every hour she could with him at the hospital. She was determined to see it through.

Enter the insurance company. The workers' compensation carrier was paying Franklin a monthly benefit. They were afraid that he might die, resulting in a large death claim. They decided it would be better if Franklin was transferred to a town across the state that had a large medical complex. That way, in the event that he needed special care, he would be close to good facilities. His wife didn't agree. She and Franklin had grown up in their small town and felt comfortable there with all their friends and relatives. She didn't want to pick up and move to a strange location, even if the medical care was superior.

The insurance company didn't like that. They went to Franklin's brother in this other town and offered him a lump sum of money plus a monthly stipend if he would petition for guardianship of his brother. Each side had their own attorneys. They went through all the legalities: interrogatories, depositions, briefs, etc. The Saturday evening before the Monday when the hearing was scheduled, Blanche dropped dead of a heart attack! Her doctor said she had been in perfect health and didn't have any heart problems. He surmised that the stress killed her.

This is but one of many tragic stories played out across this country every day. Most people feel comfortable in thinking that nothing bad will ever happen. Well, bad things do happen. Read on.

Mildred and Paul Hansen lived a happy and secure life. Mr. Hansen was a successful businessman and provided his family with a comfortable lifestyle. They had two children, who at the time were 14 and 20. One evening, Mr. and Mrs. Hansen were in a automobile accident. Mr. Hansen died immediately. Mrs. Hansen was in serious condition at the local hospital. The older child came home from college to care for his sister. The only problem was the children didn't have any money. Their father's assets were tied up in his estate. The mother was incapable of doing anything with her money because of her medical condition. They didn't even have money to pay for food. Luckily, however, their aunts and uncles helped out. The cemetery wanted cash for the burial plot for their father. Again, they didn't have any funds. Mortgage payments had to be paid. Utilities. Car payments. But they had no money. But, again, their aunts and uncles chipped in and made the necessary payments. When Mildred was released from the hospital, she repaid her brothers and sisters.

You can see that this isn't one of those disaster stories where someone got kicked out of his home. Nobody starved for lack of food. The electricity wasn't turned off. But it did create unnecessary hardship. The family just didn't plan because they never dreamed that it would happen to them. Remember, *we don't think we have a problem until we have a problem*. But you can bet they are planning now. Since that episode, Mrs. Hansen has structured her entire estate so this can't happen again. The children, now grown, realize what must be done to avoid these types of problems. They don't want to put their children through what they went through.

> *Darla and Sam Estes had been married over 45 years when Sam suffered a major stroke and ended up in a nursing home. Since all the property had been in Sam's name, she had to go through living probate to be appointed his guardian. Although an unpleasant experience, it was a piece of cake compared with what came next. Since she was guardian of his property, it could be used only for his benefit, even though she needed support. The court told her she couldn't use it for taxes. She couldn't use it for food. She couldn't use it for her benefit at all. She was in a terrible fix. Her attorney could not convince the probate court that she should receive some money. They kept coming back to the fact that she was guardian over **his** property, and as such, it could only be used for **him**. This was certainly not acceptable to her, so she hired another attorney. This one took a different tact: he threatened the court that Darla would divorce Sam. According to the rules of their state, she would then be able to get half his money. Although the thought distressed Darla, she realized this was her only hope. Thankfully, that wasn't necessary. The court gave in and became more reasonable. Nevertheless, the entire episode took a terrible financial and emotional toll on Darla.*

This story illustrates the problems faced by so many. If only people planned properly, tragedies such as these would not occur.

> *Back to the Johnson case discussed on page 223. As noted previously, Ruth had some problems. She was handcuffed financially since all their property was in joint tenancy. She met with an attorney who advised her that the best course was to get her husband declared incompetent by the court and be appointed*

*guardian.   The attorney filed a petition before the court and
alleged that Mr. Johnson was incompetent. After a period of time,
the court held hearings.   Mrs. Johnson's lawyer introduced
affidavits by the doctors attesting to Jack's incompetence. Mrs.
Johnson was appointed guardian. The court required a bond for
the full amount of the estate and further required that Mrs.
Johnson file a return with the court annually and account for every
penny.*

*But that only solved part of her problem. She still wanted to sell
some stock. The brokerage firm wouldn't allow it without court
approval. Therefore, her lawyer again petitioned the court for a
hearing on the sale of the stock. After 30 days, the hearing was
held and no objections were raised. The stock could be sold
with the proceeds placed in an FDIC-insured bank.*

*As discussed earlier, she also wanted to sell her home. Her
attorney told her to go ahead and get a contract for the sale.
Once obtained, the attorney again filed a petition before the court
for a public hearing. Again, in 30 days the hearing was held, the
contract submitted, and the sale approved. As before, the funds
had to be deposited in an FDIC insured bank.*

You can see from the Johnson's case that living probate
was not an attractive proposition. It put the surviving spouse in
the very difficult position of having to answer to the court, not
to mention the expense involved.   While every state has
different procedures, the methods of obtaining guardianship or
conservatorship are similar. Somebody has to be appointed
guardian, and only the court can do it.

HANDLING INCAPACITY

Durable Power of Attorney

Many people use a power of attorney to avoid potential
incapacity problems. A power of attorney permits one person
to act for another. In most states, this "general" power of
attorney becomes invalid upon the disability of the maker.
Therefore, a "durable" power of attorney, which is valid even

upon the disability of the maker, is necessary.

A power of attorney is the easiest, and most dangerous, solution to the problem of disability. The reason it is so easy is because it costs virtually nothing to draw up and is usually relatively simple to work with. You can find the necessary forms at most office supply stores. On the other hand, it contains some real and very dangerous dragons:

- Some institutions might choose not to accept it. Many times a bank will refuse to accept a power of attorney. Clients have told me that many financial institutions require that you use only their forms. This can get cumbersome, especially if you are constantly moving your CD's from one bank to another.

- Attorneys may not choose to accept it for a real estate closing. Most closing attorneys will require that the power contain specific language pursuant to that particular piece of property. Most powers don't contain this.

- Brokerage firms may refuse the power. Again, most brokerage firms will require specific language relative to their holdings. Some firms will accept only their form.

- An older power might not be accepted. Many financial institutions put a time limit on the validity of a power of attorney. For example, they may choose not to honor a power if it has been longer than eighteen months since it was signed. You can imagine the liability of an institution or an attorney who acts on a power of attorney that, unbeknownst to him, had been previously revoked. You might consider having your power of attorney updated periodically, such as every eighteen to twenty-four months.

- In the wrong hands, a power of attorney is a dangerous document. If you are trying to take care of all eventualities, you must give your agent broad powers. But those same powers give that person the right to do anything he or she wants, anytime he or she wants. We have all heard of situations where a child with a power of attorney has withdrawn money from his or her parent's account, or sold stocks and bonds and pocketed the money.

- A power of attorney dies when the person giving the power dies. Therefore, while it might solve some problems at the disability of Mr. Johnson, it will not be helpful after his death.

- A power of attorney won't solve all problems, though it might have been helpful in the Johnson's case. But what would have happened if they both had become disabled, or if one had died and the other had become disabled, as in the case of Mildred and Paul Hansen? The power of attorney would not have done any good. The only other solution would have been to give each of their children a power, and I don't know how comfortable they would have felt with that.

Another type of power that many attorneys recommend is a "springing" power. It does not become effective until a certain "event" occurs, such as your disability. This solves the problem of having current powers floating around among family members.

Like joint tenancy, many people use a power of attorney as an inexpensive method of avoiding proper estate planning. In the right situation, a power of attorney can ease the planning process. Recognize, however, that you are giving unlimited power to your agent. And acceptance of the power is not automatic. It is only worth something if the institution is willing to accept it. Furthermore, since you are giving so much power, it is very possible that it could backfire. As a result, trying to save some money by planning yourself could be costly in the long run.

Living Trust

Another alternative to living probate and the problems with a power of attorney is the living trust. In the trust you name a trustee or trustees to handle your affairs. You include instructions for your own care in the case of disability. Property is titled into the trust so the trustee can perform his duties without difficulty. The trust lists the powers granted to the trustee. Let's revisit Mr. and Mrs. Johnson and see what might have happened with better planning.

- *Mr. Johnson began receiving his monthly disability check. Their living trust would have included a "special durable power of attorney" which would have allowed only one thing: for the trustee (Mrs. Johnson) to deposit Mr. Johnson's property into the trust. She could have used this power to deposit his checks into the trust checking account.*

- *They owned stocks and bonds through a local brokerage firm. Whenever Ruth needed money, she would have called her broker. The brokerage account would have already been titled in the name of the trust and the brokerage firm would have had an "affidavit of trust" outlining the applicable parts of the trust. The broker would have sold the stock and issued a check, which she would have deposited into the trust checking account.*

- *After a while, whenever Ruth needed to sell property, she could have done it as trustee. The closing attorney would have wanted proof she was the trustee and further proof that Jack was disabled. She would have presented the applicable parts of the trust along with a letter from her physician.*

Conclusion

You can see the difference between the two scenarios. One of the advantages of a living trust over a simple power of attorney is that the trust has limitations on the powers of the trustee, whereas a power of attorney is effectively a blank check to the holder. Additionally, the trust provides contingencies in the event the trustees cannot, or will not, serve.

Again, which course is best for you will depend upon your particular situation. Nothing works for everybody all the time. If you are concerned about the points mentioned above, then a living trust might be a good solution. However, if you have absolute confidence in the person to whom you are giving power, and if you don't expect any of the above problems, then consider a power of attorney as a possible solution. Just make sure you are comfortable with your choice.

23

HOW CAN I HANDLE THE NURSING HOME PROBLEM?

One area of planning which causes a tremendous amount of concern today is that of a nursing home stay. Even if you aren't currently involved with someone facing a prolonged nursing home stay, statistically someday you may be. This is not meant to scare you - it's just fact. But if it does frighten you, great, because this is a scary subject. It is one of the most devastating problems many people will ever face. And unlike many of the concepts we have discussed that can cost you money, **this one can wipe you out financially.**

There is no doubt that the aspect that concerns most people is the cost of a prolonged stay in a nursing home. The people who are most at risk financially are the middle class. Whereas the government will care for the poor, and the more affluent have the cash flow and assets with which to pay, it is the group in the middle whose assets are at risk. They are too rich to be poor and too poor to be rich.

> *Sarah Middleton is concerned about a nursing home stay. Her health, while still fairly good, is starting to decline. Her assets total $105,000. She has checked various nursing homes and figures it will cost her $2800 per month, which is about average. Her current income from Social Security and her late husband's retirement is $1350.*

She knows that while the cost of nursing care will continue to escalate, her income will not keep pace. What can she do? Her choices are very limited.

- Obviously, she could pay the shortfall between the cost of the nursing home and her income by selling assets. Depending upon the length of her stay, however, she could very well run out of money. If that were to happen, Medicaid would pay for her nursing home stay.

- She could buy nursing home insurance. While this can be expensive, depending on many factors, it is a viable alternative.

- She could give her assets away, thus qualifying her for Medicaid while preserving her estate for her children.

Before reviewing the alternatives, examine the following graph. It shows exactly where the money for nursing homes comes from. Notice the fact that Medicare, the health insurance on which most senior citizens rely, provides virtually no benefit for nursing home care. Most payments are made either by the patient or Medicaid.

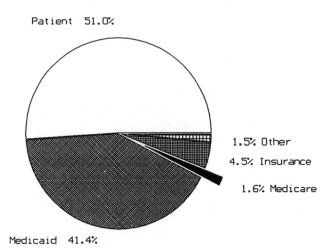

Let's review Mrs. Middleton's various alternatives.

PAY IN CASH

It goes without saying that the cost of a nursing home stay is expensive and getting even more so. For Mrs. Middleton, the cost of a nursing home is $1450 per month more than her monthly income. Assuming prices stay the same, which they won't, she could be wiped out financially in only six years.

Mrs. Middleton could take her chances and hope that (1) she doesn't go into a nursing home; (2) if she does, her assets will be sufficient to pay; (3) if she goes in, she will not stay in too long; or (4) if she does go in, there will still be an inheritance for her children upon her death.

You can see that Mrs. Middleton has a real problem. Taking her chances leaves her with a big question mark, because she has no idea what will really happen. Like most "non-planning", it leaves everything up to chance.

Considering the statistics, which indicate that a person over the age of 65 faces a 40-50% chance of a nursing home stay, doing nothing is not a sensible alternative. If you have sufficient income and/or assets, you probably could afford the cost of a nursing home stay. However, if your assets are in the $50,000 - $400,000 range, you need to do some serious planning. Unfortunately, the "plan" most people choose is "to do nothing."

Paying in cash means that Mrs. Middleton could deplete all her assets and leave nothing for her children. That's not what she has in mind. She and her late husband worked hard their entire lives to be comfortable and leave something for their children. The thought that all their life's efforts may go to a nursing home is not comforting.

BUY NURSING HOME INSURANCE

One alternative, then, is to purchase nursing home insurance. This is a tricky one. While the idea of buying insurance to cover nursing home costs sounds good, it is a minefield full of dragons. You are faced with a number of agents and companies trying to get premiums for coverage of questionable value, often offered by some pretty weak companies. I don't mean to insinuate that all companies offering nursing home insurance are bad. Nor am I saying that the coverage isn't worthwhile. It's just a fact that I have seen the results of marketing efforts by agents and organizations offering policies to the elderly, and I don't like it.

I can't tell you how much money is wasted on various health insurance programs, most of which are totally unnecessary. So many people buy insurance that is merely a duplication of other coverage. They have not one, but two or more medicare supplement policies. They have intensive care coverage. Cancer coverage. Emergency room coverage. Policies that pay a stated amount per day for stays in the hospital. Physician's coverage. Surgical coverage. So much money is spent on unnecessary coverage that it sickens me. And the people who can least afford it pay the most.

First understand that any coverage provided by **Medicare** and **Medicare Supplement** policies for a nursing home stay is very limited. You can't depend on this to be of any benefit for a nursing home, no matter what you have been told. As we saw from the graph, only 1.6% of nursing home expenses are paid by Medicare. This is not an alternative.

However, long-term care (nursing home) insurance **is** available, but you must be extremely careful. There are only a few companies I would consider recommending, and even then, you must be sure you know what you are getting and how much it is costing you. Let's look at the decisions you will have to make.

Coverage

What type of basic coverage are you going to buy? There are two areas of coverage.

- Nursing home coverage - this will cover you while you are a patient in a nursing home only.

- Home health care - this will cover you for nursing services in your own home.

Some companies offer these separately, and some offer them in one package. Think about your economic concerns and priorities before making any choice. Many times the home health benefit is so restrictive that it is of little benefit. If you choose nursing home coverage, make sure it covers skilled, intermediate, as well as custodial care.

Daily benefit

How much coverage do you want? There is a wide range available here and the companies will give you a choice that falls within their minimums and maximums. Some might pay from $30 a day to $140 a day; others from $60 a day to $120 a day. Some offer different benefit amounts for nursing home and home health care. The larger your benefit, the higher your premium. Because costs will be rising in the years ahead, most companies offer some sort of inflation-adjusted benefit that will increase your daily benefit over the years.

Elimination period

How long do you want to wait before benefits begin? Most insurance companies offer a variety of choices. For example, you might want coverage that starts the first day, or 21st day, or 45th day, or 100th day, etc. The alternatives are numerous. And obviously your premium will reflect this. The shorter the elimination period (which means the sooner the insurance starts paying), the higher your premium.

Benefit period

How long do you want to receive benefits? Again, you have a choice, depending on the company. For example, you may have a choice between receiving benefits for two years, three years, four years, five years, or the rest of your life. The longer the benefit period, the higher the premium. In many cases, we recommend a three-year benefit period because of the 30-month rule discussed in the following chapter.

The premium

The price you pay will depend upon all the above factors. The higher the benefit, the higher the premium. The shorter the elimination period, the higher the premium. The longer the benefit period, the higher the premium. The older you are, the higher the premium. What makes it so difficult is that it is impossible to know what is best for you. Nobody knows how many days, if any, you will spend in a nursing home. In most cases, the coverage chosen is a matter of affordability.

Factors you need to consider

If you decide to consider private nursing home insurance, here are some things to look for.

- The policy should be **guaranteed renewable.** That means that the company does not have the right to cancel your coverage, no matter what. The only time your coverage can end is when you (1) stop paying the premiums or (2) exhaust your benefits.

- The policy should provide for **level premiums.** You should know, in advance, the amount of your premiums. But remember, this is health insurance. And as with your medical insurance, the premiums can be increased. But make sure this can only be done if the company raises the premiums of everyone in your state that has the same policy.

- The policy should include **waiver of premium.** That means that if you start receiving benefits, your premiums will cease. Most policies state that the premiums will be waived after 90 days of benefit payments.

- The policy should have no limitations for **pre-existing conditions.** This means that the company should not have the right to deny coverage if you enter a nursing home due to a condition that you had previously. This is a perfect way for a company to deny coverage. Either you are approved for coverage, or turned down, nothing in between.

- Most policies exclude coverage for mental, nervous, and psychotic disorders. Make sure that **Alzheimer's** and similar forms of senility or dementia are specifically covered in the policy. Don't take the agent's word. Don't accept some vague wording. It should be clear to you that this is covered.

- Do not accept a policy that is subject to **underwriting after a claim.** A few companies have tried to get cute by offering coverage subject to underwriting after a claim is submitted. That's like buying car insurance and letting the company decide if they want to cover you after you have had an accident. You don't want any problems once you submit a claim.

- There should be **no prior hospital stay** required. You don't want to get into a situation where a company will only pay if you are going into a nursing home directly from a hospital. Today, most people go directly into a nursing home without having first been in a hospital.

- Make sure the company is **A+ rated** by A. M Best and, ideally, top rated by another rating service. The same guidelines that we spoke about in the chapter on life insurance apply here. Don't get involved with the lower rated companies, no matter how much the agent may try to reassure you.

- Answer **every medical question** honestly. Make sure that the agent writes down your answers. Don't leave the insurance company any room to deny your claim.

- When you receive the policy, **review it** carefully, making sure that everything you understood to be in the policy is really there. Don't take the agent's word for it. Nothing should be subject to interpretation. If it doesn't meet your approval, don't accept it. The company will refund your money if done within a set number of days.

As you can see, there is a lot to consider when dealing with nursing home insurance. But if you are careful, and follow those guidelines above, you should be able to purchase coverage to suit your needs.

Conclusion

For many people, the discussion ends here. They are either able to pay for nursing home expenses from their income and/or assets, or they can afford long-term care insurance. However, for many, the problem remains: "If I don't have the money to pay for a nursing home, and/or I can't afford or qualify for insurance, then what can I do? How can I make it through a nursing home stay while still leaving some money for my children?"

The answers to those questions are found in the following chapter.

24

HOW CAN I PROTECT MY ASSETS
FROM A NURSING HOME STAY?

In the previous chapter, we discussed the problems you face with a prolonged nursing home stay and reviewed two ways to pay for it: cash or insurance.

However, for many, those alternatives aren't applicable. Let's review Mrs. Middleton's dilemma:

Sarah Middleton is concerned about going into a nursing home. Her health, while still fairly good, is starting to decline. Her assets total $105,000. She has checked various nursing homes and figures it will cost her $2800 per month, which is about average. Her current income from Social Security and her late husband's retirement is $1350.

Mrs. Middleton is not in a position to pay in cash, because her income is insufficient to cover a nursing home bill. That shortage in today's dollars is $1450 per month. On the other hand, at her age she cannot afford nursing home insurance, either. What else can she do?

LETTING THE GOVERNMENT PAY

In the previous chapter, we covered the first two alternatives. Let's now look at the third: letting the government pay. For some people, this is their only choice: they just don't have any money and can't afford or qualify for nursing home insurance. That's Mrs. Middleton's situation. But she doesn't want all her assets devoured, either.

The dilemma

This is where we run into a real moral dilemma. Some people say that divesting yourself of assets by giving them to your children just to qualify for Medicaid is immoral and perpetrates fraud on the system. Medicaid was designed for the truly indigent, not those who make themselves so by giving away assets. Why should the government support those who are not truly needy?

On the other side are the people who say that preserving their assets for their children is a part of proper planning. They have worked hard their entire lives and have been responsible citizens, paying taxes and contributing their fair share. Why, after all this work, should they end up in the same position as the people who have spent their lives living off the government?

But there is also an in-between position that most people don't consider. If you allow your assets to be totally consumed by the nursing home, then you eventually will have to rely 100% on Medicaid. However, if you are able to preserve some assets, and draw a monthly income from them, then you will only need Medicaid to cover the shortfall. Additionally, I think most people will agree that you will receive better nursing home care if you are able to pay at least part of the cost, and not totally rely on Medicaid. I am sure you have seen, and heard, the horror stories concerning the care of people on Medicaid. It's a tragedy that must be averted.

It is not my intent to take sides here, but I do have my opinion. Let's go back to our definition of estate planning:

"During my life and after my death, I want to control and distribute my property in the manner I desire, minimizing

*all fees, taxes and court interference, **preserving for myself,
my family, and those I choose, the estate I have worked so
hard to create.***"

Part of our definition **requires** that we preserve our
estate. That means ensuring that it isn't consumed by a prolonged nursing home stay. If you don't have sufficient assets to
see you through, and if you can't qualify or afford nursing home
insurance, then the only remaining choice is either give it to the
government or take steps to preserve your estate. The latter
involves qualifying yourself for Medicaid.

One other point in this matter. In my experience, people
treat the nursing home problem the same way they look at
justice. While they think that someone else who breaks the law
should be punished, they think they themselves should get a
break. While they get upset if a person gets off on a technical-
ity, they will try every trick in the book to free themselves.
They think the DUI laws are too lax - until they get picked up
for it. And they think that people shouldn't take advantage of
the Medicaid system - unless it's one of their relatives. That's
the way we are, and nothing is going to change it!

THE RULES

What is Medicaid?

Medicaid is a combined federal and state program that
pays the cost of a nursing home for anyone who is destitute.
The issue, then, is the definition of "destitute." Since that
definition is a function of a person's assets and income, we need
to review specifically what Medicaid considers assets and
income. This is the centerpiece of nursing home planning.

What is an asset?

According to Medicaid, basically everything you own is

an asset: bank accounts, home, stocks, bonds, retirement plans, personal belongings, other investments, life insurance cash values, businesses, etc.

What is income?

Medicaid's definition of income is not unlike what yours might be: anything you receive as payment is income. This includes retirement benefits, interest, investment income, social security, etc. In most cases, if you have sufficient income with which to pay the nursing home bill, regardless of your asset structure, you will have to do so. If your income comes up short (as does Mrs. Middlebrook's), then Medicaid will make up the difference if your asset structure qualifies.

Before proceeding further, let me make a very important statement: laws vary from state to state. Since this is a joint federal/state program, it is subject to interpretation by each individual state. Don't take any of the following rules as gospel. They can, and do, vary. Additionally, the interpretation and rules are in a constant state of flux.

What can you keep?

Medicaid doesn't require that you be "flat broke." Being the kind-hearted people they are, you can still keep some assets and income and still qualify for benefits. Let's take a general look. But remember, the laws are complicated and each state can, and does, vary.

- **Assets** - Those assets which are not counted by Medicaid include approximately $2,000 in cash (depending on your state), a home, personal effects such as jewelry (some states have limits) and furniture, a pre-paid funeral and burial account, an automobile used for transportation of the person in the nursing home, and a small amount of cash value in a life insurance policy.

- **Income** - If you have sufficient income to pay the cost of a nursing home, you must do so. Any shortage, assuming you don't go over the asset limit above, will be paid by Medicaid. Nevertheless, you are allowed, over and above, to keep a minimal amount of "spending money." Be aware, however, that there are some states that **disqualify you for Medicaid if your income is a certain level, even if that income is insufficient to pay your nursing home bills.** This is just another tragedy of being part of the middle class.

What about the home?

This is a very interesting problem because the laws seem to constantly change. There is a great deal of confusion here. It has been said that the home is protected (in most states) as long as the person entering the nursing home indicates, in writing, his or her intent to return to that home. Some people have been advised to put every penny in a home, including the furnishings. I have heard of people being advised to buy the most expensive home possible and fill it with Van Gogh paintings.

This question is so difficult that even national "experts" have given incorrect information to people in various states because of the ever evolving nature of the rules. You can even check from county to county and get conflicting answers.

Some say don't worry about the house - just sign the intent to return and it will be protected. Some say that if you do this, Medicaid can take it at your death to reimburse itself for your nursing home expenses. Some say it has to be left vacant while you're in the nursing home. Others say rent it out. And worse, what might work today might not work tomorrow.

In some states, the government has a right to put a lien on your home if you enter a nursing home and apply for

Medicaid. In other states, they won't do that if you indicate you plan to return. (Rules for a married couple differ, as we will see shortly.)

I won't begin to suggest what you do in this case - that's the job of an attorney specializing in elder law in your state. The safest approach in the states that might place a lien seems to be to treat the home like any other asset. Don't assume it will be protected. Include it with your other shielded assets.

What about the stay-at-home spouse?

This is a tricky issue because you face a totally different set of problems when you are married. One of the problems occurs because Medicaid considers all assets of a husband and wife to be owned equally. That means that you can't protect your assets by having them in the name of the stay-at-home spouse. So transferring them into the other spouse's name won't help. That's where we begin.

Under *current* law, and I emphasize the word "current", the stay at home spouse may keep a relatively small amount of assets. As a rule, that amount is one-half the total assets of both spouses (it doesn't matter how they are owned). At this time, they can keep a minimum of $13,296 and a maximum of $66,480. These figures are adjusted annually for inflation. In addition, as stated above, the nursing home spouse may usually keep an additional $2,000. This is difficult to explain simply because each state has its own figures, ranging between the minimum and maximum stated above. So while in California you are able to keep $66,480, in Oregon a spouse is only permitted to keep $13,296. Make sure you check with your local authorities to find out what your state currently permits.

We talked about the house previously. In the case of a married couple, Medicaid currently does allow the stay-at-home spouse to keep the home. And unlike other assets, Medicaid does allow it to be transferred into the name of the stay-at-home spouse. Although the stay-at-home spouse may not transfer it as long as the other spouse is in the nursing home, the house may be conveyed at the death of the stay-at-home spouse.

On the other hand, if the stay-at-home spouse dies while his or her spouse is still in the nursing home, then the home will most likely pass to the confined spouse. When that spouse dies, then in some states Medicaid will try to collect what it has paid. In other states, the home won't be touched as long as the confined spouse had signed a certificate saying that he or she planned to return to the home. You can see that since the rules differ from state to state, a generalized discussion is impossible.

I know that sounds confusing, and it is. There are exceptions to the above discussion, and state laws differ.

PROTECTING YOUR ASSETS

If you want Medicaid to pay, you must remove the balance of your assets from your estate. The two ways most people choose to do this is either by giving them away or putting them in an irrevocable trust. Before we look at each, let's look at the general rule Medicaid follows concerning removing assets.

You can't just give everything away, go into a nursing home, and expect the government to pay. There is a 30-month rule that stands in your way. This rule effectively says that any assets you have given away within 30 months of your applying for Medicaid will be counted against you.

Jack Blevin's children knew their father's health was failing. They realized that he would have to go into a nursing home shortly. Just before Jack entered the nursing home, the children used their powers of attorney to transfer all his assets into their names. Therefore, when he entered the nursing home, he had nothing. However, because he gave away the property within 30 months of entering, the transfer was invalid for Medicaid purposes. He, or rather the children, will have to pay his care for 30 months (or until the value of transferred assets are spent for nursing home care) before he will be eligible for Medicaid.

• • •

Martha Stanton transferred her $70,000 in assets to her two children on January 1, 1990. On January 5, 1991, she entered a nursing home. Her care costs $2,500 per month. She has no income. The gift was made 12 months ago. The 30 month rule would require that she pay 18 months of care before Medicaid would take over. That means she must pay for 18 months times $2,500 per month, or a total of $45,000. The children may retain only $25,000 of the $70,000.

Again, the exact way this is calculated can vary from state to state. But you can see the importance of planning in advance. The solution, then, is to build a fence around your assets. Let's talk about doing that by looking at the two primary ways of removing assets.

Giving your assets away

The first alternative is to give your assets away, presumably to your children. This can be done by writing them a check, transferring the title on your property from your name to theirs, etc. However, this brings up several problems.

- If the transfer is for less than fair market value and is made within 30 months of your entering a nursing home, you will run up against the rules noted above.

- Once you give those assets away, you have no right to them whatsoever. You are not entitled to any part of them. Those assets belong to your children to do with as they see fit.

- You may run into the gift tax problems discussed earlier in the book. However, if your estate is under $600,000 and you haven't used any of your exemption previously, this will not cause a problem. But you will have to file a gift tax return.

There is an exception to the transfer rule. And that has to do with "intent." If you can prove that the transfer was not made with the intent of qualifying the person for Medicaid, you might be able to avoid the 30-month rule. This is most easy to argue in a case where an individual is in great health, does not anticipate a nursing home stay, and makes the transfer for valid reasons. But those exceptions are rare and difficult to prove.

Putting them into a Medicaid Trust

The use of a special Medicaid trust is a method that seems to work better for many people than just giving their assets to their children. Remember from our earlier discussions that there are three parties to a trust: the trustmaker (or grantor); the trustees; and the beneficiaries.

One aspect that differentiates this from other types of planning is that the benefits must be very limited. It is recommended that the trust must be drawn so you receive the income only, no principal. The reason for this is another one of Medicaid's many rules. If you, as beneficiary, are entitled to receive income, **plus** principal at the discretion of the trustee, then all that principal must be expended for your care before Medicaid will pay. But if you are entitled to income-only, then the principal can be protected. But don't forget, if you are entitled to income-only, that money will be used to pay for your nursing home care.

Arthur Madden transferred his $200,000 estate into an irrevocable trust, with his children, Fran and Howard, as trustees. Of the $200,000, $120,000 was in government bonds paying 8.5%. He was entitled to income-only from the trust, which amounted to $10,200 per year. If he enters a nursing home, the home will be entitled to that $10,200. The difference, assuming he qualifies for he 30-month rule, will be paid by Medicaid. Upon his death, all the assets in the trust will be divided between Howard and Fran.

An irrevocable trust, however, is not a panacea.

- Those assets are subject to the 30-month rule.

- The transferred assets are subject to gift tax ramifications (see below).

- You must give up control over the assets. You are entitled only to receive those amounts permitted under the trust.

- You cannot receive any of the principal. Remember, if you are entitled to receive the principal, so is Medicaid.

- If you enter a nursing home, they are entitled to receive any income that is paid to you.

- The rules can change at anytime, as can the interpretation. Remember, we're dealing with the government. Nothing in this discussion is etched in stone.

Gifting

One point concerning the gift tax ramifications. Remember from our earlier discussion that in order to qualify for the $10,000 gift tax exclusion, a gift must be of a "present interest". In other words, it must be a "no strings" gift. If you transfer your assets into an irrevocable trust but provide no right for your children to withdraw the money, then you cannot use your $10,000 annual exclusion to shelter any of the gift. However, you can use your $600,000 lifetime exemption to shelter the gifts. Since most people who set up Medicaid trusts have less than $600,000 in assets, gift taxes aren't a consideration.

The home

Because of varying laws and constant changes regarding

keeping your home, many attorneys recommend you put it into an irrevocable trust. However, there is one drawback. If you do this within 30 months of entering a nursing home, your home will be drawn into the calculation. In most states, however, if you indicate that you want to keep your home when entering the nursing home, you should be able to keep it. On the other hand, by indicating you want to return, it means that the home cannot be sold until your death, and that could be many years.

A trust in which you have no rights

Some people choose to give all their assets to their children by placing them in an irrevocable trust in which they (the parents) maintain no interest. They are not entitled to interest or principal. This protects the entire estate (including income) for the children. However, if you do this, you are relying totally on the children for all your income, which can be risky.

This same thing can be accomplished without a trust by just giving your assets to the children. However, many people prefer the trust because it allows all the children work together in the event money is needed for the parents.

What doesn't work

Let's briefly review those steps that cannot do much to protect your assets from a long-term nursing home stay.

- It won't do any good to use a living trust. By its nature, the trust is revocable, which means you could get to your assets back. And if you can get your assets, so can Medicaid.

- You can't protect them by giving everything to your spouse, because Medicaid will only allow you to protect a certain amount of those assets. In addition, what happens if your spouse goes into an institution?

- A joint account, while it might technically protect assets, is not as practical as it might sound. If you enter a nursing home and are joint tenant with another party, it's possible that you wouldn't be able to, or wouldn't want to, agree to sell that asset. While that would protect the asset from Medicaid (at least at that point), it would freeze the asset for the other party as well. Then, when that asset is eventually sold, there may be a lien on it by Medicaid for any amount they paid on your behalf. Additionally, if the other joint tenant dies, the asset passes to you as joint tenant, which means that Medicaid could get it.

What many people do is use nursing home insurance in conjunction with giving away their assets. They purchase a policy with a three year benefit to cover the 30-month time frame. Then, upon entering a nursing home, they give their assets to their children or establish a trust. As a result, the 30-month clock starts ticking and, in the meantime, insurance is paying the bills. However, you need to plan ahead to do this. You can't wait until you are in bad health.

Conclusion

As you can see, a nursing home stay poses problems with few good solutions. However, as bad as the alternatives may sound, they are still better than doing nothing. You risk your entire asset base by refusing to plan. If you wait too long, it may be too late.

This is such an important and specialized area that it **requires** proper planning with the proper advisor. Don't try to do it yourself. Don't rely on friends for advice. Unfortunately, there are only a limited number of attorneys who understand the problems and the solutions. But find one. You need professional assistance. Please, don't wait and hope.

25

WHAT ABOUT LIVING WILLS AND HEALTH CARE POWERS?

Our definition of estate planning starts out with the words, "During my life......." This chapter deals with several planning methods that take care of you during your life: the living will and health care powers.

Living Will

The living will often gets confused with the living trust, but they have no similarities. The **living will** is the document in which you indicate your desire **not** to be kept alive by life support equipment. I don't need to tell you that medical technology has increased life expectancy. Living longer, however, doesn't necessarily mean the quality of life has improved. There are many cases when people are kept alive solely by life support equipment.

The Supreme Court has ruled that if you want "live or not live" decisions made for you, you must have that permission clearly indicated. The living will allows you to do that. Unfortunately, only 20% of the population has one.

The purpose of the living will (also known as an advanced directive or advanced medical directive) is to allow you to let your desires be known concerning life support equipment. In other words, a living will indicates that you do not wish to be kept alive only by a machine. It effectively says "If I am only being kept alive by a machine, unplug it."

Understand that the laws vary state to state. In fact, many states have their own living will form that must be followed. Check with your attorney and make sure that your living will conforms to your state guidelines. If you spend time in other states, you might also want to check on their requirements. This is an extremely important issue and well worth the time and effort on your behalf.

Health Care Powers

While the living will makes a lot of sense, it does have its drawbacks. It does not address the issue of medical decisions that may or may not prolong one's life.

> *Grace McIntyre was in the hospital with a stroke. She wasn't given much of a chance to live, but the doctors felt they had to do all they could for her. Although there was virtually no chance for improvement, the doctors tried operation after operation. She had a living will, but that didn't help - she was not being kept alive by life support equipment. She was just being put through a number of operations that had little chance for success, operations that depleted her assets. All her suffering, and that of her family, was for naught. She ran out of money about the same time that she passed away.*

This is an example of a situation where a living will had no benefit. The decision was not one of unplugging a machine. The decision was about performing operations that had little hope of helping her.

As a result, about 80% of the states have adopted some form of a new document: The Durable Power of Attorney for Health Care (called Health Care Proxies in certain states).

With this document, you actually appoint someone to make medical decisions for you. That person has the authority to turn down a surgical procedure that is of questionable value.

While it is your physician's duty to keep you alive, many procedures don't have much of a success rate. The Durable Power for Health Care addresses that issue.

As with the appointment of the trustees of a trust, you will want to appoint successor agents. You never know when one person can't, or won't, be able to make the necessary decisions.

In some cases, you can leave specific instructions about what you do and do not want done to or for you. You can discuss such issues as feeding, transfusions, transplants, etc. If your state allows it, leave as many instructions as you can.

In some states, the health power replaces the living will, since it is a more comprehensive form. In other states, you need both forms. As with the living will, many states have their own forms and sets of rules concerning the durable power for health care. You cannot assume that what is acceptable in Missouri is acceptable in Maine. In some cases, the legislature has determined the exact language that must be used. As with the living will, check with your attorney for the rules in your state.

Caution

One problem with these documents is that they don't do much good if you don't have them with you when you go into a hospital. The doctor, absent any other instructions, is obligated to do whatever he or she can to keep you alive. And once they have started, it's difficult to reverse the process. There are several ways you might solve this problem.

- Have "duplicate originals" of the form filed with your physicians, local hospitals, agents (those who can make decisions for you), and attorney. Make sure your patient records reflect your wishes.

- Consider carrying a form when you travel. While it might not be honored in another state, it will at least contain your wishes.

- Carry a letter or note in your wallet indicating that you have a form and where it can be found.

Another important point is to make sure that the persons you appoint as your agents will follow your wishes. There are many people who would never, under any circumstances, make the decision to end one's life, even if it is what that person wanted. Having the wrong person in the decision making position will totally invalidate the benefit of the form.

Finally, check with your attorney about the expiration date of the form. Some states have specific requirements dealing with this aspect. It may be valid forever - it may be valid only three years.

This is a very difficult issue to address. Many people ignore it and hope it will go away. But you know better than that. Modern medicine, with all its fantastic advances, can be a burden on you and your family. Take the initiative and make your wishes known. You may only have one opportunity to do it - do it now!

26

HOW CAN I PROTECT MY ASSETS FROM A LAWSUIT?

by Kelly R. Burke, Attorney-at-Law

How many times have you heard about a businessman who files bankruptcy but does not seem to lose anything in the process? Bankruptcy was formerly a devastating, last gasp step. Now bankruptcy is commonplace, even planned for in the future (as in the case of TWA). Most doctors, lawyers, architects, engineers, business owners, real estate developers, and other professionals (called the "provider" for this discussion) would not consider bankruptcy, except in the most drastic of situations. But if they could subject only a small portion of their assets to creditors, surely they would do so, right? Providers have become fairly knowledgeable about risks, and seek to limit exposure using a variety of methods. One way is by allowing their spouses to have complete dominion and control over the "protected" assets. Another way is limited partnerships, often seen as liability proof. As we will see, however, these strategies, and others, often have significant flaws.

Estate planning contemplates that you have an estate for which to plan. The loss of an estate prior to the death of the provider, or after the death of the provider, is a familiar occurrence. There are a variety of methods available for asset protection; some are good, and some are bad.

I have always felt that the best explanation of legal principles is to avoid citing case law, statutes, and I.R.S. regulations. Instead I think the best explanation of asset protection is by example. Because state law varies tremendously, realize that this discussion is only general in nature.

> *Paul, a successful securities defense lawyer, had built up a large portfolio of assets and had a net worth of five million dollars. While Paul was one of the best in his field, he had no experience or education in estate planning. Paul and his wife, Ann, were looking forward to Paul's retirement so that they could tour the world. Over the years Paul had titled all of his assets in his name. Shortly before his retirement, Paul made an error on a new issue of stock, thus resulting in liabilities and SEC fines of millions of dollars against him and his firm. Paul had professional liability insurance, but due to the trebling nature of the SEC fines, his assets were subject to the judgment which followed and rendered him virtually penniless.*

● ● ●

> *Bill, a prominent local businessman and president of the chamber of commerce, was married to Carol, twenty years younger than he. Bill had assets of approximately three million dollars plus his business which was worth another one million. Bill, being a do-it-yourselfer, decided he would "protect" his assets from liability by placing all of his assets in Carol's name. So Bill retitled all of his personal assets into his wife's name and set up a closely held corporation (owned entirely by Carol) to hold his business equipment, inventory and land, which in turn leased everything back to Bill's business. Bill had no control over his assets upon his death, which is another matter altogether. The real problem was Bill had no control over the assets **while he was alive.***

> *Bill, in his capacity as president of the chamber of commerce, took a month long trip to Europe to scout for business. Carol could not go, having "prior commitments". Bill returned home and looked for his lovely wife at the airport. Not finding her, Bill called home only to be told the phone had been disconnected. The chauffeur took Bill to his house. The current residents expressed shock that Bill thought he owned this house. After all, they had just closed on it last week. Where was the lovely Carol? She and the club tennis pro were having the time of their lives in Rio.*

At least Bill had his business, right? Well, Carol needed the assistance of a lawyer to help her dispose of her assets quickly. It seems that the lease payments were his fee. Can't happen? Think again.

• • •

Warren, a real estate developer, concerned about liability, placed his assets in his wife's name. His wife, Shirley, was a kind woman who was too generous with their two children, neither of whom were very responsible. Warren titled all their property in Shirley's name for creditor protection, but he realized that he had no ability to stop his children from mooching off their mother.

• • •

Ron, an architect, was approached by a friend about investing in a metal plating business. Ron, not wanting liability, made a $10,000 investment through a limited partnership arrangement. Unfortunately, the business floundered and was unprofitable. Ron decided to cut his losses and sold his limited partnership interest. The business was sold three times over the next six years, before finally filing bankruptcy. Upon inspection of the premises, the EPA found a toxic waste hazard existed on the property, which hazard had developed for a number of years due to the procedures used by the company. The environmental protection laws provide for joint and several liability, so a letter was sent to Ron detailing what the government wanted from him. Ron, like most of us, figured this could not apply to him, as he had only been a limited partner six years ago. So Ron ignored the letter, which ultimately resulted in him owing the government over $3,000,000 for the cleanup of the sight. Ron and his wife owned all their property jointly. Therefore, he had no choice but to pay the cost of cleanup. (As far as I can determine, there is no insurance coverage for this type of situation).

Historically, providers retain control of their assets because "control" is part of their lives. Those who attempt asset protection usually do so by titling their assets in the name of their spouse. But as reflected in Bill's case, that can be hazardous. Other alternatives (limited partnerships, irrevocable trusts, close corporations) are becoming less and less attractive as the courts and laws circumvent their effectiveness in planning.

What method remains for protecting assets from malpractice and creditor judgments while allowing the provider to maintain control?   I have found that a properly structured revocable living trust can be the answer in many cases. Remember some basic tenets of living trusts: assets are placed in a trust by a trustmaker; trustees are appointed to manage these assets; beneficiaries reap the benefits of the trust. Under normal circumstances, all three positions are occupied by the same person, usually the husband and wife. However, with that structure, **none** of the assets are protected from creditors.

Thus, the only way to possibly protect those assets is **not to** occupy all three positions (again, due to varying state laws, advice of legal counsel is always required). Normally, a couple places their joint and individual property into a joint trust, and each spouse is co-trustee with some degree of control over the property. Another method is separate trusts for each spouse. Let's review how a provider might set up a trust.

- Separate trusts are established; one for the spouse with liability concerns (called the "provider") and one for the other spouse (called the "spouse").

- Both spouses are co-trustees of the spouse's trust.

- Only the provider is trustee of the provider's trust.

- The provider conveys his or her property to the spouse, who then places the property into his or her separate trust. Thus, the trust property is the "property" of the spouse, and is not subject to the creditors of the provider. It is just as though the spouse had full ownership.

The difference, and the advantage, of the revocable living trust over regular ownership is that the provider still maintains control over the property by virtue of being co-trustee of the spouse's trust.   Remember that the trustee controls and manages the property in the trust estate for the benefit of the beneficiaries. But the trustee has no right to the trust assets, only the right to exercise management over the trust assets.

The beneficiaries are the only persons entitled to use, spend and enjoy the trust assets since the trustees have no right to the benefit of the trust property. This brings up the other major complaint from most providers, "I don't want to give up my assets, I worked hard for this." That is why an irrevocable trust is generally out of the question, except in certain limited situations. Yet the provider **can be the beneficiary of the spouse's revocable living trust!** A revocable living trust can name both spouses, children, parents, etc., as the beneficiaries. The provider gets to enjoy the fruit of his or her labor, yet because ownership is in the spouse's trust, the provider need not worry about losing his or her assets to the birds of prey (i.e. vultures) patrolling the local courtrooms.

Recall the examples set out earlier? How would those situations have been affected by a properly drawn, revocable living trust? Let's look:

> *Paul, the securities lawyer, lost his fortune because he owned his assets in his name. If Paul had given the assets to his wife, and a living trust was created in Ann's name with both of them as joint trustees, Paul would have protected "his" assets from the S.E.C. fines and malpractice claim because he would have had no ownership interest in the assets. Yet he would have had control over the assets as joint trustee with his wife. Paul would have been able to take that trip around the world upon his retirement.*

This same technique could be helpful for any professional concern with a malpractice suit. By titling the assets in the spouse's name, they would not be part of the professional's assets. Yet, if the professional is co-trustee of that trust, then he or she can still maintain some control.

> *Bill was the businessman with the young wife. He could have placed his personal assets in his wife's name, with the assets immediately going into a living trust with Bill and Carol as joint*

trustees. All the assets would have been creditor free, at least from Bill's liability claims (Carol's creditors would have been another thing, but the risk/benefit has to be in Carol's favor). Since Bill would have been a joint trustee with Carol, she would not have been able to sell the house from underneath John when he went to Europe. Carol might have left with the club tennis pro, but at least not with Bill's money in tow.

Not all joint trustees have to co-sign each check. The rules can be adjusted for different circumstances, just like corporate checks. One can set up a procedure where checks for less than $500 (or whatever figure you desire) can go through without two signatures. Bankers can provide the type of check writing privileges needed for a trust.

Warren, the developer with the impossible children, was able to rectify his by establishing a separate living trust for his wife with him as co-trustee. Accordingly, his signature is required on the checks. The kids will have to figure out some other way to mooch off of Shirley.

•   •   •

Ron, the architect, could have approached it differently. Since he knew the metal plating business had some liability (though he had not thought of environmental problems), he could have purchased his interest through his living trust. All their other assets could have been titled in his wife's trust, with both of them as co-trustees. As with everyone else the EPA had sought out, Ron would have been judgement proof when the EPA came calling.

Normally, not all of the assets belonging to the provider will be placed in the spouse's name. Depending on state law, some assets have to be "owned" by the professional (i.e., professional corporation stock). Another consideration is the use of the $600,000 federal estate tax exemption. The provider needs to pass his or her $600,000 to someone other than the surviving spouse (this is where the Family Trust comes into play) in order to maximize estate tax planning. That might be done by passing assets with minimal value to litigious parties to the Family Trust. For example: the closely held stock, life insurance proceeds, retirement plan assets, etc. By limiting the amount subject to creditors to $600,000, and making those assets the hardest type of assets against which to collect, the provider has deterred the collection of the judgement and might encourage a settlement with the creditor. These "owned" assets may still be placed in the spouse's trust, so probate is avoided.

However, a living trust is not perfect. First, the trust-making spouse can "fire" the co-trustee, thus creating the possibility that the spouse can fire the provider and do whatever he or she wants to do anyway. The properly drawn trust will have some type of notice provision (typically thirty days) that requires notice to the "fired" trustee (provider). This will at least give the liable spouse time to take appropriate action to thwart the coming storm.

Further, since the trust is revocable, which is more often beneficial than detrimental, it can technically be canceled by the spouse while the provider is on a trip. In practice this is very complex and unrealistic. Virtually every stock brokerage firm, bank and real estate lawyer would require notice to the non-consenting trustee. A joint trustee clause on a stock brokerage account is an "and" account, requiring both signatures. Did you ever try to close or clean out an "and" account without both signatures? If you got lucky and did so, the entity which allowed it might be liable if you were without proper authorization. Most institutions, likewise, would subscribe to the rule that when revoking a trust, both trustees have to consent to transfers or major dispositions of assets. Therefore, it is, as a practical matter, inconceivable that the spouse could revoke the trust and disburse assets without proper authorization from the other trustee. At a minimum, he or she would have to be in compliance with the notice provisions stated earlier.

Finally, depending again on state law, and to some extent federal law, the transfers to the revocable living trusts contemplated above would generally need to be created two years or more before the liability (or as lawyers, say "cause of action") arose. Thus, you can not create a trust after you know of the liability. In order to take advantage of the trust benefits as to liability, you need to create the trust now, before these future problems arise. This is very similar to insurance: you can't buy life insurance once you have been diagnosed as having a terminal condition. A lot of people wait until the problem occurs before doing anything, but in each of the examples set out above, the providers did not realize they had problems until it was too late. That is why this is called estate **planning**.

Weighing the good against the bad, the advantages of a revocable living trust far outweigh the drawbacks. No matter what, it certainly beats the alternatives. You will complicate the search for personal assets by litigious claimants, protect against the disappearing spouse (at least disappearing with your money!), and you will, I suspect, be able to sleep a little better at night. There is no substitute for peace of mind. Trusts don't solve every problem, but they do solve most.

One final word of caution. Ever wonder why they call it the "practice" of law? There are some in my profession who do "practice" on their clients. Despite possessing insufficient training and experience and despite not possessing the requisite legal knowledge, many lawyers will draw up a will or even a trust. So be sure to get competent legal advice. Don't let the lawyer practice on you; you have worked too hard to get where you are.

Another major complaint from the public is that lawyers draw up documents that only lawyers understand. (Yet, if that was true, why would negotiated contracts end up in court being argued over what the contract means? Thus, even lawyers sometimes do not know what their own verbiage means, which is why they make such good Senators.) Lawyers can, if forced to, make a document easily readable. So make sure you understand what the trust says and means, every single word of it.

PART V

SPECIAL PLANNING SITUATIONS

27

WHAT HAPPENS TO MY BUSINESS UPON MY DEATH?

One of the more difficult issues I encounter when working with business owners/doctors/farmers is the question of what will happen to their businesses/professional practices/farms upon their deaths. They want to ensure that their heirs will receive full value and that estate taxes won't eat up the asset. This is an area that is very complex because it brings together so many factors and involves a myriad of planning issues. Unfortunately, like so many of the issues we have discussed, the complexity and amount of thought required means that most people don't plan at all.

Why is planning so important?

Small businesses represent a vital cog in our economic cycle, although you'd have a tough time telling it from the way Congress treats the small businessperson. Family businesses generate 40% of the gross national product. They represent 95% of all businesses in this country. They employ a significant portion of the work force. Yet, because of improper planning, fewer than 33% survive the second generation, and of those, only 50% make it to the third generation. Considering the amount of work that went into the business by the founder, that's a sad commentary. Even sadder, however, is the fact that this is completely unnecessary. Proper planning could dramatically increase those statistics.

What will happen at your death?

Many people have devoted the bulk of their lives to building a business/professional practice/ farm. They have spent untold thousands of dollars making that endeavor a success. Yet, very little time is expended on considering what will happen to that business/practice/farm upon the death of one of the principals.

Michael Law was a general surgeon who had been in solo practice for many years. He always felt the value of his practice was based on his ability as a surgeon. He realized that he had no equipment of consequence for his wife to sell. His practice didn't provide a flow of repeat patients. As a result, his planning was based upon having sufficient life insurance to take care of his wife, while assuming the value of his practice would be virtually nothing. However, there was one thing he didn't plan on: his wife dying first. Then, upon his subsequent death, his heirs received their inheritance. They also received a shock when they learned that the value of his medical practice was included in his estate. This resulted in unexpected estate taxes. Even though the practice had no ongoing value to the heirs, the IRS didn't agree that it was worthless. In fact, the IRS attached such a high value that the bulk of Dr. Law's estate was eaten up by estate taxes.

● ● ●

C. B. Franklin owned a farm that had been in his family since the early-1900's. It had survived the depression and all the activity that occurred around it as a major metropolitan area continued to spread. The farm had been passed down from generation to generation. When C. B.'s brother died several years ago, C. B. inherited his half. While he never thought about any estate taxes that might be due at his brother's death, the real problem occurred when the IRS ruled that his farm did not qualify as an active farm because less than half the land was used for farming. Therefore, it was valued at its actual market value, which was high due to the fact that it could be developed for residential use.

● ● ●

Roger Adamson was a 25% stockholder in Midwest Manufacturing Company. It was a closely-held corporation in which his other partners owned 40%, 20%, and 15% respectively. While they had thought about succession planning, it never was of much concern. The corporation was profitable. All the partners realized that they could continue the business upon the death of any of the others. So, when Roger died, his wife inherited his stock. She had no interest in participating in the business, and his former partners certainly didn't want her involved. However, she soon found out that the company had made no plans for this eventuality. They all soon realized that the worst was yet to come.

●   ●   ●

Hank Warren, a widower, was sole owner of a successful service company. He had three children, Jonathan, Ben, and Wendy. Jonathan worked with him in the family business; Ben and Wendy were each married and living in other cities. Hank had always assumed that Jonathan would take over the business. He had a good head on his shoulders and a feel for what it took to be successful. The company had borrowed substantial amounts of money. Hank was on all the notes; Jonathan on some. When Hank died, his will was read. He left everything to his children, one-third each. All of a sudden, Jonathan was a minority stockholder in the business his father wanted him to have.

These are just a few cases illustrating the problems that individuals face upon their deaths. As the statistics stated previously indicate, these cases are not unique.

VALUATION

If your heirs are going to receive full value for your business/practice/farm, you first need to determine the value. This is an inexact science if there ever was one. What you think it is worth can be vastly different from what the IRS thinks. What you can sell it for today may not be an indication of its true value. Its current use may not be representative of what the IRS decides. The operative organization here is the Internal Revenue Service. It pronounces the final verdict - the only one that matters.

Since we are talking about businesses, medical and dental practices, and farms, let's explore each and look at the valuation problems and issues.

Closely held business

A "closely held" business differs from a public company, such as Wal-Mart, in that there is no readily established market value for the stock. Whereas Wal-Mart is traded on the New York Stock Exchange and is easy to value at any given time, the same isn't true with Midwest Manufacturing Company (our first example of this chapter). Because there is no ready market for the stock, meaning no exchange where the stock is bought and sold, valuation is difficult.

But before talking about the problems, let's first see why there is a question of valuation in the first place. Why is it so important?

Beyond the obvious answer that valuation is important for financial planning reasons, there are two factors that are important from the standpoint of this book.

- Upon your death, or the death of any of the stock-holders, the deceased's interest is usually sold. Proper valuation helps determine that price and makes any transition less of a burden.

- Upon death, the value of the deceased shareholder's stock is included in his or her estate for federal estate tax purposes. It is important to know what this valuation is for estate tax liquidity purposes.

Because several valuation methods are used, precise figures are difficult. For example, the value might be based on book value, capitalization of average earnings, book value plus goodwill, or fair market value plus a multiple of past earnings. Since there are so many different methods, many planners and

CPAs average the various methods together to reach a final figure.

Further, it is important to take advantage of any special valuations that are permitted under our tax code. For example, special gift tax valuation rules are permitted in situations in which business interests are transferred to members of one's family. It is important to seek knowledgeable counsel in this area.

Farm

The case earlier in this chapter reflects several good reasons why it is so important to properly value farms in advance. In situations where I have worked with farmers, they have tended to downplay the value of their farm. They usually complain about the problems they have making money and assume that factor will have a major bearing on the valuation of their farm. And while it is a consideration, it is not necessarily the overriding one.

On the other hand, there are some breaks for farmers or ranchers that will help them from an estate-tax standpoint. Included in this is a "special use valuation" which allows the valuation on its "current" use rather than on the basis of "highest and best" use. However, there are restrictions and limitations that must be taken into consideration. Unfortunately, this didn't help in our example.

Medical/Dental Practice

The medical and dental professions are unique. While most businesses have a tangible product which gives value to the business, the professional only has himself or herself. As a result, valuing a practice can be difficult. Unlike a business, which has value beyond one or two individuals, a medical or dental practice is based almost solely on the reputation and competence of the individual practitioner. Once again, it is important to work with advisors who specialize in this area to help you with your valuation.

POTENTIAL PROBLEMS

In dealing in this area, there are some problems that constantly crop-up. They are not unique. They need not be a surprise. They are just the result of lack of planning.

Like so much we have discussed thus far, problems can be resolved when they are anticipated. But business people, farmers, and doctors are so busy running their businesses or professions that they rarely take the time to do meaningful planning. Hopefully, this will change.

Unforseen estate taxes

Dr. Law's children were faced with a surprise. The sole practitioner rarely considers estate taxes because he or she doesn't regard the practice as having sufficient value to cause concern. As a result, he usually goes ahead with his financial plans and lets the chips fall where they may.

Nevertheless, estate taxes can be an issue. Normally, this is not a problem if the practitioner is survived by a spouse, because no estate taxes are due at the first death. By the time the surviving spouse is gone, the practice is long forgotten and not a tax issue.

But if the practitioner has no spouse, or if both spouses die simultaneously, there is a potential problem that must be addressed. That practice, at least as far as the IRS is concerned, has value, even though in reality that practice is limited once the sole practitioner has died. But try to tell that to the IRS. They will value it as they see fit.

Dr. Michael Law survived his wife. The value of his estate, not *including his practice, was $2,000,000. At his death, the IRS valued his practice at $750,000. As a result, this valuation increased his federal estate taxes from approximately $588,000 to $965,500.*

Even though his practice had no value to Dr. Law's children, they had to pay significant taxes. However, proper planning, as discussed below, could have avoided this problem.

For C. B. Franklin, taxes were a complete surprise. While he had considered that there might be some taxes due, he certainly couldn't predict the disastrous results.

C. B. Franklin's farm is located in a fast growing section of a major metropolitan area. There are subdivisions and office parks surrounding his one hundred plus acres. And, due to his age, he is farming very little of the land. The IRS says the land should be taxed at its actual market value. That means that Mr. Franklin's brother's estate will have to pay over one-half million dollars in estate taxes - liquid cash that is just not available.

Lack of funds

The case of Roger Adamson is not unique. Many business people and medical practitioners with whom I counsel never make any plans for the death of one of the stockholders. That was the case at Midwest Manufacturing.

The stockholders were too busy making money to think about potential problems. Everything seemed to be going so well. And since they were all relatively young, they never anticipated a death. So when Roger died, his wife inherited his stock. She was now a minority stockholder in a closely-held corporation. And she was willing to sell her stock back to Midwest......for a price. She certainly wasn't greedy, she just wanted fair value. She retained an attorney, and a settlement was negotiated. Midwest, being a fast growing company, didn't have the cash with which to pay her. So her attorney drafted an agreement whereby she would be paid monthly for a period of five years. She signed over her stock to the corporation in exchange for a promissory note, collateralized by that very stock and certain equipment and inventory. All of a sudden, the corporation had a debt on its balance sheet. It also had a cash flow drain - she was getting money and contributing nothing for it. They also had to hire someone to take Roger's place. This changed the entire picture within the corporation. The situation caused a strain on everyone that could have been easily avoided at a minimal expense.

No provisions for the family business

For Jonathan Warren and his sister and brother, things couldn't have been worse. They all became equal owners of a business that only Jonathan understood and cared about. Ben and Wendy had established their own careers. They just weren't interested in the family business. But they did feel they were entitled to their portion of their father's estate. Since together they were majority stockholders, Ben and Wendy wanted a voice in the business - and some income from it. It turned into a total disaster. The bankers were scared enough when Hank died. Now they panicked. The kids never got along too well anyway. Now they were continually feuding. The bankers saw what was happening to the business and, one by one, they called the loans. The company had to sell equipment to pay back the banks. Finally, the business filed bankruptcy. It is a business no more.

Loan guarantees result in gift and estate taxes

As discussed previously, if you guarantee a loan for another, that act is now interpreted by the IRS as a gift to that person. Any guarantee over $10,000 (your annual gift exclusion) will require that you file a gift tax return and reduce your $600,000 lifetime exemption for guarantees over your annual exclusion. This is true even if the guarantee is never exercised.

In addition, those guarantees can have adverse estate-tax consequences if you wish to leave property to a spouse under the unlimited marital deduction. For a complete discussion of this problem, refer to Chapter 17.

SOLUTIONS

All these cases have one thing in common: lack of

planning. In the Law case, the family ended up paying needless taxes. In the Franklin case, this nice gentleman is faced with losing his farm. In the Adamson case, the business ended up paying out money needlessly. In the Warren case, no provisions were made for passing the business. The sad fact is that each and every one of these cases could have been avoided with some simple planning.

The bulk of this book has been spent discussing smooth transitions, usually from family member to family member, and eliminating unhappy surprises. Remember our definition:

> *"During my life and after my death, I want to control and distribute my property in the manner I desire, minimizing all fees, taxes and court interference, preserving for myself, my family, and those I choose, the estate I have worked so hard to create."*

Did any of our examples accomplish this? No. Because, once again, all the people planned for the best by not planning at all. What are the possible solutions? Let's look.

BUY-SELL AGREEMENTS

One of the easiest ways to solve many business succession problems is with a buy-sell agreement. That was certainly true in the case of Midwest Manufacturing.

A buy-sell agreement is a written agreement whereby one party agrees to sell and another party or parties agree to buy it. The sale takes place at a predetermined price (or based on a predetermined formula) and takes effect upon death of one of the stockholders. It is the ideal vehicle to guarantee continuity.

There are three types of buy-sell agreements.

- **Cross-purchase** - This agreement is entered into between the various shareholders. Each partner agrees with the other to purchase his share for (typically) a predetermined price. This agreement is binding on all the parties, including the heirs. In our case, Roger's share would have been purchased in proportion by each of his surviving partners.

  This type of agreement has the advantage of creating a market, which previously didn't exist, for the stock. In addition, it helps set a value for buy-out purposes. For future income tax purposes, it helps the surviving partners increase their cost basis in the corporation. One of the primary disadvantages, especially in this case, is the involvement of so many parties, as we shall see shortly.

- **Entity-purchase** - This agreement, also called a stock-redemption plan, is an agreement whereby the corporation itself redeems the shares of the deceased stockholder. In this case, Roger's stock would have been purchased from his wife by the corporation instead of the surviving partners.

  One of the advantages of this type of plan is the minimum of paperwork, especially when there are more than two stockholders. There are further advantages if the plan is funded with insurance. On the other hand, there are several disadvantages. First, this type of plan can result in an AMT (Alternative Minimum Tax) problem for the corporation. (However, if it is an S Corporation, there is no AMT problem.) In addition, there is no step-up in the cost basis as with the cross-purchase plan. And finally, the entity-purchase plan may significantly change the ownership status for the remaining shareholders. For example, the person who was a fifty percent stockholder may now end up owning a controlling interest.

This was the most popular plan until 1986. Due to changes in the tax laws resulting in the alternative minimum tax, it is no longer as popular as it once was.

- **Wait and see** - This is a relatively new type of agreement whereby the parties "wait and see" until there is a death to determine which type of buy-sell agreement (entity purchase or cross purchase) to use. As a general rule, at death, the surviving stockholders have the right of first refusal to purchase the stock. If they choose not to do this, it reverts to an entity purchase, and the corporation purchases the stock.

Leaving your business to a family member

If it is your intent to leave your business to a family member, then you might consider making that provision in your will or trust. There is no reason for the heir to pay for something that he or she will inherit anyway. In addition, the business will receive a stepped-up basis for tax purposes. This might create an estate-tax problem, however, that you need to consider.

LIFE INSURANCE IN BUSINESS SITUATIONS

Throughout this book, I have indicated that the proper use of life insurance can solve many planning problems. I hate to sound like a broken record, but, once again, life insurance comes into play here. All of the problems we have discussed in this chapter have one thing in common: the need for ready, liquid cash. As in so many other situations, only life insurance can provide the needed cash at the lowest possible cost.

Let's look at how life insurance fits into the various business situations.

Buy-sell agreements - The use of agreements is great, except for one minor fact: how will the company afford to buy out the deceased stockholder's estate? While many business owners think they can afford to finance this purchase over time, it is not a reasonable solution. Most individuals and companies have enough problems without having to spend precious cash paying off heirs. Why not consider shifting the burden to the insurance company and let it do what it does best? Let's look at each type of agreement.

- **Cross-purchase** - Each partner would own and be the beneficiary of a policy on each of the others. In our example, Roger would have had a policy on each of the other three stockholders, and each of the other three stockholders would have a policy on each of the others. When Roger died, three policies would have paid benefits to the surviving partners. Each partner would have then purchased Roger's stock from his wife. However, as you can see, this could be cumbersome because there would have had to be twelve separate policies.

- **Entity-purchase** - In this case, the corporation would be the owner and beneficiary of a policy on each stockholder. At Roger's death, Midwest Manufacturing would have received the death benefit and purchased his stock from Mrs. Adamson with that money. Only four policies would have been needed - one on each stockholder. But the corporation would have faced AMT ramifications.

- **Wait and see** - In this situation, the insurance would have been structured as if it were a cross-purchase agreement. Therefore, twelve policies would be used. At Roger's death, the surviving shareholders would have had the right of first refusal. If they decided they didn't want to buy the stock, the corporation would have purchased it. To provide the needed cash, each of the surviving shareholders would have loaned the money they received from the insurance on Roger to the corporation. This would have avoided the AMT problems. The corporation would have then purchased the stock.

The primary advantage of using life insurance is that it provides liquidity that is normally absent. Additionally, as we saw in the previous discussion about paying estate taxes, it allows the resolution of a potential problem for a fraction of what the cost might have been.

A new type of insurance that works well in this type of situation is a "first-to-die" policy. This is the opposite of the "second-to-die" policy which is used for estate taxes. The first-to-die covers several insureds, but only pays the death benefit when the first insured dies. Since only one death benefit has to be paid, the premiums are lower than for two separate policies.

Family business continuation - Life insurance could have played a major part in keeping the Warrens' business out of bankruptcy court. The business faced two problems: bank loans and ownership succession. In the former, the company could have taken out term insurance on Hank's life that would have provided sufficient liquidity to retire the bank debt. This would have relieved Jonathan from worrying about paying off that debt.

Additionally, life insurance could have been used to equalize Hank's estate. Since Ben and Wendy weren't interested in the business, it didn't make sense to leave them stock, let alone make them majority owners. Instead, Hank could have left the stock entirely to Jonathan and taken out life insurance payable to the other children. This would have equalized the estate between the three. If he had done that, the business would still be in operation today. Jonathan would be happy because he would have the business. Ben and Wendy would be happy because they would have an equal amount in cash.

Farm estate taxes - The problem of estate taxes on the farm is not unlike other situations discussed earlier in the book. With proper planning and the use of life insurance, C. B. Franklin would have received sufficient cash at his brother's death to pay the estate taxes. Had he done this, he would be assured of keeping the farm.

Why isn't planning with insurance done more often? A primary reason is the common prejudice against life insurance agents, coupled with a lack of understanding of how to properly use life insurance. Nevertheless, life insurance, properly used, is the only sensible way to solve these tremendous problems to everyone's satisfaction. It is also the cheapest way.

VALUATION FOR ESTATE TAX PURPOSES

In the past, it was possible to use a buy-sell agreement to value a closely-held business for estate-tax purposes. However, recent IRS rulings have changed that. Currently, a buy-sell agreement cannot be depended upon to set the value of the business for closely-held businesses. However, there are exceptions. If the agreement meets all of the following, then the valuation set in the agreement can be used for estate tax purposes.

- The agreement must be part of a bona fide business arrangement.

- It must not be used to transfer property to family members for less than full consideration.

- The terms must be comparable to similar arrangements entered into by persons in an arm's length transaction.

If all three conditions are met, then the value can be used.

NOTE: There have been recent tax changes that drastically affect business continuation planning. Provisions affecting estate freeze rules, recapitalization, grantor retained income trusts (grits), etc., have been changed. Check with your advisors before taking any action.

DISABILITY

Don't think that death is the only problem you face with business succession. The disability of one or more of the owners can result in disastrous consequences.

Randy McConnell was a 50% owner in a small distribution business. While his partner handled all the business aspects, Randy took care of the warehousing and transportation of the products. One day, while working in the warehouse, he was struck by a fork-lift and severely injured. He was unable to walk without the aid of a walker, unable to stand for extended periods of time, and obviously unable to lift. As a result, the company had to hire an employee to take his place.

Of course, as with most people in this situation, Randy continued to get paid. But then the company was made aware of a very disturbing fact: because they had no Qualified Sick Pay Plan, **the wages paid to Randy were not deductible to the business, but they were taxable to him.** This was a shock!

This was a bad situation all around. The company was making payments to Randy that it couldn't afford. A replacement had to be hired. It was causing dissention because Randy's partner got sick of making payments for nothing. And all the tax benefits to the company were lost.

Qualified Sick Pay Plan

The easiest way to have solved this problem would have been with a Qualified Sick Pay Plan. This is a plan that is established **before** an accident or sickness occurs and contains the following information:

- who to pay;

- how much to pay;

- when to start the payments;

- how long to pay.

As long as this is included, you have a qualified plan, and the payments will be tax-deductible to the company. But that still doesn't resolve the other problem: where is the money going to come from with which to make those payments? The answer is (surprise) insurance.

The proper use of a disability insurance plan, such as that discussed previously, will provide the company with the needed funds with which to make those payments. As a result, the company can make the premium payments when everything is going well, and the insurance company will pay when it is needed. There are many IRS regulations that must be met, so this must be handled properly.

Disability buy-out

In addition to the buy-sell agreements we covered earlier, you can also have a disability buy-out agreement. This will allow a disabled stockholder to be bought out much the same as would happen at death. Once again, by using insurance to fund this agreement, the financial burden is shifted from the business to the insurance company.

AVOIDING TAXES ON THE SALE OF YOUR BUSINESS

Although we have discussed disposition upon death, we need to talk about what will happen if you choose to sell your business/practice/farm while you are alive. There are many privately-held businesses sold every day for a variety of reasons.

In many cases, a sale results in hefty capital gains.

Jesse Langhorn, a widower, owns a successful electronics firm that he founded in 1965. A sole stockholder, he is now ready to retire. Nobody in his family has any desire to take over the business. Coincidentally, a large firm has offered him $2.1 million for the business. It is an answer to his prayers. Since his cost basis is virtually nil, it is also an answer to the IRS's prayers. After all, he would have to pay income taxes on over $2,000,000 of capital gains!

The idea of selling his business makes a lot of sense to Jesse. He could take the proceeds, buy government bonds, and receive a comfortable income for the rest of his life. But after looking at the numbers with his CPA, he was concerned that so much of his life's work would go to taxes. Here is what the analysis showed:

Sales Price	$2,100,000
Cost Basis	80,000
Gross Profit	$2,020,000
Income Taxes	767,600
Net Profit	$1,332,400
Estate Taxes	732,820
Net to Heirs	$ 599,580

You can see that **over 70% of the value of his business would be lost to income and estate taxes!** This means if Jesse sells the property, pays the capital gains, reinvests the money, and spends the income, his children would receive only $599,580 at his death. This results in a substantial shrinkage in the value of the business.

Needless to say, Mr. Langhorn is not thrilled with this scenario. He hasn't worked all these years just to have the government absorb 70% of his business. However, once he saw how a Charitable Remainder Unitrust could solve his problem, he felt better. (For a complete discussion of charitable trusts, refer to Chapter 21.)

Instead of selling his business to the new owner, he could establish a Charitable Remainder Unitrust and donate his stock to it. **Exhibit 12** illustrates how it would look in Mr. Langhorn's case. Remember, everyone's numbers will differ due to age, tax brackets, marital status, etc.

Step 1.   Mr. Langhorn could contribute his stock in the business to his charitable remainder trust. That stock would then be sold to the new owners by the trust. There would be no capital gains to be paid since it would be sold by a tax-exempt entity.

Step 2.   He would receive a tax deduction of $492,094, resulting in income tax savings of $186,996.

Step 3.   Since his children would receive no benefit from the trust upon his death, he would take $40,000 from the tax deduction for the first year's premium on a $1.5 million life insurance policy in an irrevocable life insurance trust.

Step 4.   The $2.1 million from the sale of his business would be invested in government bonds yielding 8% annually. This would give him over $2 million in income over his life expectancy.

Step 5.   He would take part of that annual income for life insurance premiums. That amount would total $760,000, based on current projections.

Step 6.   Upon his death, the charities would receive $2.1 million dollars.

Step 7.   Additionally, his children would receive (based on current projections) $2,447,769 estate and income tax free.

Exhibit 12

Charitable Remainder Unitrust Plan Diagram

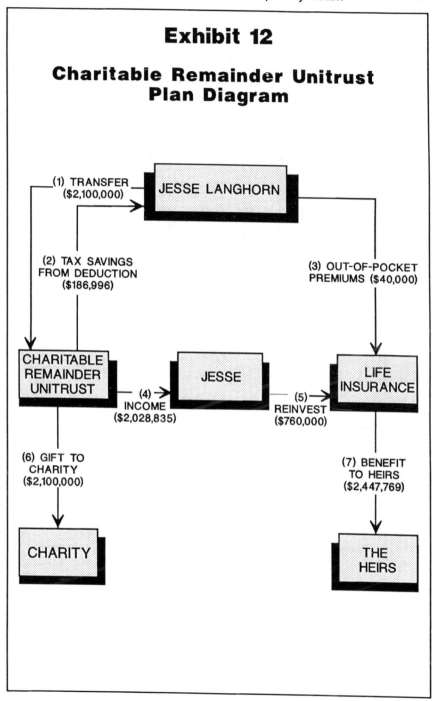

Let's compare two alternatives:

Alternative #1. Mr. Langhorn **sells his business** as he would have normally. He pays the capital gains taxes and reinvests the remainder in government bonds at 8%. At his death, the money, after estate taxes, goes to his children.

Alternative #2. Mr. Langhorn **contributes the stock** to his Charitable Remainder Unitrust which sells it and reinvests the proceeds at 8% in government bonds. He receives the income from the bonds, then takes some of that money and purchases a life insurance policy in a wealth replacement trust. At his death, the insurance proceeds go to his children while the balance of the CRT goes to his favorite charities.

	1. Without CRUT	2. Using CRUT
CONTRIBUTIONS		
Market Value	$2,100,000	$2,100,000
Savings from Tax Deduction	0	186,996
Capital Gains Tax on Sale	767,600	0
Net to Invest	$1,332,400	$2,286,996
CASH FLOW		
Income During Life	$1,287,247	$2,215,831
Less: Insurance Premiums	0	800,000
Net Spendable Income	$1,287,247	$1,415,831
ESTATE FOR HEIRS		
Gross Value of Estate	$1,332,400	0
Plus: Life Insurance	0	$2,447,769
Less: Estate Taxes	732,820	0
Net Estate for Heirs	$ 599,580	2,447,769
SUMMARY OF BENEFITS		
Net Income	$1,287,247	$1,415,831
Estate for Heirs	599,580	2,447,769
Amount to Charity	0	2,100,000
TOTAL BENEFIT	**$1,886,827**	**$5,963,600**

After looking at this, can you think of any **valid** reason why Jesse wouldn't choose this route? It provides more income for him while he is alive. It leaves his children more than four times as much as they would have received. It provides his favorite charities with over two million dollars! And he would still control where the money is invested. This is an amazing benefit to all parties involved.

This is just one way Jesse could structure it. If he wanted more income, he could put less into the life insurance trust. If he needed less income, he could put more into the trust. Or he could put only half his stock into the trust and keep the other half out. That way he would save capital gains on part and still leave himself with plenty of "play money." The important thing to realize is that it is a flexible plan that can be structured to his particular situation. And it certainly meets our definition of estate planning:

> *"During my life and after my death, I want to control and distribute my property in the manner I desire, minimizing all fees, taxes and court interference, preserving for myself, my family, and those I choose, the estate I have worked so hard to create."*

He certainly worked hard to create his estate. Doesn't it just make sense to preserve it for himself and his family?

As I have warned so often, this is a technique that must be done correctly and with professional guidance every step of the way. The trust must be in place before an agreement is made to sell the business. You must have proper administration of your trust. And you must have the right advisors handling the plan. If done correctly, tremendous benefits can be realized.

This works for stock market profits, too

This same technique can be used to shelter capital gains

on common stock. There are many people who are reluctant to sell a stock because the gain will result in substantial taxes. The Charitable Remainder Unitrust can be used just as effectively in the case of common stock as it was in Jesse Langhorn's case.

Conclusion

Many business owners, farmers, and doctors ignore succession and valuation problems. They think that everything will somehow work out satisfactorily. I don't have to tell you that they usually don't. It is a shame to see how many people allow all their hard work to go down the drain for lack of planning.

28

HOW CAN I PROVIDE FOR MY HANDICAPPED CHILD?

Through the years, we have become more sensitive to the problems faced by handicapped, or "special" children. However, nothing can match the responsibility that the parent of a special child faces.

Unfortunately, unlike so much of our planning, we are dealing with an issue that has no good solutions. There is no magic wand that can be waived which will solve all your problems. But there are some steps you can take to mentally sort out possible solutions to your concerns.

THE NEEDS OF THE SPECIAL CHILD

Planning for special children is unusually difficult. In our discussion of minor children, we assumed that a distribution could be made when the child reached a certain age. Such an assumption cannot be made in the case of special children. They have needs that could last beyond your lifetime or your physical ability to handle them. They may outlive their brothers and sisters. Someone has to care for your special children, and that should be part of the planning.

When planning for the special child, some basic questions must be answered concerning care. How are you going to provide for this child for the rest of his or her life? Who is going to be the responsible party?

These are not questions that prompt easy answers. They involve the consideration of various financial assistance programs and the involvement of other family members. However, the biggest mistake is the refusal of parents to face the facts and make the difficult decisions. It is such a strenuous subject to address that many people just procrastinate until it is too late. This is unfair not only to the child but to the other members of the family. Who better than you is in a position to take action and make the arrangements? Certainly not the probate court.

GOVERNMENTAL ASSISTANCE PROGRAMS

The federal government provides several basic programs through Social Security and Medicaid. In addition, you will undoubtedly find some local programs to provide assistance.

Social Security Disability Benefits

Disability benefits are available to special children if an eligible parent becomes disabled, retires, or dies. For the parents to be eligible for social security, they must have met the normal social security requirements based on work hours. For the child to qualify, he or she must have been disabled prior to age 22 and have been, and still be, unable to work. Social Security's definition of disability is very simple: if you can't work at any job, you are disabled.

Supplemental Security Income

This program, also through Social Security, is for disabled individuals and is based on need. While under the age of 18, the child must qualify based on the assets and income of his or her parents. Once past that age, he or she qualifies based on his or her own assets and income. The rules are very stringent, and the child is allowed very little in the way of property. As of this writing, the child may have $2,000 in non-exempt property in addition to property specifically exempted, which includes a home, a car, and life insurance.

Medicaid

If the special child is eligible for Supplemental Security Income, he or she qualifies for Medicaid. Medicaid is the program that pays for care not covered under Medicare. You may recognize this program from our discussion of long term care for the aged. Medicaid is the program that pays when the person lacks the resources to do so. You will want to check the current rules for this program in your state.

GOVERNMENT ASSISTANCE - YOUR DECISION

In your planning, you must make one basic decision: **do you or do you not want your child to qualify for governmental assistance?** Lets explore the ramifications of each choice.

Yes, I want my child to qualify for governmental assistance.

If this is your choice, you have three ways to approach it: totally disinherit your child, leave the money to another family member to care for the child, or use a trust.

Disinheriting - means that upon your death, you leave nothing to the child. Since the child has no funds, he qualifies for the programs mentioned above and becomes a ward of the state. In some cases, he will bounce from institution to institution. In others, he will get buried in the system. His care will be affected by the opening and closing of various government programs. You have no control over his welfare and don't know what may happen to him.

Leaving the money to another family member - means that all your assets belong to that person, not your special child. As a result, you aren't assured that your child will be cared for in the manner you prefer. Any number of things can happen to destroy this plan, such as death of the other party, divorce, financial problems, disagreement; all of those dragons that we have spoken about continually. Remember, that money belongs to the person to whom you leave it, to use as he or she sees fit. There is no guarantee that the child will be any better off than with disinheritance.

A "Special" Trust - allows you to leave your instructions for the care of your special child while keeping the assets uncountable for governmental assistance purposes. This trust grants the trustee the power to give what he or she deems appropriate to the child for his care to the point that it will not disqualify him for governmental assistance. For example, the trustee can provide better housing, grant additional spending money, or buy items for the child. But the trustee won't duplicate what the government provides. You can include provisions for disposition of the assets of the trust should the child become independent and be able to care for himself.

No, I don't want to qualify my child for governmental assistance

If this is your desire, then there are several routes to take.

No Planning - I hate to list this as an alternative, but it is the course that most people take. They are uncertain as to the proper direction to take and don't feel they can make the tough decisions that we are talking about here. As a result, they do nothing. Obviously, this is the worst thing you can do. All the bad things we talked about earlier in the book come home to roost. Every dragon in the closet finds his way out. The special child ends up inheriting property. But, as with minors, he cannot legally own it. As a result, the child is under the jurisdiction of the probate court. Guardians, who may or may not have a great concern for your child, are appointed. Remember, there are only two reasons for wanting to gain guardianship: love and greed. You've got a living probate process that milks the estate of valuable funds. Nobody knows what action to take. Where should the child live? Where should he go to school? What medical care does he need? What should be his standard of living? It's an unacceptable alternative.

Simple Will - Although it is hard to believe, special children are often left money in a simple will. The parents, in a futile attempt to do something, have an attorney draft a will naming a guardian and leaving money to the child. This is only a little better than number one above. The only difference is that a guardian is named. All the other problems with leaving property to minor children happen when you leave property to special children, only they are magnified. As above, the simple will just isn't a good mechanism for leaving the necessary instructions.

Trust - As in so many cases, a trust will take care of many of the problems. Because of the flexibility, the trust itself, raises many questions. But first things first. A trust, either as a part of the will (testamentary) or in the form of a living trust, allows you to leave instructions upon your death. You can name a trustee for your child's funds. You can leave detailed instructions concerning important issues. Assuming you leave sufficient funds, you can care for the needs of your special child for the rest of his life. The same issues of a testamentary vs. living trust are encountered here.

YOUR OTHER CHILDREN

This is such a touchy issue when special children are involved. Along with all these other difficult decisions, you must resolve how to treat your other children in relation to your special child.

If you decide to disinherit your special child to qualify him for governmental assistance, or if you decide to leave all your money to your other children to care for their sibling, then there are no further decisions to make. You can stop reading at this point.

However, if those choices are not attractive, then we need to look at what else you can do. This time I am going to make the assumption that you agree that some type of trust is necessary, whether it be to qualify your child for governmental assistance or otherwise. Now your decision comes down to this: **am I going to create one trust for all my children or am I going to create separate trusts?** Let's look at the issues:

One Trust - the creation of one trust for all the children puts all your assets in one pot at the death of you and your spouse. Utilizing this trust, your trustee would follow your instructions in handling the finances for the children. You could give the trustee discretion in disbursing the funds, with the emphasis on your special child. At his death, the special child's trust would be dissolved and all proceeds distributed. While this has the advantage of being able to direct the necessary assets to your special child's needs, it also means that your other children, if the assets are totally consumed by the special child, may never receive their inheritance. Additionally, they will have to wait until the death of the special child before receiving anything.

Separate Trusts - the creation of a separate trust for the special child means you can specify funds for your special child knowing that those dollars can not be diverted to any of the other children. At the same time, you can either create another trust for your other children or provide for them to receive their inheritance outright. In either case, the money is theirs and cannot be used for your special child. Upon the death of the special child, his funds can be distributed to his brothers and sisters. While this sounds good in theory, it is difficult to know how much to put in the special child's trust - with the concern being that he may run out of funds before he dies.

Which type of trust to use

Decisions, decisions, decisions. It seems this chapter will never end and the choices will go on forever. But, fear not. We are getting close to the end. By now we have narrowed the decision making process, and hopefully we have triggered your thinking in the appropriate direction. Assuming you feel the trust is the only route to take, another choice must be made: **will the trust be a revocable living trust, an irrevocable living trust, or a testamentary trust?**

The **irrevocable living trust** involves setting up a trust and transferring property into it. However, the transfer of property to an irrevocable living trust constitutes a gift and must be considered in that light. Once you establish the trust, the terms cannot be changed, so while it does have the advantage of possibly reducing estate taxes in the future by "freezing" the value of the gift, the property cannot be reclaimed.

A **revocable living trust** involves setting up a trust and titling your property into it. As discussed previously, the revocable trust is totally under your control (assuming you are the trustee) and can be canceled or changed anytime you wish.

A **testamentary trust** is established at your death as a result of your will. While your will (and thus your trust) can be changed during your life, it becomes irrevocable upon your death. It carries with it the advantages and disadvantages discussed earlier.

Funding the trust

One final decision must be made: **how are you going to fund the trust in order to be fair to all your children?**

Fairness is a really thorny issue when it comes to families with special children. In these families, not much is fair. The other children usually feel they are getting the short end of the stick as more attention and funds are directed to the special child. This is not right or wrong; this is reality. Fortunately in most households, the other children understand and support the position of the parents. Nevertheless, you still have the problem of how to distribute your assets to your children, and that comes down to a function of money.

Repeating what was said at the beginning of the chapter, there are no good solutions to this problem. It is just that some are better than others. If you set up separate trusts, then the special child may run out of money. If you set up one trust for all the children, the other children may never receive their inheritance.

If you don't have sufficient assets to care for the special child while allowing the other children to receive the inheritance you desire, then the most equitable solution to the dilemma is the use of life insurance. Separate trusts can be set up with life insurance used to fund either the special child's trust or the trust of your other children, or both. If you are especially concerned with the special child but have sufficient assets, you can leave your assets to him and fund the other children's trust with life insurance. If you can possibly estimate a dollar amount the special child might need, you can fund that trust with life insurance and leave the remainder of your property to the others. And with the irrevocable life insurance trust we discussed earlier, these dollars can pass outside your estate.

Conclusion

The fact is that planning can be accomplished to take care of **all** your children, but it must be done carefully and with compassion. The worst thing you can do is ignore the problem and hope it goes away. The best thing you can do is take care of the problems **in advance** by doing some planning that takes into consideration the needs of each and every one of your children.

29

WHAT ARE THE RULES FOR NON-U.S. CITIZENS?

The United States has long been the land of opportunity. This fact has attracted many people from other countries who have chosen to go to school or work in this country.

While the opportunities to make money may be equal regardless of nationality, the privilege of passing that money is anything but equal. There is a different set of rules when it comes to residents who are not citizens of the United States (aliens). These rules are very complicated, and I recommend that you work with a competent estate planning attorney. What is presented here is only a broad overview.

Passing property to a spouse

As previously covered, the general rule is that one spouse can pass property to the other under the unlimited marital deduction. However, for **resident aliens to pass property under the unlimited marital deduction, the surviving spouse must be a U. S. citizen.** In general, there is <u>no</u> marital deduction for the surviving spouse who is not a citizen of the United States. However, it is not all bad news. There is still the $600,000 exemption equivalent that allows you to pass property at your death, regardless of your citizenship.

To recap, the big difference is that U. S. citizens are able to leave $600,000 to any one person or groups of persons, (or to the family/bypass trust) and the balance to the spouse, thus avoiding all estate tax at the first death. In the case of a spouse who is not a U.S. citizen, only $600,000 can be left estate-tax free; the balance is taxable.

Qualified Domestic Trust (QDT)

One planning technique that can be used is the Qualified Domestic Trust. Although just a temporary solution, this special trust allows the surviving spouse to receive income during his/her life, as long as certain criteria are met.

- At least one of the trustees must either be a citizen of the United States or a domestic corporate fiduciary (for example, the trust department of a bank).

- The surviving spouse must be entitled to income from the trust.

- Any distribution from the principal is contingent on the U. S. trustee's right to withhold any estate tax that might be due on that distribution.

Most attorneys with whom I work feel that, because of a quirk in the law, non-probate property is better suited toward the QDT than probate property. This is because the surviving spouse is permitted to place the inherited property in a QDT up to the day before the estate tax return is due. However, that is only allowed when the property has passed to the surviving spouse directly (not through probate). That means that non-probate assets, such as joint property, life insurance benefits, retirement benefits, and property in a living trust, are best suited for the QDT.

Estate tax must eventually be paid

Like the unlimited marital deduction with U. S. citizens,

you must "pay the piper" estate taxes. Two events will cause taxes to be due: when a distribution of principal is made from the trust to the surviving spouse, or when the surviving spouse dies.

You can see that Congress has designed the trust to hold assets rather than disburse them. While the surviving spouse can receive income, there will be tax due if the spouse attempts to utilize principal. So while a U. S. citizen can deplete assets, the non-citizen spouse cannot do so without incurring tax liability.

While on the surface the QDT might sound pretty good, the reality is that it only delays the taxing process. Better planning might include a regular program of gifting.

Gifts

Whereas the U.S. citizen has an unlimited marital deduction, a spouse may gift up to $100,000 to the non-citizen spouse per year. That means, through a periodic gifting program, the non-citizen spouse can have assets in his/her name at the death of the first spouse on which no taxes have been paid. This is in addition to the $600,000 exemption. To qualify under the gift exclusion, the gift must meet those same "present interest" requirements that were discussed in previous chapters.

Estate Taxes

This is one area that really hits the non-citizen. Unlike the U. S. citizen who has the unlimited marital deduction, only $600,000 can be passed estate-tax free to the non-citizen spouse. If the estate exceeds that figure, there is tax on the death of the first-to-die.

In addition, there will probably be estate tax due on the second-to-die. And, unlike with citizens, the growth in the estate of the second-to-die is added to the estate of the first to die for total calculation. Also, remember that anytime principal is taken out of the QDT, that, too, is estate taxable.

Leveraging the gift with life insurance

Once again, life insurance provides opportunities that are not available with traditional planning. Because of the limitation in passing property to a non-citizen spouse, many planners like to use life insurance in an irrevocable trust to maximize the gift exclusion. We have spoken earlier about the tremendous leverage you can realize with the use of life insurance. By using your annual gift exclusion, you can maximize that gift to the ultimate benefit of your family.

> *Dr. Yogesh Smaha is a citizen of the United States, but for business reasons back home, his wife is not. He is concerned that estate taxes will take the majority of his estate at his death. While he has done the necessary planning, he is still limited in what he can do. To replace the lost value, he is gifting $25,000 a year to an irrevocable trust through his wife. The trust will, in turn, purchase a $1,500,000 life insurance policy on his life. He would like to pay the premium for no more than 20 years and wants an increasing death benefit. By using proper procedures, this can provide funds to his wife that are estate-tax free.*

Properly established, this can provide more funds estate-tax free than any other method.

Conclusion

The best advice I can give is to become a citizen of the United States. As long as a non-citizen becomes a citizen before the death of the first spouse, then he/she can qualify for citizen rules. If your estate is large enough, it is certainly a worthwhile exercise. The next best alternative would be the use of life insurance to maximize your $100,000 annual exclusion.

30

HOW CAN I PROTECT MY FAMILY IN A SECOND MARRIAGE?

A generation ago, it was rare to see second marriages. Now, second, third, and fourth are common. And with these additional families come additional problems, especially in the estate planning field.

Let's look at the typical scenario in a second marriage:

Bill and Nancy Glenn had been married five years, and both had children from a previous marriage. They had their attorney draw up a will. As is typical, Bill's will left everything to Nancy, if living, otherwise to his children. Nancy's will left everything to Bill, if living, otherwise to her children. This scenario is carried out every day of the year in different towns across America.

Bill died in a tragic accident. Nancy received his property according to his will (and the balance of the property by virtue of her being the surviving joint tenant and beneficiary). As time goes by, one of two things will happen to Nancy: either she will remarry before her death, or she will remain single until her death. In either case, what about Bill's children? They're living with their mother. Nancy doesn't have much to do with them anymore. But she has all their dad's property.

Most likely, they will end up with nothing. And vice versa. If she dies first, Bill ends up with it all, and his will leaves everything to his kids. Her kids are out in the cold.

This is a problem that very few people recognize, and it

brings up the Rosenberg Law of Second Marriages: the children of the first to die lose! Not a very comforting thought.

Concerns in a second marriage

But how else can it be handled? Let's look at Bill's concerns.

- He loves Nancy, and wants to make sure that she is taken care of if he dies first, so he can't leave everything outright to his children.

- Since Bill has minor children and their natural mother has custody, he doesn't want to leave money to the children, otherwise his ex-wife will have control of it.

- If the children are in college when he dies, he wants to make sure they have money for their education, but he doesn't want all the money to go to them in a lump sum.

Use of a trust

What's the solution? By now you should know: a trust. Either a testamentary trust as part of the will, or a living trust. The trust will specify that certain property will go into a Q-TIP trust for Nancy's benefit. She can have the interest off the property, and if she needs money for emergencies, the trustee can give it to her. But upon her death, the property goes to Bill's children. The same is done in Nancy's trust.

Bill can also leave separate funds in a trust for the children and name a trustee. If he has confidence in his exwife, he can name her as trustee for the children. He can indicate how and when the children should receive their property.

In other words, with some planning, everyone can be taken care of. The beauty of using a trust is that it can be structured to meet all their goals. If they have "his, hers, and ours" children, the trust can provide for the care of all of them.

Ray, age 67, is married to Leslie, age 40. Ray has three children, ranging in ages from 25 to 41. He has some very real planning goals: he wants to take care of Leslie; he doesn't want his children to have to wait until Leslie dies before they receive any inheritance; and he feels that the longer he is married, the more he will want to leave Leslie. Ray entered the marriage with about $1.5 million in property, Leslie with $5,000. Additionally, Ray's younger son is somewhat irresponsible, so Ray doesn't want him to receive his share all at once.

It was determined that a living trust would be best for several reasons. Ray and Leslie's estate would avoid both living and death probate. Ray could be initial trustee and could name successor trustees, which would include one of Ray's children, to take care of him if he became disabled. The trust would help them reduce their estate taxes. The trust could establish sub-trusts to take care of Leslie; and they could easily change the terms as the marriage matured. This would also serve to equalize the estate, since previously, if Leslie died first, she wouldn't have had $600,000 to put into the Family Trust. If they used a testamentary trust instead of a living trust, Ray would have to title property in Leslie's name alone, which he is uncomfortable doing at this point in their marriage.

At Ray's death, $600,000 will go into a family trust for his children. The two older children will get their money immediately. The youngest will receive his over a period of time. Two other sub-trusts will be established for Leslie. The Marital Trust will consist of a certain amount of money, with the balance going into the Q-TIP Trust. She will have full access to the marital trust, which will include the home. She will receive income from the Q-TIP with principal as needed for health. Leslie, along with Ray's daughter (with whom she has good rapport), will be co-trustees of that trust. After Leslie's death, Ray's children will get the balance of the property.

Leslie's instructions in the trust are different, since Ray wants access to the money if she dies first. She realizes that all the assets coming into the marriage are from Ray, and she isn't greedy. She is happy that he cares enough to take care of her so well after such a short period of time. And, knowing Ray as I do, he will make the terms more liberal as the years pass.

This is just one example, but it shows how proper planning can accomplish your goals, no matter how complicated they may seem. Some situations take a lot more planning and thinking than others, but those are the most fun to work on. What may seem overwhelming to you is merely an exciting challenge to a professional.

Conclusion

Thank you for allowing me to share these very important estate planning concepts with you. As you know by now, proper planning is vital to your financial security and that of your loved ones. You are now familiar with enough concepts to start taking necessary action. That process begins by reviewing your situation, determining your goals, choosing the proper techniques, and meeting with the necessary legal and financial advisors.

Let's take one last look at our definition.

"During my life and after my death, I want to control and distribute my property in the manner I desire, minimizing all fees, taxes and court interference, preserving for myself, my family, and those I choose, the estate I have worked so hard to create."

If you want to achieve that definition, the questions that now arise are, "Where do I go from here? What is the next step? How do I go about it?"

Take a glance at the Rosenberg Planning Path on page 313. You will see how all the pieces we have discussed fit together. Thoughtful goal setting, followed by proper planning, can help you accomplish all you desire.

As stated previously, this is not a do-it-yourself book. With all the tools and techniques available, improper execution can cause disastrous results. Hopefully, you will use this opportunity to seek out **professionals** who can help you effect meaningful planning. But that may be easier said than done.

Therefore, at the suggestion of the publisher, I have made arrangements to help you achieve your goals in the easiest manner possible. Those opportunities are explained on pages 307-309. I wish you the best no matter which course you choose.

From The Publisher

The subject of estate planning never ends. It continues to evolve as your situation transforms and the laws change.

Nevertheless, it is time for you to put theory into action. This book was designed to provide the necessary information to help you achieve your particular goals. If you do nothing, then you will have accomplished nothing more than learning about estate planning. We strongly implore you to take steps today to resolve any potential problems and structure your estate in the manner you desire....don't procrastinate!

As frequently stated by Stephen Rosenberg, this book is not a do-it-yourself guide. This subject requires professional advice. If you can receive that locally, we urge you to pursue it. If you are not aware of professionals locally that can assist you, Stephen has assembled a select package of services that can help you to achieve your estate planning goals. The following are a few of those services and programs.

1. **Personalized Estate Analysis** - Exclusive arrangements have been made with Estate Planning Specialists, a nationally recognized firm headquartered in Chandler, Arizona, to provide you with a personalized, comprehensive estate analysis. This confidential analysis comes in a handsome binder and brings together a wealth of information, neatly organized into easy-to-follow sections. It includes calculations which graphically show your potential estate tax liability; wealth-creation ideas that will help you build your estate; and specific recommendations on the most cost-effective methods to reduce the cost of your estate taxes by up to 90%.

Estate Planning Specialists has agreed to provide this analysis to purchasers of this book for just $69. To give some idea of the value, Mark Skousen, one of the most highly respected financial consultants in the world, said they should be charging at least $300 per analysis. In addition, Estate Planning

Specialists has agreed to refund 100% of your money if you are not completely satisfied. To receive your personalized analysis, delivered within ten working days, just complete the form on pages 311 and 312 and mail it to the address at the bottom of the second side. If you have any questions about this program, call (800) 223-9610, extension 274.

2. **Book on Tapes** - Stephen Rosenberg has professionally recorded a dynamic discussion of <u>Keep Uncle Sam (and Cousin George) From Devouring Your Estate</u> on a series of audio cassette tapes. Let Stephen be your personal estate planner by providing you with your own private seminar! The series is divided into three planning areas:

Unit 1 - *Basic Techniques Of Estate Planning:* covers methods of ownership; workings, advantages and disadvantages of wills, probate and trusts; an explanation of estate taxes; plus working with minor and adult children.

Unit 2 - *Estate-Tax Savings*: provides a review of estate taxes; gifting; irrevocable insurance trusts; charitable giving; life insurance; and ways to reduce the cost of estate taxes.

Unit 3 - *Special Planning Situations*: covers protecting against disability; nursing home protection; living wills; health care powers; selling a business/farm/practice; providing for handicapped children; planning for non-U.S. citizens; and second marriages.

The tapes are specifically designed for the person who cannot take the time to read the book and would rather listen to an absorbing explanation of this important subject. The cassettes are attractively packaged and perfect for gifts. Each unit consists of two 90-minute tapes and retails for $16.95, plus $2.50 shipping and handling. The complete set of three is available for $44.95, plus $5.00 shipping and handling. They can be purchased at your local bookstore or by phoning (800) 847-4483 [(800) VIP-GIVE] and charging them to you credit card.

3. **Free Newsletter** - If you purchased this book at a seminar or bookstore, you are entitled to receive, at no cost, *Rosenberg's Estate Alert!*, a periodic newsletter on important tax and law changes. (Mail order purchasers need not call - you will automatically receive this newsletter.) *Rosenberg's Estate Alert!* will keep you abreast of news vital to your estate planning and preservation needs, inform you of important seminars in your area, and provide useful planning ideas. To have your name added (at no cost) to the subscriber list, call Mr. Rosenberg's office at (800) 777-0867.

4. **Speakers Program** - Stephen Rosenberg is available to speak on matters of estate planning to your association, convention, conference, company, or group. His programs can be specifically tailored in time and content to your particular audience. Stephen has achieved acclaim from people across the country for his unique ability to take a complicated subject and make it fun and easy to understand. For a free media kit describing his programs, call his office toll-free at (800) 777-0867. Or write to him at 2517 Moody Road, Suite 100, Warner Robins, GA 31088.

5. **Consulting Service** - The Rosenberg Financial Group is available to provide consulting services to those who would like to discuss their concerns with leading professionals on the cutting edge of estate planning. For information concerning this service, call Mr. Rosenberg's office at (800) 777-0867. Or express your concerns in writing to him at the above address.

PERSONAL ESTATE PLANNING PROFILE (ESTATE ANALYSIS) – *CONFIDENTIAL*

IF YOU ARE SINGLE, WIDOWED OR DIVORCED, SIMPLY PROVIDE YOUR PERSONAL INFORMATION AND DISREGARD ALL REFERENCES TO A SPOUSE.

CLIENT'S FULL NAME			SPOUSE'S FULL NAME		
DATE OF BIRTH / /	SMOKER? ☐ YES ☐ NO	CITIZENSHIP	DATE OF BIRTH / /	SMOKER? ☐ YES ☐ NO	CITIZENSHIP
WITHIN THE PAST FIVE YEARS HAVE YOU CONSULTED A PHYSICIAN, MEDICAL PRACTITIONER OR BEEN CONFINED TO A HOSPITAL, CLINIC OR MEDICAL FACILITY? ☐ YES ☐ NO IF YES, PLEASE GIVE DETAILS:			WITHIN THE PAST FIVE YEARS HAVE YOU CONSULTED A PHYSICIAN, MEDICAL PRACTITIONER OR BEEN CONFINED TO A HOSPITAL, CLINIC OR MEDICAL FACILITY? ☐ YES ☐ NO IF YES, PLEASE GIVE DETAILS:		
HOME ADDRESS		CITY, STATE, ZIP	HOME PHONE ( )		BEST TIME TO CALL
MAILING ADDRESS		CITY, STATE, ZIP	WORK PHONE ( )		BEST TIME TO CALL

INCOME

JOINT ANNUAL GROSS EARNED INCOME $ _____ JOINT ANNUAL GROSS INCOME FROM INVESTMENTS $ _____

CHILDREN (LIST ALL LIVING CHILDREN: C = CLIENT   S = SPOUSE   J = JOINT

NAME	AGE	SEX ☐ M ☐ F	PARENT ☐ C ☐ S ☐ J	NAME	AGE	SEX ☐ M ☐ F	PARENT ☐ C ☐ S ☐ J
NAME	AGE	SEX ☐ M ☐ F	PARENT ☐ C ☐ S ☐ J	NAME	AGE	SEX ☐ M ☐ F	PARENT ☐ C ☐ S ☐ J

LIFE INSURANCE & ANNUITIES (PLEASE LIST ADDITIONAL POLICIES ON SEPARATE PAPER)

COMPANY	INSURED	OWNER	BENEFICIARY	FACE AMOUNT	CASH VALUE

ASSETS & LIABILITIES • KEY: USE THE FOLLOWING TO INDICATE HOW TITLE IS HELD:

H = HUSBAND'S SEPARATE   W = WIFE'S SEPARATE   CP = COMMUNITY PROPERTY   JT = JOINT TENANCY   TC = TENANCY IN COMMON   TE = TENANCY BY THE ENTIRETY

DESCRIPTION OF ASSETS	FAIR MARKET VALUE	LIABILITY	NET VALUE	HOW TITLE IS HELD
RESIDENCE				
OTHER REAL ESTATE				
STOCKS & BONDS				
BUSINESS INTERESTS				
CASH IN BANKS (CDS, MONEY MARKETS, ETC.)				
NOTES RECEIVABLE				
PERSONAL EFFECTS (AUTOS, BOATS, ETC.)				
RETIREMENT PLAN (NOT IN SETTLEMENT)				
OTHER ASSETS				
OTHER ASSETS				
OTHER ASSETS				

PAYMENT PREFERENCE

☐ MY CHECK OR MONEY ORDER FOR $69 MADE PAYABLE TO ESTATE PLANNING SPECIALISTS IS ENCLOSED.

☐ PLEASE CHARGE TO MY CREDIT CARD (CHECK ONE):   ☐ MASTERCARD   ☐ VISA   CARD # _____   EXPIRATION DATE _____

SIGNATURE _____

PLEASE DON'T PUT THIS OFF — SEND FOR YOUR ESTATE ANALYSIS TODAY
ESTATE PLANNING SPECIALISTS · 3200 N. DOBSON RD., BUILDING C · CHANDLER, AZ 85224 · 1-800-223-9610

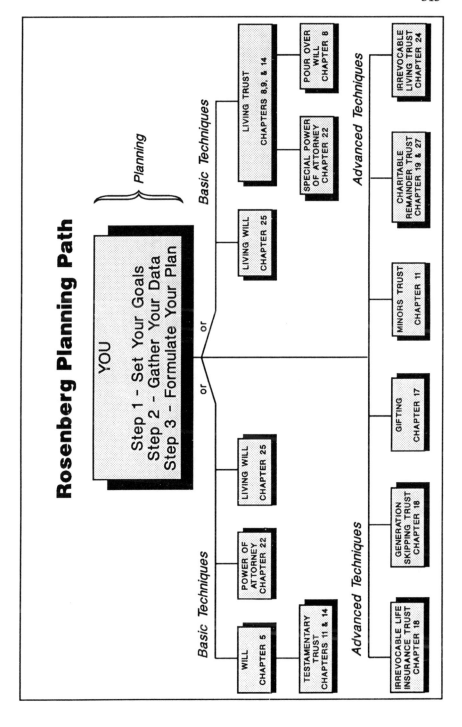

Rosenberg Planning Path

YOU

Step 1 - Set Your Goals
Step 2 - Gather Your Data
Step 3 - Formulate Your Plan

Planning

Basic Techniques

LIVING TRUST
CHAPTERS 8,9, & 14

POUR OVER WILL
CHAPTER 8

SPECIAL POWER OF ATTORNEY
CHAPTER 22

LIVING WILL
CHAPTER 25

Advanced Techniques

IRREVOCABLE LIVING TRUST
CHAPTER 24

CHARITABLE REMAINDER TRUST
CHAPTER 19 & 27

MINORS TRUST
CHAPTER 11

GIFTING
CHAPTER 17

GENERATION SKIPPING TRUST
CHAPTER 18

IRREVOCABLE LIFE INSURANCE TRUST
CHAPTER 18

Advanced Techniques

LIVING WILL
CHAPTER 25

POWER OF ATTORNEY
CHAPTER 22

WILL
CHAPTER 5

TESTAMENTARY TRUST
CHAPTERS 11 & 14

Basic Techniques

INDEX

A-B trust, (See Family trust)
Affidavit of trust, 142-143
Aliens, (See Citizens, foreign)
Ascertainable standards, 88-89
Assets, transferring, 69, 143-149

Banks, as trustees, 84
By-pass trust, (See Family trust)
Business, 267-288
    passing at death, 267-288
    sale of, 282-287
    valuation, 269-272
Buy-sell agreements, 275-277

Changing titles, 69, 143-149
Charitable giving, 205-218
Charitable remainder trust,
    205-218, 282-288
Children, adult, 121-124
    provisions for, 122-124
    joint tenancy with, 31-32
Children, minor, 103-120
    custodial accounts for, 115-
      117
    as life insurance benefici-
      aries, 105-107
    gifts to, 115-117
    guardians of, 110-111
    providing for, 112-113
    selecting guardians, 110-111
    selecting trustees, 111-112
    trusts, 115-120
    Uniform Gifts to Minors,
      115-117
    wills and, 38
Citizens, foreign, 54, 297-300
Community property, 24-26
    rules, 24-26
    states, 24

Cost-basis, 159-160
Co-trustees, 82-84
Cross-ownership of life
    insurance, 167, 202
Crummey provisions, 172-174
Court-fees, (See probate)
Custodial accounts, 115-117
Custodians, (See Guardians)

Disability, 40, 221-232
    and living trusts, 221
    and wills, 40
    planning for, 223-232
    insurance, 221-223
Divorce, 32
Durable power of attorney,
    228-231

Economic Recovery Tax Act,
    1981 (ERTA), 44
Estate tax, 53-62, 87-102, 183-
    195
    calculation, 55-57
    citizens, foreign, 54
    ERTA, 44,
    federal, 57
    life insurance and, 165-195
    state, 60-61
    reducing cost of, 72, 87-102,
      183-195
    paying, 183-195
    rules of, 54-55
Executor (executrix), 37, 46-47
Exemption, ($600,000), 65

Family trust, 88-90
    definition of, 88
    estate tax planning, 88-90
    purposes of, 88-90

Farm, (See Business)
Federal gift taxes, (see Gifts
    and gifting)

Generation-skipping, 279-181
Gifts and gifting, 25-26, 31,
    155-163, 205-218
    annual exclusion, 155-157
    between non-spouses, 31
    in contemplation of death,
        168
    citizens, foreign, 299
    charitable giving, 205-218
    community property, 25-26
    cost basis, 159-160
    Crummey provisions, 172-174
    definition, 155
    ERTA, 44
    present interest, 156
    taxes, 157-158
Goal setting, 9-12
Grandchildren, 179-181
Guardians, 39, 110-111

Handicapped children, 289-296
Health care powers, 254-255

Incompetency, (See Disability)
Inheritance tax, 60-61
Insurance,
    disability, 222-223
    life, 165-179, 197-204
    long-term care, 236-240
    nursing home, 236-240
Intestate, 35-37
IRAs (See Retirement plans),
Irrevocable life insurance trust,
    170-179
Irrevocable living trust, 22-24,
    295

Joint tenancy, 16-18, 24-33
Joint trusts, 82

Keogh, (See Retirement plans)

Lawsuits, protection, 257-264
Life estate, 19-20
Life insurance, 165-179, 197-204,
    277-280
    and agents, 200-201
    choosing a company, 198-200
    buy-sell agreement, funding of,
        277-280
    citizens, foreign, 300
    Crummey provisions, 172-174
    federal estate planning, 176-
        179
    irrevocable insurance trust,
        170-179
    three year rule, 167-168
    mistakes, 201-203
    transferring a policy, 167-168
Living trusts, (See Revocable
    living trusts)
Living will, 253-254
Loan guarantees, 162-163
Long term care insurance, (See
    Nursing home)

Marital deduction, 154
Marital trust, 90-91
Minors, (See Children)
Medicaid, (See Nursing home)
Medical practice, (See Business)

Nursing home, 241-252
    assets, defined, 244
    income, defined, 244
    insurance, 236-240
    Medicaid, 241-252
    Medicaid trust, 241-252
    rules, 243-244

Pension plans, (See
    Retirement plans)
Pour-over will, 72, 142

Powers of attorney, 228-231
  durable, 228-231
  general, 228-229
  special durable, 231
Present interest gifts, 156
Probate, 45-51
  advantages of, 48-49
  appointing guardians or
    custodians, (See Guardians)
  avoiding, 46
  creditors, 48
  disadvantages of, 49-51
  joint tenancy, 46
  life insurance proceeds, 46
  process of, 47-48
  public records of, 50

Qualified Terminal Interest
  Property (Q-TIP), 91

Real estate, (See Property)
Retirement plans, 61-62, 147-148
  beneficiary designations, 147-
    148
  excess accumulation tax, 61-62
  excess distribution tax, 61-62
  living trusts, 147-148
  using charitable unitrust for,
    214-218
Revocable living trusts, 20-22,
  65-78, 133-152, 295-296, 301-
  304
  affidavit of trust, 142-143
  advantages of, 69-74
  community property states, 81
  contesting, 70-72
  cost, 74-75
  defined, 67-68
  disability, 231
  disadvantages of, 74-77
  estate tax savings, 72
  funding, (See Transferring
    property)
  handicapped children, 295-296

income tax consequences, 73
  minors, 72
  pour-over will, 72, 142
  structuring, 79-86
  transferring property into, 69,
    143-149
  trustees, choosing, 82-86
  trustees, duties, 84-86
  second marriages, 301-304
Rosenberg Planning Path, xiv,
  313

Sole ownership, 14-15
Sprinkle provisions, 90
State laws, 24-26, 35-37, 60-61
  community property, 24-26
  intestacy, 35-37
  state inheritance tax, 60-61
Stepped-up basis, 156-160
Successor trustees, 82-83

Taxes, (See Estate taxes)
  gift, (See Gifts and gifting)
Tenants by the entirety, 18-19
Tenants in common, 15-16
Testamentary trusts, 125-130,
  295
  compared with living trusts,
    125-130
  handicapped children, 295
  probate, 126
Titles, 13-33, 143-149
  changing, 143-149
  property, 13-26
  life estate, 19-20
  irrevocable living trust, 22-24
  joint tenants, 16-18, 24-33
  revocable living trust, 20-22
  sole owner, 14-15
  tenants by the entirety, 18-19
  tenants in common, 15-16
  types of, 13-26
Transferring property, 63, 143-
  149

Trustees, 80-86
  choosing, 82-86
  co-trustees, 82-84
  defined, 80
  institutions, 84
  responsibilities of, 84-86
  successor, naming of, 82-86
Trustmaker, 80
Trusts, 88-91, 103-120, 170-179,
    205-218, 282-288, 295
  charitable remainder, 205-218,
      282-288
  family, 88-90
  irrevocable life insurance, 170-
      179
  irrevocable living trust, 22-24,
      295
  marital, 90-91
  minor children, 103-120
  Q-TIP, 91
  revocable living trust, 20-22,
      65-78, 133-152, 295-296,
      301-304
  testamentary trusts, 125-130,
      295
  2503 (b) trusts, 117-119
  2503 (c) trusts, 119-120

Uniform Gifts to Minors Act,
    115-117
Uniform Transfers to Minors
    Act, 115-117
Unlimited marital deduction,
    154

Wills, 35-44
  advantages of, 38-39
  children in, 38-39
  definition, 37
  disability, 40
  disadvantages, 39-42
  contesting, 41-42
  costs, 39
  intestate, 35-37

pour-over, 72, 142
probate, 40
public documents, 40-41
self-proving, 43-44